Fifty Days

The Divine Disclosures During a Holy Sufi Seclusion

Shaykh Muhammad Hisham Kabbani

Introduction by

Shaykh Muhammad Nazim al-Haqqani

Institute for Spiritual and Cultural Advancement

ISBN: 978-1-930409-72-9

Library of Congress Control Number: tbd

Published and Distributed by:
Institute for Spiritual and Cultural Advancement
17195 Silver Parkway, #201 Fenton, MI 48430 USA
Tel: (888) 278-6624
Fax:(810) 815-0518

Available for purchase online at ISN1.NET
Email: staff@isn1.net

Shaykh Muhammad Nazim Adil al-Haqqani (right), world leader of the most distinguished Naqshbandi-Haqqani Sufi Order, with his representative, and author of this book, Shaykh Muhammad Hisham Kabbani.

بِسْمِ اللَّهِ الرَّحْمَنِ الرَّحِيمِ

الرَّحْمَنُ عَلَّمَ الْقُرْآنَ خَلَقَ الْإِنسَانَ عَلَّمَهُ الْبَيَانَ

*The Most Merciful has made known the Qur'ān;
He Created humankind; He Taught him eloquence.
Sūratu 'r-Raḥmān [the Merciful], 55:22*

Contents

PUBLISHER'S NOTES **10**

INTRODUCTION **12**

FOREWORD: BY SHAYKH NAZIM AL-HAQQANI **13**

PART ONE: THE SECLUSION WRITINGS **21**

Endless Attacks of Shaytan 28

Disciplining the Ego 30

Three Dangers of Seclusion 35

The Key to the Journey is Patience 42

Knowledge Uplifts the Seeker 45

The Prophet Reached the Highest Hidden Realities 46

Seeking a Divinely-Ordained King 49

The Ark of the Muhammadan Nation 53

The Kings of the Heart Demolish All Its Idols 54

Abase One's Self and Be Raised by the Lord 61

Pride: the Worst Satanic Trait 64

Levels of Discipleship 67

PART TWO: THE COMMENTARIES **69**

AUTHENTIC SECLUSION 70

Seclusion is a Test from the Shaykh 71

Reclaiming the Throne of the Heart 74

The Trials of Seclusion 75

PRAYING FOR A KING 79

Reflecting on Allah's Creation 80

Accountability to the Creator 83

The Value of Seclusion 85

DANGERS OF SECLUSION 87
Overcoming the Three Dangers 91
Prerequisites of the Authentic Seclusion 95
Seclusion Requires a Perfect Shaykh 96
WAR AGAINST THE EGO 97
Allah Wants Us to Repent 99
Distractions of *Dunya* 101
Declare War on Your Enemy 102
Shaytan Does not Accept Defeat 103
How to Win the War Against Shaytan 106
Seclusion Requires Support of the Shaykh 108
Importance of Pacing 110
THE STAFF OF MUSA 113
Secret Meanings of the Letters of the Holy Name 114
The Station of Oneness and the Station of Uniqueness 121
Allah's Generosity and Majesty 123
THE PROPHET IS THE CENTERPOINT OF CREATION 125
The Children of Israel and Talut 126
Ark of the Covenant 129
THREE LEVELS OF TRANQUILITY 131
Tranquility of the Heart: 131
Tranquility of the Prophets 133
Tranquility of the Prophets' Inheritors 134
ARK OF THE KNOWERS 139
The Snake that Devours Untruth 143
PURIFICATION OF THE HEART AND THE THREE LEVELS OF THE SELF 147
The Heart of the Believer is between the Two Fingers of the Lord 148

Two Types of Believers 150
Seclusion unlocks the Six Secrets of the Heart 152
Secrets of Talut and Powers of the Saints 153
NECESSITY FOR A GUIDE 157
Kings Despoil the Land 158
Saints Cast Down the Idols of the Heart 161
You Must Earn Your Trust 167
Accept the Authority of the Shaykh 170
SHAYTAN'S TRAPS 177
HIDE YOUR ASCETICISM 181
Use the Best of this Life for the Next 183
Titles of Self-Aggrandizement 184
Stealing Another Shaykh's Disciples is a Grave Sin 185
Ten Excellent Character Traits 188
THE WORST TRAITS: PRIDE AND ARROGANCE 191
Fire Comes from Dumps 192
Fire of Intimacy 193
The Heart's Boiling Pots 196
Humility Defeats Shaytan 196
Be a Dump 197
Keep Your Love to Your Shaykh Alone 198
THREE LEVELS OF SPIRITUAL ATTAINMENT 203
First Level 204
Second Level 205
Third Level 207
EXERCISE AND ITS RESULTS 209
ADAM AND THE TREE OF LIFE 215

Choose Your Goal 219
Human Beings are Built on Mistakes 221
The Tree of Life 222
PROPHET MUHAMMAD IS ALLAH'S CALIPH 225
The Meaning of *Huwa* 227
The Divine Essence is Utterly Unknowable 230
DIVINE BLUEPRINTS 235
Power of the Kidney 236
Heavenly Coma 237
Heavenly Pictures 239
How Do We Repay Our Lord? 243
THREE LEVELS OF FRUITFULNESS 247
Consult Others 247
Honor the Prophet 249
Levels of Fertility 251
Level of *Murid* 253
EXEMPLARS OF HUMILITY 257
Attacks by the Delegations of Pride 260
Endless Oceans of the Divine Essence 261
Tasting Will Make You Progress 262
The Light of the Absolute Essence and the Station of the Gnostics 264
BITTERNESS TRAINING 267
The Shaykh's Disdain Raises You 268
EXEMPLARS OF GUIDANCE 271
Bayazid al-Bistami 271
Spiritual Poverty 278
Station of Slavery 280

Publisher's Notes

This book is specifically designed for readers relatively familiar with Islamic and Sufi terms. However, to accommodate those who are not, we have often accompanied Arabic terminology with English translations.

Qur'ānic quotes are centered, highlighted in bold and italics and footnoted, citing chapter name, number and verse. The Holy Traditions of Prophet Muhammad ﷺ (known as *hadith*) are offset, italicized and footnoted referencing the book in which they are cited. Every attempt has been made to be precise and comprehensive in citing sources.

Universally Recognized Symbols

Muslims around the world typically offer praise upon speaking, hearing, or reading the name "*Allāh*" and any of the Islamic names of God. Muslims also offer salutation and/or invoke blessing upon speaking, hearing or reading the names of Prophet Muhammad, other prophets, his family, his companions, and saints. We have applied the following international standards, using Arabic calligraphy and lettering:

ﷺ *ṣall-Allāhu 'alayhi wa sallam* (God's blessings and greetings of peace be upon him) following the names of the Prophet ﷺ.

۶ *'alayhi 's-salām* (peace be upon him) following the names of other prophets, angels, and Khiḍr.

۶ *'alayhā 's-salām* (peace be upon her) following the name of Mary, Mother of Jesus.

۶/۶ *raḍīy-Allāhu 'anhu/'anhā* (may God be pleased with him/her) following the name of a male or female companion of the Prophet ﷺ.

ق *qaddas-Allāhu sirrah* (may God sanctify his secret) following the name of a saint.

Transliteration

To simplify reading the Arabic names, places and terms are not transliterated in the main text. Transliteration is provided in the section on the spiritual practices to facilitate correct pronunciation and is based on the following system:

Symbol	Transliteration	Symbol	Transliteration	Vowels:	
				Long	
ء	'	ط	ṭ	آ ى	ā
ب	b	ظ	ẓ	و	ū
ت	t	ع	ʿ	ي	ī
ث	th	غ	gh	Short	
ج	j	ف	f	َ	a
ح	ḥ	ق	q	ُ	u
خ	kh	ك	k	ِ	i
د	d	ل	l		
ذ	dh	م	m		
ر	r	ن	n		
ز	z	ه	h		
س	s	و	w		
ش	sh	ي	y		
ص	ṣ	ة	ah; at		
ض	ḍ	ال	al-/'l-		

Introduction

This book is what emerged from the heart of Shaykh Muḥammad Hishām Kabbānī after spending fifty days in a seclusion prescribed by his guiding master, Shaykh Muḥammad Nāẓim al-Ḥaqqānī. During the course of his time, ensconced by himself and isolated in Shaykh Nāẓim's empty home in Damascus, a short walk from Grandshaykh ʿAbd Allāh al-Fā'iz ad-Dāghestānī's mosque and burial place (*maqām*), Shaykh Hishām underwent incredible experiences.

With the permission of his master, Shaykh Hishām began to put pen to paper to engrave some of the holy inspirations (*wāridāt*) that were pouring into his heart from the holy connections, built up during normal life through worship and divine service, but enhanced and amplified during the isolation and spiritual focus of the "forty plus ten" days. This seclusion is traditionally observed according to the traditional Sufi calendar during the Muslim holy month of Rajab, known as the month of God, for its special spiritual character, and one-third of Shaʿbān, known as the month of the Prophet, for in it the Night Journey and Ascension to the Divine Presence of the Prophet took place, a peerless spiritual journey whose appearances permeate and invigorate the seeker during all of the month's holy days.

The first chapter of this book is a translation of writings that Shaykh Hishām penned near the end of his fifty-day seclusion from Rajab to mid-Shaʿban of 2005. The remainder of this book are the subsequent commentary Shaykh Hishām made on those writings in discourses made during the month of fasting. These teachings expand on those inspirations and reveal the depths of meaning behind them, and are based on associations (inspired talks) given to students of the shaykh after the pre-dawn prayers every morning in Ramadan 2005.

Foreword

The Purpose of Shaykh Hisham's Seclusion

Bismillāhi 'r-Raḥmāni 'r-Raḥīm

There is permission for seclusion, *khalwah,* and to practice for forty days (*al-arbaʿīn*). But we have not been ordered to assign anyone other than Shaykh Hisham, to enter into a complete seclusion for forty days while leaving all people, family and children and renouncing utterly all worldly interests (*dunyā*) and country in order to embrace the service of Allāh as much as possible.

In this year, they[1] sent us a signal to inform the servant who is poor before Allāh the Wealthy, Shaykh Nāẓim, who has the titles of al-Ḥaqqānī an-Naqshbandī, that I should commission Shaykh Hisham to enter into the forty days seclusion in this year 1426 H. (Aug 2005) to be cut off from *dunyā,* children, family, country and work and to give his heart and to make himself available only for his Most Glorified and Exalted Lord's service. I was informed in this matter to commission one of the deputies of our Master, the Sultan of Saints and the teacher of the ummah Shaykh ʿAbdAllāh al-Fā'iz ad-Dāghestānī (May Allāh raise his station continuously) and specifically that I should commission Shaykh Hishām al-Kabbānī, who is known (within the circle of saints) by the titles as al-Haqqānī, and who is also known as Madadu 'l-Ḥaqq.

Allāh is granting him a special support in order to sever disbelief from its roots and in order to open the way for truth, for the appointment of the True One and for protecting the people of truth and to overpower the kingdom of Iblīs and to bring about its ruin.

---

[1] "They" here refers to Shaykh Nazim's spiritual headquarters, his Grandshaykh, who in turn receives his orders from the Prophet (s).

I was given the signal and the glad tidings that I should commission one of the deputies of Mawlana Shaykh ʿAbdAllāh al-Fā'iz ad-Dāghestānī, Shaykh Hishām al-Kabbānī ar-Rabbānī al-Ḥaqqānī, to enter into seclusion from the beginning of the month of Rajab al-Murrajab until the tenth of Shaʿbān al-muʿaẓẓam and to accomplish as much as possible in terms of the perfection of the seclusion by practicing spiritual focus, *tawajjuh*, wayfaring, *sulūk*, and standing in worship at night, *qiyām*, to be, as much as possible in the service of al-Malik al-Āʿlām, the Knowledge-dispensing King.

That is why I called him to come here to our presence in order for me to assign him this duty. According to our insight he will assume the station for which a promise was made on the Day of the Promise and the Covenant, Yawm al-ʿAhdi wa 'l-Mīthāq, to devote himself to the service of the Lord of servants; to conquer disbelief (*kufr*) and invalidate and bring it to ruin and to abolish the kingdom of Satan and *abālisah* (devils).

May Allāh unveil to him from His Secrets and support him with a special support. Since the time is near for the blessed month, the month of Rajab al-Murrajab 1426 H. by Allāh 's leave Shaykh Hisham will direct himself in obedience to what they have asked of us and what we have received that we should cast this assignment upon his shoulders to carry the responsibility of this service. Our honorable masters saw that this important task is only suitable for Shaykh Hishām al-Kabbānī, titled ar-Rabbānī, and that he should make himself available to achieve and to apply himself with ardor to pave the way for the appearance of the "Owner of this Time" *Sayyīdinā* Mahdī ؑ. And they have revealed that he should reign with the governance he is given according to what is required of him right before the time of *Sayyīdinā* al-Mahdī ؑ, during his time and after his time.

We wish that Allāh will facilitate this matter and we are reminding him that everything which the servant does solely for his Lord, may He be glorified, even if it is difficult, will be made easy. The servant in whose deed the ego takes its share will be made tired and that will be the cause for him not to receive support from the angelic realm to complete his service.

In summary he will intend after 'Aṣr prayer, next Thursday, the fourth of August, he will shower for welcoming the blessed month of Rajab al-Murrajab and he will enter seclusion[2] with the intention of subduing the ego and its evil from his self, *nafs*, and from all the selves of the members of the Ummah.

We want him to erase the evil of the egos from the servants and to free them up and to bring them to the service of (Allāh according to the verse):

أَلَا لِلَّهِ الدِّينُ الْخَالِصُ

Alā lillāhi 'dīnu 'l-khāliṣ

Is it not to God alone that all sincere faith is due.[3]

In his seclusion he will be busy with his master and mine, Shaykh 'AbdAllāh, the teacher of the ummah. Then he will ascend in the company of Mawlanā Shaykh 'AbdAllāh to the service of the Prophet of the Last Days, the Beloved of Allāh, our Master Muḥammad ﷺ and then he will intend to raise the flag of peace between the east and the west.

Allāh Almighty said:

كُلَّ يَوْمٍ هُوَ فِي شَأْنٍ

Kullu yawmin hūwa fi shān

And every day He tends to a different matter.[4]

Then he will supplicate and ask on behalf of the Ummah that the Lord send a Sultan, as was indicated by the Lord of Glory when He said:

---

[2] The seclusion was performed in Shaykh Nazim's home in Damascus.

[3] Sūratu 'z-Zumar [The Groups], 39:3.

[4] Sūratu 'r-Raḥmān [The Most Merciful], 55:29.

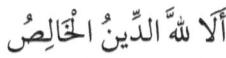

يَا مَعْشَرَ الْجِنِّ وَالْإِنسِ إِنِ اسْتَطَعْتُمْ أَن تَنفُذُوا مِنْ أَقْطَارِ السَّمَاوَاتِ
وَالْأَرْضِ فَانفُذُوا لَا تَنفُذُونَ إِلَّا بِسُلْطَانٍ

Yā ma'shar al-jinni wa'l-ins in istaṭ'atum an tanfudhū min aqṭār as-samāwāti wa'l-arḍi f'anfudhū lā tanfudhūna illa bi sulṭān.

O ye assembly of Jinns and men! If it be ye can pass beyond the zones of the heavens and the earth, pass ye! Not without authority shall ye be able to pass, a Sultan.[5]

There is no need to interpret the meaning of the word Sultan. Its meaning is apparent. If there was any difficulty in understanding a word we may then go to interpretation.

In this case everybody knows the meaning of the word Sultan or of *illa bi-sulṭān, "except through a Sultan."* Why then do they want to interpret and add things by saying it means "Sultan of knowledge"? Why don't they say "Sultan of men" or "Sultan of the angelic realm", or "Sultan of the earth"?

This (seclusion) must be (intended) for correcting what is happening on the face of the earth. This cannot be accomplished without a Sultan. (As the Almighty Lord said,):

O ye assembly of Jinns and men! If it be ye can pass beyond the zones of the heavens and the earth, pass ye! Not without authority shall ye be able to pass, a Sultan.

The Sultan is the shadow of Allāh on His earth. Whoever honors him, similarly will Allāh honor. And whoever humiliates him, Allāh will abase. This is the service, the one who enters it must... What I mean is that the focus of this seclusion, is to ask for the Sultan, because the people are under hardships such as cannot be described, the likes of which have not been seen before. And the people are confused, they do not know how to escape from

[5] Sūratu 'r-Raḥmān [The Most Merciful], 55:33.

this difficulty. This difficulty is like being in a tunnel. There is no way out except through a Sultan.

"The Sultan is the shadow of God on earth." The people left him (the Sultan), and they followed the misguidance of devils, and they fell into their trap. They do not know how to be delivered from this doom or how to be delivered from this disaster.

This is the original purpose: only to ask for this matter, we don't want anything else.

For what other purpose is this seclusion? Oh my Lord I seek refuge with Allāh .

أَلَمْ تَرَ إِلَى الْمَلَإِ مِن بَنِي إِسْرَائِيلَ مِن بَعْدِ مُوسَى إِذْ قَالُواْ لِنَبِيٍّ لَّهُمُ ابْعَثْ لَنَا مَلِكًا نُّقَاتِلْ فِي سَبِيلِ اللّهِ

Alam tara ila al-malāi min banī isrāīla min baʿdi mūsā idh qālū li-nabīyyin lahum 'ubʿath lanā malikan nuqātil fī sabīlillāhi

Have you not turned your vision to the Chiefs of the Children of Israel after (the time of) Moses? They said to a Prophet ﷺ (that was) among them: "Appoint for us a king, that we may fight in the cause of Allāh."[6]

That was in order to teach the servants. He did not mention that they asked directly "send us a king" for they never did that.

When they faced hardship, the Children of Israel went to their prophet. To those devils who deny intercession through saints and prophets, this is the best example and proof of the validity of intercession. Why did they go to their prophet? Why didn't they directly say "Oh our Lord, send a king to us."

They went to their prophet and asked him " ask from your Lord." *"When they said to their prophet, 'appoint for us a king'"* it means, "your tongue is pure. You ask on our behalf from your

[6] Sūratu 'l-Baqara [The Heifer],2:246.

Lord. We have made you our intercessor (*wasīlah*). You ask from your Lord, to send us a king."

Who owns the land and the people? The king. When they were righteous, the king was righteous. When they deviated, the king deviated. That is it.

Every night in the last third before dawn, Shaykh Hisham will be in the station of intimate discourse with his Lord. After completing the special *awrād,* recitations and the *ṣalawāt,* praise on the Prophet and recitation Shaykh Hisham has been assigned for this seclusion, and with which he will be busy 24 hours, every night, at the most favorable time for Allāh's acceptance of supplication, Shaykh Hisham should request Allāh to send us a king—a king who will struggle in Allāh 's Way. His supplication in this manner and in this state will be so effective, it will be the same as that of 124,000 saints engaged in supplication for forty days without cease.

They are asking the Lord of servants to send them a king. That is why we are sending Shaykh Hisham Effendi, whom we know very well. The others saints, we do not know them.

For this purpose he must not enter into any other activity. Other things are not important. He must ask this only; it is the summary and distillation of the forty days and the ultimate purpose is this consultation with the Prophet ﷺ.

He must be present, spiritually with the Prophet ﷺ , and ask, "Oh Prophet of Mercy! Oh Prophet of Mercy! Oh Prophet of Mercy! Ask your Lord to send us a king so that we may struggle in Allāh's way, *fī sabīlillāh.* Ask for the one of whom you gave us the glad tidings, Oh Prophet of Mercy! *Yā Nabī ar-Raḥmah!"* And we are looking to see the results.

What I advised him regarding his physicality, is so that he does not become weak and in order for him to complete the service, so that he is neither carrying too much nor too little, for the best of ways is the middle one.

I advised him regarding eating and drinking, and whatever he does it is alright. Most important is that after that he ask "Oh our Lord, send us a king. Make the hardships that burden us, O Allāh, as if it did not exist. O our Lord erase their evil through Your Men of God. And it is for You, for You, for You Alone, O my Lord to sever their roots:

فَقُطِعَ دَابِرُ الْقَوْمِ الَّذِينَ ظَلَمُواْ وَالْحَمْدُ لِلّهِ رَبِّ الْعَالَمِينَ

Fa quṭiʿa dābiru'l-qawmi 'Lladhīna ẓalamū w'alḥamdulillāhi rabbi'l-ʿālamīn

severed were the roots of the oppressors and praise be to the Lord of the worlds.'"[7]

That is the main task with which we are ordered. He will afterwards begin to receive, little-by-little, openings to his heart during the seclusion. At first a little, then more and then excessive outpourings will come to him during the seclusion.

The wisdom of the assignment of Shaykh Hisham for this task in this year just now became apparent. The real purpose has just appeared with this step... then afterwards he is free to do as he likes. Regarding this matter, in his task he will receive inspirations continuously to his heart and he will respond to them.

He will be like a tower for the airport: Air Traffic Control. He will be a beacon, *minārah,* that is continuously turning, perceiving in all directions. More inspirations will come, but harmful thoughts will also attack. When such thoughts attack, he should renew his ablution, *wuḍū,* and pray two *rakaʿts.* In this matter, it is up to him to read the Holy Qur'an; as much as possible to read more. He does not need to read other books, because inspirations will be coming related to the intricate meanings (of the Qur'an), and he has permission to write them down. And surely he is an ocean in knowing what is coming from

[7] Sūratu 'l-Anʿam [Cattle], 6:45.

the unseen according to the signals we received, from the people of signals (vision).

We understood that the intensity of the hardship required in order to invoke God to bring about the appearance of the Mahdī ﷺ has just been reached. The people have reached their limits of carrying hardship from the overwhelming extent of oppression and darkness.

May Allāh remove it from existence: all oppression, transgression, tyranny, and denial (of truth) through the blessings of the Prophet ﷺ and the sanctity of Sūrat al-Fatiha.

Hishām Effendi, there will be a continuous ongoing connection, *rābiṭah,* from your heart to ours. A line running from our direction to you, will support you in this important endeavor. That is the honorable connection (*rābiṭah sharīfah*).

Sulṭān al-Awlīyā Mawlānā Shaykh Nāẓim ʿAdil al-Ḥaqqānī

August 3, 2005 (28th Jumāda II 1426)

Part One:

The Seclusion Writings

Bismillāh ir-Raḥmān ir-Raḥīm

وَتَحْسَبُونَهُ هَيِّنًا وَهُوَ عِندَ اللَّهِ عَظِيم

You consider the matter lightly, but for Allāh it is a grave matter. [8]

All of us think that seclusion is an easy endeavor. But if the seclusion is coming through a direct order from the shaykh by permission of the Sulṭān of Saints, my master Shaykh ʿAbd Allāh al-Fā'iz ad-Dāghestānī, by permission of the Prophet ﷺ; then one must give serious consideration to it.

It is the seclusion of antagonists inconflict , the seclusion of solitude in which the servant—by order of the shaykh—is completely severed from family, children, country and wealth.

To those who have never experienced seclusion, it may seem that it is no great exertion for the servant to spend time alone, busying himself with the remembrance of Allāh, recitation of the Holy Qur'an and *ṣalawāt* on the Prophet ﷺ for the duration of his seclusion. But experience proves otherwise.

My master, Shaykh Nāẓim, told me before I entered the seclusion that involuntary thoughts would attack me from every side. I tried to console myself, hoping these thoughts would not really be so bad. I asked God to protect me from such assaults. However, Mawlana knows the inner thoughts of the ego, its poisons and its faults and his warning proved true.

Seclusion is not only for remembrance, reading Qur'an and *ṣalawāt*. We have to understand that the purpose of the seclusion is to demolish the evil-commanding ego, to destroy that tyrant who is sitting like the king on the throne of your heart. The throne of your heart is greater than the throne of Bilqīs. It is loaded with hatred and envy, ornamented with all kinds of flagrant and hidden sins. It is possible to know some of these sins—the sins of

[8] Sūratu 'n-Nūr [The Light], 24:17.

the hidden idolatry, which the Messenger ﷺ described in this narration:

أخوف ما أخاف على أمتي الشرك الخفي

Akwafu mā akhāfu ʿalā ummattī ash-shirk al-khafī

"What I fear most for my nation is the hidden idolatry."[9]

This kind of idolatry turns you away from reflecting, contemplating and observing the True One. It turns you instead toward matters that are vile and low, matters related only to the material world. These worldly affairs have crowned themselves as your king.

That is why my master told me at the beginning of my seclusion to commit myself to *munājāt,* an intimate discourse, with my Lord during the last third of the night. He said that I must come to the spiritual presence of the Prophet ﷺ, accompanied by the Sulṭān of Saints, and ask our Prophet ﷺ: "O Prophet of Mercy, O Prophet of Mercy, O Prophet of Mercy, ask your Lord to send us a king so that we can fight in the way of Allāh ﷻ"

أَلَمْ تَرَ إِلَى الْمَلَإِ مِن بَنِي إِسْرَائِيلَ مِن بَعْدِ مُوسَى إِذْ قَالُواْ لِنَبِيٍّ لَّهُمُ ابْعَثْ لَنَا مَلِكاً نُّقَاتِلْ فِي سَبِيلِ اللّهِ

Alam tara ila al-malāi min banī isrāīla min baʿdi mūsā idh qālū li-nabīyyin lahum 'ubʿath lanā malikan nuqātil fī sabīlillāhi

Have you not seen how the people from the children of Israel asked their prophet: "Send us a king so that we can fight in Allāh's Way?[10]

Mawlana said, "Ask your Lord to send us king, a king who owns the land and its inhabitants."

---

[9] Āḥmad in his *Musnad,* Ibn Mājah in his *Zuhd,* al-Ḥākim in his *Mustadrak,* al-Bayhaqī in his *Shuʿb.*

[10] Sūratu 'l-Baqara [The Heifer],2:246.

Here, he means a physical king who will hold the reins of all affairs, meaning *Sayyidinā* al-Mahdī. However, he was also telling me to ask our Lord to send us a spiritual king who will expel the king of the disobedient ego from the thrones of our hearts. The phrase *who owns the land and its inhabitants* means he will own our selves and all our faculties, that he will command us to seek closeness to our Lord through the different stations of absolute worship of Allāh, as manifested in this holy verse:

الا لله الدين الخالص

Alā lilāhi ad-dīn al-khāliṣ

For Allāh alone is the pure religion.[11]

The ego is divided. In order to ascend in the Stations of Closeness, you have to be firm in keeping your tranquil self, *an-nafs al-muṭma'inna*, away from the worship of your evil-commanding self, *an-nafs al-ammārah*. This is the purpose of seclusion—to separate the two manifestations of ego, the one that commands you to evil and the one that seeks peace and tranquility through the worship of its Lord.

In seclusion, it is necessary to fight the four enemies and prevent them from overpowering the content self. These enemies are:

Nafs, the evil-commanding ego,
Dunyā, the material world,
Hawā, lustful desires,
Shayṭān, Satan.
So, understand if you are clever!

How can we get the strength to fight Satan, to fight lustful desires, to fight the material world and to fight the evil-

---

[11] Sūratu 'z-Zumar [The Groups], 39:3.
[11] Sūratu 'z-Zumar [The Groups], 39:3.

commanding ego? How can we hope to succeed in this contest when our Father Adam, who was a prophet, succumbed to the temptations of Satan and ate from the tree of disobedience? His ego aided Satan by suggesting to him that he should eat from the tree, confirming the promise of Satan that, by eating, he would achieve immortality and gain a kingdom that would notdecline . In seclusion, we have to fight against the same Satan, aided by those same agents. They attack you in order to distract you from the purpose of your seclusion. They will make you busy with worldly affairs. They will make worldly desires beautiful to your eyes, as stated in the Qur'an:

زُيِّنَ لِلنَّاسِ حُبُّ الشَّهَوَاتِ مِنَ النِّسَاء وَالْبَنِينَ وَالْقَنَاطِيرِ الْمُقَنطَرَةِ مِنَ الذَّهَبِ وَالْفِضَّةِ وَالْخَيْلِ الْمُسَوَّمَةِ وَالأَنْعَامِ وَالْحَرْثِ ذَلِكَ مَتَاعُ الْحَيَاةِ الدُّنْيَا وَاللّهُ عِندَهُ حُسْنُ الْمَآبِ

Zuyyin li 'n-nāsi ḥubbu 'sh-shahawāti min an-nisā' wa 'n-nabīyīna wa 'l-qanāṭīra 'l-muqanṭarati mina 'dh-dhahabi w 'al-fiḍati wa 'l-khayli 'l-musawwamati wa 'l-an'āmi wa 'l-ḥarthi dhālik matā'u 'l-ḥayāti 'd-dunyā w'Allāhu 'indahu ḥusnu 'l-maāb.

Beautified for men is the love of things they covet: women, children, much of gold and silver (wealth), branded beautiful horses, cattle and well-tilled land. This is the pleasure of the present world's life; but Allāh has the excellent return (Paradise with flowing rivers, etc.) with Him.12

What do you expect will happen then when you declare war upon Satan and his agents by entering into seclusion? This will be a war in which the enemy cannot accept defeat. It is impossible for Satan to accept defeat, because he pledged to Allāh:

[12] Sūrat Āli 'Imrān [The Family of 'Imrān], 3:14.

قَالَ رَبِّ بِمَا أَغْوَيْتَنِي لأُزَيِّنَنَّ لَهُمْ فِي الأَرْضِ وَلأُغْوِيَنَّهُمْ أَجْمَعِينَ

Qāla rabbi bimā aghwaytanī la-uzayyinanna lahum fi'l-arḍi wa la-ughwīyyannahum ajmaʿīn.

He said, "My lord, with that which you have caused me to go astray; I will beautify it for them and make all of them go astray."[13]

قَالَ فَبِعِزَّتِكَ لَأُغْوِيَنَّهُمْ أَجْمَعِينَ

Qāla fabi-ʿizzatika la-ughwīannahum ajmaʿīn

He said: By Your Might, then I will surely mislead them all.[14]

إِلاَّ عِبَادَكَ مِنْهُمُ الْمُخْلَصِينَ

Illa ʿibādik minhum al-mukhliṣīn

Save Your servants amongst them who are sincere.[15]

Allāh's response to Satan is:

إِنَّ عِبَادِي لَيْسَ لَكَ عَلَيْهِمْ سُلْطَانٌ إِلاَّ مَنِ اتَّبَعَكَ مِنَ الْغَاوِينَ

Inna ʿibāḍī lays laka ʿalayhim sulṭānun illa man ittibaʿka min al-ghāwīn.

Certainly, you shall have no authority over My servants, except those who follow you amongst those who went astray.[16]

That is the reason why this war will be a war of destruction between Good and Evil. There is no doubt that Evil will perish in the end, for Good is true. It is impossible for Evil to overtake Good. Nonetheless, in order to fight Satan, you must

---

[13] Sūratu 'l-Ḥijr [The Stony Tracts], 15:39.
[14] Sūrah Ṣād, 38:82.
[15] Sūratu 'l-Ḥijr [The Stony Tracts], 15:40.
[16] Sūratu 'l-Ḥijr [The Stony Tracts], 15:42.

plan ahead for this war, and that requires that you understand the enemy's plans.

Allāh ﷻ said:

فَأَلْهَمَهَا فُجُورَهَا وَتَقْوَاهَا

Fa-alhamahā fujūrahā wa taqwāhā

He has inspired it (the self) how to be good and how to rebel.[17]

This verse means that Allāh ﷻ has taught you the methods of piety that you have to use and the methods of rebellion that the evil-commanding ego can use against you. Seclusion will make you an expert in these methods.

This is what I received of inspirations today Friday, after the ʿAṣr prayer.

Endless Attacks of Shaytan

The uncontrollable thoughts are attacking me every day between sunrise and sunset. They subside from sunset until sunrise. They subside in particular after sunset, during the night vigil prayer and during the dawn prayer up until sunrise. After sunrise, whole new waves of thoughts begin their attack: thoughts about family, about children, about wealth and about health. These thoughts will turn into an instrument in your ego's hands, steering it whichever way it likes.

This is what I was facing from the moment I began my seclusion, on Thursday 29th of Jumādā 'l-Ākhir, 1426, after ʿAṣr prayer, up to Friday the 8th of Shaʿbān.

During this period the attacks were so intense that, at times, I felt that I wanted to abandon the seclusion and flee. I felt as if I was in the midst of an ocean torrent, crushing everything in its mass of water—as if I were a victim of the tsunami, watching this wall of water destroying everything I had: my family, my children, my country and my possessions. In this small room with

[17] Sūratu 'sh-Shams [The Sun], 91:8.

closed windows and shutters and a door that I only open to renew my ablution, I felt I was a man with nothing—not even a homeland. I felt as if I was in a prison, left in solitary confinement.

The only solace I had was to read the Book of Allāh ﷻ, *Dalā'il al-Khayrāt* and to do the required liturgy of God's remembrance. These remind you that you are not alone in your seclusion, that you are with your Lord, with your beloved Master Muḥammad ﷺ, with your shaykh, your beloved Sulṭān of Saints, Shaykh ʿAbdAllāh al-Fā'iz ad-Dāghestānī and with your teacher, your guide, Mawlana Shaykh Muḥammad Nāẓim Adil al-Ḥaqqānī (may Allāh give him long life). At that moment, your thoughts become lighter for a short while, so you immerse yourself in reciting the Qur'an and performing these other acts of worship.

On Friday, after ʿAṣr prayer and during one of the more intense attacks of these uncontrollable thoughts, I received an inspiration from Mawlana Shaykh Nāẓim saying: "My son, I have been ordered to break the tip of the sword of your evil-commanding ego by giving it a little bit of what it likes." Mawlana ordered me to drink some tea in order to give my ego a little bit of something that it desired and, thereby, to diminish the strength of its desires and make it easier to subdue. Praise be to Allāh ﷻ, I quickly got up and drank some tea. At that moment, my thoughts calmed down and I began to write these inspirations.

I hope that my ego will stop at this limit, although I know that Mawlana Shaykh had informed me that this seclusion would be one of the most difficult ones, because we are living in the most difficult times. "This is the reason why," he said, "uncontrollable thoughts will attack you from every side, so be patient."

I ask that Allāh ﷻ give me patience, and relieve me from the ego's desires and from its war against me; to give me power over the ego and its devils; to take the reins off of my horse, the lordly power that is found in the Secret of Secrets of the heart, which is inspired by the signals of the Muḥammadan Lordly

Lights, the heart which is yearning to know the secret of the secrets of the divine knowledge, with which He favored some of His righteous and saintly servants:

فَوَجَدَا عَبْداً مِّنْ عِبَادِنَا آتَيْنَاهُ رَحْمَةً مِنْ عِندِنَا وَعَلَّمْنَاهُ مِن لَّدُنَّا عِلْماً

Fawajada ʿabdan min ʿibābidnā ātaynāhu raḥmatan min ʿindinā wa ʿallamnāhu min ladunna ʿilma

They found a servant from amongst Our servants whom We have given a mercy from Our presence and whom We taught knowledge from Our Divine Presence.[18]

وَاتَّقُواْ اللهَ وَيُعَلِّمُكُمُ اللهُ وَاللهُ بِكُلِّ شَيْءٍ عَلِيمٌ

W'attaqū 'Llāḥa wa yuʿallimakumullāh w'Allāhu bi-kulli shayin ʿalīm

And be aware of Allāh and Allāh will teach you, and Allāh is all knowing of everything.[19]

We ask Allāh ﷻ to teach us knowledge from His Divine Presence, and praise be to Allāh ﷻ the Lord of all worlds.

This is what came to my heart and what I wrote down on Friday the 8th of Rajab 1426. I ask that Allāh ﷻ will answer Mawlana Shaykh Nāẓim's prayer, since he asked me to engage myself in an intimate discourse with my Lord and ask Him to send us a king so that we may fight in His Way.

I finished writing this at 7:00 p.m., between ʿAṣr and Maghrib prayers. I then went out to renew my ablution and I found a cat sitting outside the door of my room staring at me. I did not know where this cat came from.

Disciplining the Ego

In the *Burdah*, it says:

---

[18] Sūratu 'l-Kahf [The Cave], 18:65.

[19] Sūratu 'l-Baqara [The Heifer],2:282.

وَالنَّفْسُ كَالطِّفْلِ إِنْ تُهْمِلْهُ شَبَّ عَلَى حُبِّ الرَّضَاعِ وَإِنْ تَفْطِمْهُ يَنفَطِمِ

فَاصْرِفْ هَوَاهَا وَحَاذِرْ أَنْ تُوَلِّيَهُ إِنَّ الْهَوَى مَا تَوَلَّى يُصْمِ أَوْ يَصِمِ

Wa'nafsu kā'ṭ-ṭifli in tuhmilhu shabba ʿalā

Ḥubbi 'l-riḍāʿu wa in tafṭimhu yanfaṭimi

faṣrif hawāhā wa ḥādhir an tuwalīyahu

inna'l-hawā mā tawallaw yuṣmi aw yaṣami

The ego is like an infant, if you neglect it,

It will grow up attached to the love of being nursed,

And be fearful of the schemes of hunger and satiation,

For truly eating food will only strengthen the desire for consumption.

There is a big difference between asking to enter seclusion and being ordered into it. Indeed, in all such things, there is a difference between asking to do something and being told to do it. When you ask for something, even something difficult, it is as if you are asking for dessert, for your enjoyment. This is because the ego has a share in that which you asked for. If you ask to enter seclusion and are granted permission to do so, it will be easy to endure because the ego is getting what it wanted. On the other hand, if the ego is suddenly confronted with an order from the shaykh to enter seclusion, it will be extremely difficult to endure because this requires subordinating the ego to the will of the shaykh. The ego will never submit to this willingly. It will attack you with all its armies and satanic methods. It will try to make the reality of the shaykh's order impossible to implement or accept.

This is the reality of the seclusion which I did not seek out. I was ordered to enter this seclusion without notice by Mawlana Shaykh Muḥammad Nāẓim ʿAdil al-Ḥaqqani. His name means "one who is just and true." I hope that with the Justice and Truthfulness of my Lord, Allāh ﷻ, will grant me success in completing this seclusion, for my Lord has full and absolute control over my evil-commanding ego and the ability to purify it from its desires, cut its attachment to the material world, protect it from the tricks of the devil and to cure it from all its ailments.

The ego is a coward, because it comes to defeat you with its countless wild battalions of vile, worldly thoughts and devils marching under its banner. In this way, it is able to defeat you—unless the perfect master is educating, directing and training you. He will be like a roaring lion protecting his cubs from any harm. We hope that, with the blessings of our master Shaykh Muḥammad Nāẓim ʿAdil al-Ḥaqqani, we will enjoy peace and calm from the attacks of the ego, which is scheming against usincessantly .

اعْلَمُوا أَنَّمَا الْحَيَاةُ الدُّنْيَا لَعِبٌ وَلَهْوٌ وَزِينَةٌ وَتَفَاخُرٌ بَيْنَكُمْ وَتَكَاثُرٌ فِي الْأَمْوَالِ وَالْأَوْلَادِ كَمَثَلِ غَيْثٍ أَعْجَبَ الْكُفَّارَ نَبَاتُهُ ثُمَّ يَهِيجُ فَتَرَاهُ مُصْفَرّاً ثُمَّ يَكُونُ حُطَاماً وَفِي الْآخِرَةِ عَذَابٌ شَدِيدٌ وَمَغْفِرَةٌ مِّنَ اللهِ وَرِضْوَانٌ وَمَا الْحَيَاةُ الدُّنْيَا إِلَّا مَتَاعُ الْغُرُورِ

Iʿlamū annamā'l-ḥayatu 'd-dunyā laʿibun wa lahwun wa zīnatun wa tafākhurun baynakum wa takāthurun fi 'l-amwāli wa 'l-awlādi ka-mathāli ghaythin aʿjaba 'l-kuffāra nabātuhu thumma yahīj fatarāhu muṣfarran thumma yakūnu ḥuṭāman wa fi'l-ākhirati ʿadhābun shadīdun wa maghfiratun min'Allāhi wa riḍwānun wa mā'l-ḥayātu'd-dunyā illā matāʿu 'l-ghurūr

Know that the life of this world is only play and amusement, pomp and mutual boasting among you, and rivalry in respect of wealth and children, as the likeness of vegetation after rain, thereof the growth is pleasing to the tiller; afterwards it dries up and you see it turning yellow; then it becomes straw. But in the Hereafter (there is) a severe torment (for the disbelievers, evil-doers), and (there is) Forgiveness from Allāh and (His) Good Pleasure (for the believers, good-doers), whereas the life of this world is only a deceiving enjoyment.[20]

سَابِقُوا إِلَى مَغْفِرَةٍ مِّن رَّبِّكُمْ وَجَنَّةٍ عَرْضُهَا كَعَرْضِ السَّمَاءِ وَالْأَرْضِ أُعِدَّتْ لِلَّذِينَ آمَنُوا بِاللَّهِ وَرُسُلِهِ ذَٰلِكَ فَضْلُ اللَّهِ يُؤْتِيهِ مَن يَشَاءُ وَاللَّهُ ذُو الْفَضْلِ الْعَظِيمِ

Sābiqū ila maghfiratin min rabbikum wa jannaatin ʿarḍuhā ka-ʿarḍi 's-samāwāti wa 'l-arḍi uʿiddat li'lladhīna āmanū billāhi wa rasūlihi dhālika faḍlullaāhi yu'tīhi man yashā'u w'Allāhu dhu'l-faḍli'l-ʿaẓīm

Race one with another in hastening towards Forgiveness from your Lord (Allāh), and towards Paradise, the width whereof is as the width of heaven and earth, prepared for those who believe in Allāh and His Messengers. That is the Grace of Allāh, which He bestows on whom He pleases. And Allāh is the Owner of Great Bouny.[21]

مَا أَصَابَ مِن مُّصِيبَةٍ فِي الْأَرْضِ وَلَا فِي أَنفُسِكُمْ إِلَّا فِي كِتَابٍ مِّن قَبْلِ أَن نَّبْرَأَهَا إِنَّ ذَٰلِكَ عَلَى اللَّهِ يَسِيرٌ

Mā asāba min muṣībatin f i'l-ardi wa lā fī anfusikum illā fī kitābin min qabli an nabraahā inna thālika ʿalā Allāhi yasīr

No calamity befalls on the earth or in yourselves but is inscribed in the Book of Decrees (Al-Lawḥ al-Maḥfūẓ), before We bring it into existence. Verily, that is easy for Allāh .[22]

---

[20] Sūratu'l-Ḥadīd [Iron], 57:20.
[21] Sūratu'l-Ḥadīd [Iron], 57:21.
[22] Sūratu'l-Ḥadīd [Iron], 57:22.

لِكَيْلَا تَأْسَوْا عَلَى مَا فَاتَكُمْ وَلَا تَفْرَحُوا بِمَا آتَاكُمْ وَاللَّهُ لَا يُحِبُّ كُلَّ مُخْتَالٍ فَخُورٍ

Likay lā tā'saw ʿalā mā fātakum wa lā tafraḥū bimā ātākum w'Allāhu lā yuḥibbu kulla mukhtālin fakhūri

In order that you may not be sad over matters that you fail to get, nor rejoice because of that which has been given to you. And Allāh likes not prideful boasters.23

الَّذِينَ يَبْخَلُونَ وَيَأْمُرُونَ النَّاسَ بِالْبُخْلِ وَمَن يَتَوَلَّ فَإِنَّ اللَّهَ هُوَ الْغَنِيُّ الْحَمِيدُ

Alladhīna yabkhalūna wa yā'murūna 'n-nāsa bi 'l-bukhli wa man yatawalla fa inna Allāha huwa 'l-ghaniyyu 'l-ḥamīd

Those who are misers and enjoin upon people miserliness (Allāh is not in need of their charity). And whosoever turns away (from Faith), then Allāh is Rich (free of all wants), Worthy of all praise.[24]

Imagine that you would give all your wealth and all that you have in the material world in return for one day you spent in this world reflecting and contemplating upon Allāh's creation.

الَّذِينَ يَذْكُرُونَ اللَّهَ قِيَاماً وَقُعُوداً وَعَلَىَ جُنُوبِهِمْ وَيَتَفَكَّرُونَ فِي خَلْقِ السَّمَاوَاتِ وَالأَرْضِ رَبَّنَا مَا خَلَقْتَ هَذا بَاطِلاً سُبْحَانَكَ فَقِنَا عَذَابَ النَّارِ

Alladhīna yadhkurūna Allāha qiyāman wa quʿūdan wa ʿalā junūbihim wa yatafakkarūna fī khalqi 's-samāwāti wa 'l-arḍi

[23] Sūratu'l-Ḥadīd [Iron], 57:23.

[24] Sūratu'l-Ḥadīd [Iron], 57:24.

rabbanā mā khalaqta hādhā bāṭilan subḥānaka faqinā ʿadhāba 'n-nār

Those who remember Allāh (always, and in prayers) standing, sitting, and lying down on their sides, and think deeply about the creation of the heavens and the earth, (saying): "Our Lord! You have not created (all) this without purpose, glory to You! (Exalted be You above all that they associate with You as partners). Give us salvation from the torment of the Fire."[25]

To be ordered into seclusion is a mercy for you from your guide. He is giving you forty days to be alone with your Lord, your Prophet and your masters, in the remembrance of Allāh ﷻ.

Three Dangers of Seclusion

There are three main types of antagonistic and destructive thought patterns that attack the seeker, individually or in unison, when he is in seclusion. They are:

1. Boredom

Boredom is like a person who is always present in the room with you, trying to prevent you from focusing on your Lord. He makes the place of seclusion seem gloomy and makes you feel as if you are wasting your time, sitting and doing nothing. When boredom sees you in a state of remembrance, it sends negative thoughts to your heart. It does all this to prevent you from being in seclusion with your Lord, to prevent you from achieving a state of intimacy with Him, to prevent you from ascending to the stations of the gnostic way and unlocking their secrets. Boredom wants to make your seclusion a prison. It does not want you to rise through the stations of divine knowledge, which cause you to shine and ascend to the knowledge of taste.

Those secrets include many sorts of knowledge: universal knowledge, worldly knowledge and heavenly knowledge; knowledge of inanimate and animate things; knowledge of

[25] Sūrat Āli ʿImrān [The Family of ʿImrān], 3:191.

speaking and silent things. This knowledge causes the mind utter bewilderment, because it is the door to the presence of the "Secret of the Secrets of the Essence" سرّ سرّ الذّات which is أنت الله "You are Allāh ." This station will only open to the people of remembrance who are asking insistently to reach this station, as we have mentioned earlier:

Those who remember Allāh (always, and in prayers) standing, sitting, and lying down on their sides, and think deeply about the creation of the heavens and the earth, (saying): "Our Lord! You have not created (all) this without purpose, glory to You! (Exalted be You above all that they associate with You as partners). Give us salvation from the torment of the Fire."[26]

It is hidden in the Secret of the Essence of Divine Knowledge in the Name الله Allāh ﷻ, the Name of Majesty that encompass all the Names and Attributes, The Name which points to Him, without any limitation. These secrets are between the أ (the "A," or *alif*), which is standing straight. This shows that everything needs the support of the *alif* to be straight. An example is: اسلام, ايمان, احسان, أحمد (Islam, *Īmān*, *Iḥsān*, Āḥmad) they all need the station of straightness in order to exist, since their existence is established by Allāh ﷻ.

alif is the first letter of the alphabet. Nothing precedes it, but it precedes all the other letters and their meanings. That is why the opening surah of the Holy Qur'an is al-Fāṭiḥah, which begins with the أ of الحَمْدُ لله. The second surah in the Qur'an, al-Baqarah, also begins with the أ of ألم. Likewise, the Basmalah where the أ was omitted in بسم, but in reality it is ب ا سم. The name الله is spelled أ ل ل ه. It begins with the أ, and is then followed by the two لل (*Lām Lām*) within which the secrets were effaced and veiled. It veiled their meaning with the ه (*hāh*), which encompasses all knowledge and points to the القدرة النورانية "the enlightening power" that will be a witness of Divine Unity for you. All of these

[26] Sūrat Āli 'Imrān [The Family of 'Imrān], 3:191.

secrets will collectively pour into the أ and will witness the Uniqueness for you. This station begins with the أ of "أحدية" *Āḥadīyyah* (Uniqueness). The Station of Uniqueness is the station of witnessing, which is why when *Sayyīdinā* Bilāl was tortured he would cry أحد أحد *"Āḥad, Āḥad."* He was witnessing the dressings of light that were descending on him from the heavens; the dressings of light which were decorated with the majesty, beauty and perfection of the Names and Attributes that are from the light of the face of the Messenger of Allāh ﷺ; from أحمد Āḥmad, his name in the heavens. Āḥmad begins with the أ, which his Lord manifested on him. He then took it and gave it as a gift to *Sayyīdinā* Bilāl at the Station of Uniqueness with the special, pure light—pure with the beauty, intimacy and intensifying of the lights of Allāh ﷻ.

This boredom you experience in seclusion is one of the ways your ego tries to prevent you from reaching these lights and knowledge. But he is unable to be a companion or a friend who can make your loneliness easier to bear.

2.Worry

Worry is the feeling people experience when they make a mistake and their conscience makes them feel guilty about it. Through worry, failure comes. When worry attacks, a feeling of guilt sets in that causes the seeker to feel that he is failing. The way to fight worry is to be patient and to challenge yourself to improve and do better. Not being patient will cause you to fall into the claws of worldly enjoyment. This is because after acting impatiently, you will later feel feel that you have failed (your assigned task), and this feeling is one of the main ruinous traits of the lower self. If you are unable to face the challenge and persist to success, then your worst enemy will cause you to suffer a nervous breakdown. You will become harsh, disoriented and fragmented. This will lead you to believe that there is no point in continuing the struggle, because there is no hope of success. This in turn will cause you to turn away from your spiritual exertions and immerse yourself in the worldly life. When you yield to this, the material world will close in on you from every side, making you its slave.

However, if you are able to remain patient and persist until you succeed, the material world will become your slave instead. As the poet said:

فالدُنيا أميرَةَ من طلبَها وخادِمةَ من تَرَكهَا.

"The material world is a princess over those who seek it, and a servant for those who rebuff it."

فهي طالِبة ومَطلوبَةً فمن طلبَها رفضَتهُ ومن رفَضَها طَلَبَته.

"It seeks and it is sought. Whoever seeks it, it rejects; whoever rejects it, it seeks."

ألدُنيا جِسرُ الآخرة فاعبُروها ولا تَعمرُوها

"This material world is a bridge to the Hereafter, so cross over it and do not build it."

فخِلِّ الدُنيا ولا تذكُرها واذكُر الآخِرة ولا تنسَها

"Leave this world alone and do not remember it, and remember the Hereafter and do not forget it."

خُذ من الدُنيا ما يُبَلِّغُكَ الآخِرة ولا تأخُذ من الدُنيا ما يمنَعُكَ الآخرَة

"Take from this world what aids you to reach the Hereafter, and take not from this world what prevents you from reaching the Hereafter."

Or as Sayyīdinā 'Alī ؓ said:

كما قال سيدُنا علي: اعمل لدُنياكَ كأنكَ تَعيشُ أبداً واعمَل لآخرَتِك كأنكَ تموتُ غداً ثُمَ زادَ على قدرِ مقدارِكَ فيها.

> "Work for your worldly life as if you will live forever, and work for the Hereafter as you will die tomorrow; then he added: in proportion to the length of time you will stay in each."

The Prophet ﷺ expanded on this point when he took his Companions to the mountain of Uḥud. It was at the time of the sunrise; he stood behind them with his back to the east and told them to look to the mountain ahead of them. When they looked, they saw that their shadows were ahead of them. The Prophet ﷺ told them that he would give his mantle to whoever was able to catch his shadow before reaching the mountain. Out of love for the Prophet ﷺ, they all ran trying to catch their shadow, but to no avail. When they all had reached the mountain, the Messenger ﷺ asked them to turn and look at him. When they turned towards him their shadows were cast behind them. The Messenger ﷺ then asked them to run to him, and as they ran their shadows ran after them. He then told them "Whoever turns towards me, towards the Hereafter, this world will run after him; and whoever turns to this material world, he will spend his life running after it without being able to catch it."

This is why it was said:

الدُنيا جِيفة وطُلاَّبُها كِلاب

> "This world is carcass, and those seeking it are dogs."

The only things you will take with from this world are your deeds. If your deeds were done in Allāh's Way and the Messenger's Way, you have won and succeeded. If your deeds were done for other than Allāh ﷻ, for the sake of your material pleasures, then Satan has cheated you and thrown you in the filth of the sewage and garbage—and the garbage of this worldly life has such a terrible stench, the mountains would crumble were they able to smell it.

When you feel that you have failed in your spiritual endeavor, you will immerse yourself in this worldly life. You will forget to thank Allāh ﷻ for the great honor and favor He gave to you: the grant of creating you as a member of the nation of the Beloved of Allāh ﷻ, the nation of al-Muṣṭafā ﷺ. This is the greatest favor bestowed on a servant of Allāh ﷻ. That is why we have to show our gratitude by continuously thanking Allāh ﷻ. As our master ʿAlī ؓ said:

النعمةَ موصولةٌ بالشُكر والشُكر يتعلق بالمزيدا فلن ينقَطِع المزيدَ

من الله حتى ينقَطِع الشُكرَ من العبدِ

"The favor is connected to gratitude, and gratitude is connected to receiving more; receiving more from Allāh will not stop, until the servant stops thanking."

It was also said:

من عظّم النعمَة شكَرها ومن شكَرَها استوجبَ المزيد

"Whoever appreciates and honors the favor, he will be thankful for receiving it; and whoever is thankful for receiving it, he is qualified to receive more."

O servant of Allāh ﷻ, you must thank Him for Him to give you more.

وبالشكر تدومُ النِعَم

through gratitude favors are made to continue.

As our Lord mentioned:

وَإِذْ تَأَذَّنَ رَبُّكُمْ لَئِن شَكَرْتُمْ لأَزِيدَنَّكُمْ وَلَئِن كَفَرْتُمْ إِنَّ عَذَابِي لَشَدِيدٌ

And (remember) when your Lord proclaimed: "If you give thanks, I will give you more (of My Blessings).[27]

Do not let worries and failure make you forget to be thankful to Allāh ﷻ for His favors. As was said:

من لم يستغني بالله أحوجَهُ الله إلى الخلقِ ومن إستغنى بالله أحوجَ الله الخَلقَ إليهِ

"Whoever is not content with Allāh, Allāh will make him in need of created beings; and whoever is content with Allāh, Allāh will make created beings in need for him."

So always be content with Allāh ﷻ, empower yourself and fight worries and failure with a power granted from Allāh ﷻ. You need to do this in order to fend off Satan, who is always seeking you and trying to tempt you with the pleasures of this world, constantly striving to make you lose your focus on the Hereafter.

The Hereafter is المزيد *al-mazīd*, "the increase," which refers to Allāh's ﷻ abundant increase that is the life to come. If your actions are righteous, then you will find this "increase" in Heaven. This is what the Qur'an is referring to when it states:

وِمِنْهُم مَّن يَقُولُ رَبَّنَا آتِنَا فِي الدُّنْيَا حَسَنَةً وَفِي الآخِرَةِ حَسَنَةً وَقِنَا عَذَابَ النَّارِ

Wa minhum man yaqūlu rabbanā ātinā fi 'd-dunyā ḥasanatan wa fi 'l-ākhirati ḥasanatan wa qinā ʿadhāba 'n-nār.

And of them there are some who say: "Our Lord! Give us in this world that which is good and in the Hereafter that which is good, and save us from the torment of the Fire!"[28]

---

[27] Sūrah Ibrāhīm, [Abraham], 14:7.

[28] Sūratu 'l-Baqara [The Heifer],2:201.

Here, Allāh ﷻ refers to an "increase" in the blessings of both this world and the next. This is for those who remain steadfast in their pursuit of righteousness. However, for those who abandon that path after failure and worry overtake them, and turn instead to the pursuit of worldly desires, for those who become impatient with the hardships of their tests and yield to Satan and his minions, for them Allāh ﷻ has also promised an "increase":

يَوْمَ نَقُولُ لِجَهَنَّمَ هَلِ امْتَلَأْتِ وَتَقُولُ هَلْ مِن مَّزِيدٍ

Yawma taqūlu li-jahannama hali'mtalāti fataqūlu hal min mazīd.

On the Day when We will say to Hell: "Are you filled?" It will say: "Are there any more (to come)?"[29]

Thus, those who in this worldly life follow Satan will also find an "increase," but theirs will be an increase in punishment in the fires of Hell.

This is why it is important for you to seek knowledge and gnosticism, in order to avoid being ensnared by the pleasures of this material world. Knowing will keep you with a perfect master; one who is an expert in the sciences of the *ṭarīqah* (the Sufi path) and the *sharīʿah* (Islamic law). Such a master knows how to keep you from becoming easy prey for Satan and he will lead you down the Straight Path.

The Key to the Journey is Patience

This journey will be an arduous one. It will require that you learn patience. It is a journey from one shoreline to another through a tempestuous ocean. Although this ocean has no beginning and no end, you have to persist in your seeking. You must learn from what you see on this endless ocean. You must dive to its bottom and bring out its realities. All of these realities

[29] Sūrah Qāf, 50:30.

are with your master, who is aware of your states, day and night. But it is incumbent on you to learn through experience and journeying, because knowledge is not attained through books and memorizing alone. Such knowledge is only knowledge of paper "علم الاوراق"; real knowledge comes with persistence, expertise and learning through experience. Acquiring this authentic knowledge requires immense patience. Through patience, all aims can be attained.

Indeed, it has been said:

الصبر مفتاح الفرج

"Patience is the key for relief."

You have to be patient with everything your shaykh sends your way. He knows the right medicine for your condition, but he will not administer it until you become desperate.

Imam Shāfiʿī said:

تصَّبَّر على طول الجفى من مُعلِمٍ   فإن رُسوخ العِلمِ في نفَراته

ومن لم يَذُق مرَّ التعَلُمِ ساعَة   تجرَّعَ ذُلَّ الجَهلِ طولَ حياتِه

ومن فاتَه التعَليم وقتَ شبابِه   فكبِّر عليهِ أربعاً لوفاتِه

حياةُ الفتى والله بالعِلمِ والتُقى   إذا لم يكونا لا إعتِبار لذاتِهِ

Be patient with long periods of harshness towards you from the teacher

Through his distaste for you, knowledge sinks roots within you

Whoever when learning did not taste an hour of bitterness

Will drink the humiliation of ignorance all his life

The one who missed learning during his youth

Then make four *takbīrs* on him at his funeral (confirming his death)

I swear by Allāh ﷻ that the life of a youth is through knowledge and piety

And if he possesses these not, then his life has no value.

If you have this patience, they will open for you and Allāh's Divine Providence will reach you. His "Divine Breeze" will reach you. As the Sulṭān of Saints mentioned about the three nails you have to put in front of your eyes Grandshaykh ʿAbd Allāh, may Allāh sanctify his soul, often reminded us, "You must always keep three nails tacked to your forehead (remember these three rules at all times if you want to succeed in *ṭarīqah*):

If I give you a broken shovel and tell you to dig down until you reach the middle of the Earth to get your diamonds, you dig. You never ask why or complain; you just dig.

If I give you a bucket and say "Empty the ocean!" don't ask if the water will ever decrease, or argue it is impossible: just start scooping! The second you think the task is impossible, impractical, or useless, you failed that test and will have to start all over again.

If I tell the ant her sustenance is in the West and she is in the East, she will just start walking. The *murīd* must be like that ant: do not use your mind to understand how you will get your sustenance, just go! If you die trying, you die, you surrender."

Other sayings about patience and learning include:

العلمَ بالتعَلُم والعِلم بالتحَلُم

Knowledge is attained by learning, and knowledge is attained through forbearance,

العلم في الصِغر كالنَقشِ على الحَجَر

Learning during childhood is like engraving on stone,

من علَّمني حرفاً صِرتُ لهُ عبداً

Whoever taught me a letter I became his slave.

Knowledge Uplifts the Seeker

Knowledge is very important. That is why, when the Children of Israel asked their prophet to send them a king fight in Allāh's Way, he sent them Ṭālūt. When they objected to his assignment because he was not wealthy, their prophet said:

وَقَالَ لَهُمْ نَبِيُّهُمْ إِنَّ اللهَ قَدْ بَعَثَ لَكُمْ طَالُوتَ مَلِكاً قَالُوَاْ أَنَّى يَكُونُ لَهُ الْمُلْكُ عَلَيْنَا وَنَحْنُ أَحَقُّ بِالْمُلْكِ مِنْهُ وَلَمْ يُؤْتَ سَعَةً مِّنَ الْمَالِ قَالَ إِنَّ اللهَ اصْطَفَاهُ عَلَيْكُمْ وَزَادَهُ بَسْطَةً فِي الْعِلْمِ وَالْجِسْمِ وَاللهُ يُؤْتِي مُلْكَهُ مَن يَشَاءُ وَاللهُ وَاسِعٌ عَلِيمٌ

Wa qāla lahum nabīyyuhum inna Allāha qad baʿatha lakum ṭālūta malikan qālū annā yakūnu lahu 'l-mulku ʿalaynā wa naḥnu aḥaqqu bi 'l-mulki minhu wa lam yuta saʿatan mina 'l-māli qāla inna Allāha iṣṭafāhu ʿalaykum wa zādahu basṭatan fi 'l-ʿilmi wa'l-jismi w'Allāhu yutī mulkahu man yashāo w'Allāhu wāsiʿun ʿalīm.

Their Prophet said to them: "(Allāh) hath appointed Ṭālūt as king over you." They said: "How can he exercise authority over us when we are better fitted than he to exercise authority, and he is not even gifted, with wealth in abundance?" He said: "(Allāh) hath Chosen him above you, and hath gifted him abundantly with knowledge and bodily prowess: Allāh

Granteth His authority to whom He pleaseth. Allāh careth for all, and He knoweth all things."[30]

The phrase "He has increased him abundantly in knowledge" means that Ṭālūt was given knowledge from the Divine Presence, knowledge of Gnosticism, knowledge of realities, knowledge of taste, and knowledge of the power of light. He was given knowledge from the Secret of the Essence, meaning from the secret of the realities by which my master 'Abd al-Qādir al-Jilānī used to supplicate to Allāh ﷻ:

اللهم إني أسألُك بسِرِّ الذَّات وبذاتِ السِر هو أنتَ وأنتَ هو

"O Allāh, I am asking You through the Secret of the Essence and the Essence of the Secret, He is You and You are He."

The Prophet Reached the Highest Hidden Realities

His Lord had given him from the Prophet's ﷺ reality, as He also gave the prophets from the Muḥammadan ﷺ reality. He gave his saints from the manifestations of the elevated Names and Attributes of Allāh ﷻ, he gave them from the names of His beloved Chosen One, al-Musṭafā ﷺ, He gave them from the meanings of the specific intricate realities that deliver the seeker to the highest sought-after goals. This is the greatest goal, it is the station that will connect you and point you to the meaning of the eternal secrets, and the immemorial, unique Essence with its attraction to those who love it. This is so because of Its exquisite administering and due to Its being from the secret of Lordship, which is above and beyond time and space. This station is unique in relieving hardship, sins and worries. How can it be otherwise when He holds in His hand the Power, Grandeur and Omnipotence—when He causes life and death? There is nothing before Him, nor is there anything after Him. He is above causality

[30] Sūratu 'l-Baqara [The Heifer],2:247.

and the realm of causes. No one can understand the meaning at this station except "a Messenger He is pleased with," meaning Allāh's Messenger Muḥammad ﷺ.

Muḥammad ﷺ is able to reach, to understand and to know that which Allāh ﷻ desired him to reach. Allāh ﷻ raised him to the station of قابَ قوسَيْنِ أوْ أدْنى *qaaba qawsayni aw adnā, "two bows length or nearer."*[31] He revealed to him the Secret of Secrets, the contents of the unseen lights and the circumference of the circle of the universes of the Essence. He plunged him into the ocean of the light of the standing *alif*, which is not preceded by anything else. Through this letter beings were created. It is evidence for the power of administrating, because it is the first letter of Allāh's Name, which encompasses all Names and Attributes: Allāh ﷻ. It governs the rest of the letters, whether fiery, earthly, airey or watery—the four elements from which all things were created. It is like the shining sun which enters into every form, and without which there would be no human life.

(Our Lord!) Through the *alif* everything comes into existence in its inner and outer reality. It is the letter that applies Your Decree on that which does not exist, causing it to exist, and on everything which exists compelling it (to Your Will). By the Truth of Your Compelling Attributes, I ask you my Lord to send us a king to lead the struggle in Your Way, in defeating Your enemy and ours, and in defeating the devils of our egos. Please deliver us from the confusion and torments of this world. Open for us the hearing of our hearts, until we no longer hear, see or love anything that You do not love. Cause us by Your Grace, to be in Your Presence and in the presence of Your greatest Messenger ﷺ.

Our Lord, You are exalted above having partners. You are the Knower of that which is hidden in the soul and the conscience. Grant us a favor from Your Illuminating Grants, knowledge from Your Self-subsisting Knowledge, a heart from the Reality of Your

---

[31] Sūratu 'n-Najm [The Star], 53:9.

Pre-eternal Power. O Raḥmān (Most Munificent) of this World and of the Hereafter, You have been merciful without exception from the Secret of Your Name Ar-Raḥmān, which brings hearts closer together, pulling hearts together with the Compassion of Your Name Ar-Raḥīm (The Most Merciful).

These two Honorable Names have tremendous healing power and are a source of blessings for every believer asking for little or for much, for worldly or spiritual matters. O Allāh, keep our hearts in the remembrance of these two Names and for their honor, send us a king to lead us in the struggle in Your Way.

When Allāh ﷻ told the Children of Israel that He was sending them Ṭālūt (Saul) as a king, they objected because Ṭālūt was not wealthy. Their prophet told them that Allāh ﷻ had increased him in knowledge and stature. Allāh ﷻ made him a knower in their worldly affairs and in the matters of their Hereafter.

As we have said earlier, knowledge is the most important thing a servant can ask for:

وَقُل رَّبِّ زِدْنِي عِلْماً

Wa qul rabbi zidnī ʿilma

and say, "My Lord, increase me in knowledge."[32]

فَوَجَدَا عَبْداً مِّنْ عِبَادِنَا آتَيْنَاهُ رَحْمَةً مِنْ عِندِنَا وَعَلَّمْنَاهُ مِن لَّدُنَّا عِلْماً

They found a servant from amongst our servant whom we have given a mercy from Our presence and whom we taught knowledge from Our Divine Presence.[33]

وَاتَّقُواْ اللهَ وَيُعَلِّمُكُمُ اللهُ وَاللهُ بِكُلِّ شَيْءٍ عَلِيمٌ

---

[32] Sūrah ṬāḤā 20:114.

[33] Sūratu 'l-Kahf [The Cave], 18:65.

And be aware of Allāh and Allāh will teach you, and Allāh is all knowing of everything.[34]

The knowledge referred to in these verses is heavenly knowledge. May our Lord teach us from the knowledge that is stored as a hidden treasure, so that we may know You as we ought to, so that we may reach the station of:

وَفَوْقَ كُلِّ ذِي عِلْمٍ عَلِيمٌ

.. and above every knower, there is another who knows more.[35]

and manifest in us the verse:

...وَعَلَّمْنَاهُ مِن لَّدُنَّا عِلْماً

...whom we taught him knowledge from Our Divine Presence.[36]

Seeking a Divinely-Ordained King

O my Lord, You have explained in this verse the symbol of his kingship:

وَقَالَ لَهُمْ نِبِيُّهُمْ إِنَّ آيَةَ مُلْكِهِ أَن يَأْتِيَكُمُ التَّابُوتُ فِيهِ سَكِينَةٌ مِّن رَّبِّكُمْ وَبَقِيَّةٌ مِّمَّا تَرَكَ آلُ مُوسَى وَآلُ هَارُونَ تَحْمِلُهُ الْمَلآئِكَةُ إِنَّ فِي ذَلِكَ لآيَةً لَّكُمْ إِن كُنتُم مُّؤْمِنِينَ

And their prophet (Samuel) said to them: "Verily! The sign of His Kingdom is that there shall come to you the Ark of the Covenant (at-Tābūt), wherein is peace and reassurance (sakīnah) from your Lord and a remnant of that which Mūsā

---

[34] Sūratu 'l-Baqara [The Heifer],2:282.
[35] Sūrah Yūsuf [Joseph], 12:76.
[36] Sūratu 'l-Kahf [The Cave], 18:65.

(Moses) and Harūn (Aaron) left behind, carried by the angels. Verily, in this is a sign for you if you are indeed believers.[37]

It has been related that the *sakīnah* that came to them was comprised of three types.

The first is the Ark of the Covenant, which the angels brought to the Children of Israel, in which there was *sakīnah* from their Lord. This *sakīnah* is the "breeze of knowledge." It is a good and peaceful breeze that comes from the mouth of the knower of Allāh ﷻ. The sound coming from the mouth of the knower of Allāh ﷻ fills the heart of the enemies (Satan and his followers) with terror, because the knower's heart and tongue are busy with the remembrance and wisdom of Allāh ﷻ. This is the secret in *sakīnah*.

The second one is the divine inspiration that finds its way to the tongue of the knower of Allāh, for among the subtleties of the doings of the True One, al-Ḥaqq, is the casting of wisdom upon His friends, and from there to their tongues, just as an angel would cast revelation into the hearts of the prophets, fanning the secrets therein and the revealing the inner understandings that are hidden within the intimate self, enshrouded by the thick clouds of hidden idolatry. The knower of Allāh is able to disperse these dense clouds by finding that hidden idolatry and casting it out. He is able to do so through the knowledge that Allāh ﷻ bestows upon him from the Lights of His Beautiful Names and Attributes.

The third is the one that was revealed to the heart of the Prophet ﷺ and to the hearts of his inheritors. This *sakīnah* has in it light, power and spirit. It causes those who are afraid to be at peace, due to the grandeur, power, omnipotence and reverence of Allāh ﷻ. It is also a solace for the melancholy one swimming in the Godly oceans of infatuation. His thirst will not be quenched, nor will his ailment heal without this *sakīnah* entering his heart. As Allāh ﷻ revealed in this verse:

---

[37] Sūratu 'l-Baqara [The Heifer],2:248.

ثُمَّ أَنزَلَ اللهُ سَكِينَتَهُ عَلَىٰ رَسُولِهِ وَعَلَى الْمُؤْمِنِينَ

Then Allāh did send down His Sakīnah (calmness, tranquility and reassurance) on the Messenger (Muḥammad), and on the believers.[38]

From this we can observe that the Ark symbolizes something very important, something that carries the body and the form, and that is the heart.

الا في الجِسدِ مُضغَة إذا صلُحَت صلُحَ الجَسدُ كُله وإذا فسُدَت فسُدَ الجَسد كله ألا وهو القَلب

The Prophet ﷺ said:
"In the body there is a piece of flesh if it is healthy, the whole body will be healthy, it is the heart."

The *sakīnah* is the knowledge, sincerity and remembrance of Allāh residing in the heart and that causes it to be content and at peace. *Sakīnah* enters the heart of the knower when his heart becomes an abode for knowledge and loyalty. This is the secret of knowledge; it is the springboard of all knowledge of universes and of created beings.

Allāh ﷻ said:

وَعَلَّمَ آدَمَ الأَسْمَاء كُلَّهَا ثُمَّ عَرَضَهُمْ عَلَى الْمَلاَئِكَةِ فَقَالَ أَنبِئُونِي بِأَسْمَاء هَـؤُلاء إِن كُنتُمْ صَادِقِينَ

And He taught Adam all the names (of everything), then He showed them to the angels and said, "Tell Me the names of these if you are truthful."[39]

Allāh ﷻ taught Adam ﵇ the knowledge of all that He created—of all that is other than Allāh . He taught Adam the place

[38] Sūratu 'l-Anfāl, [The Spoils], 8,

[39] Sūratu 'l-Baqara [The Heifer],2:31.

and station of everything. He taught him about the reality of His beloved al-Muṣṭafā ﷺ when He informed him:

لو لاك لو لاك ما خلقت الافلاك

> "If it was not for Muḥammad ﷺ, I would not have created any of My Creation."[40]

This is why Adam ؑ sought the intercession of Muḥammad ﷺ when he repented to Allāh ﷻ. Allāh accepted his repentance, because of the intercession of the Messenger ﷺ. This is important information for us to use whenever we are faced with any hardship or calamity, and whenever we are seeking to be closer to Allāh ﷻ.

Thus, our understanding of what is signified by the words of our Lord *"The sign of His Kingdom is that there shall come to you the Ark of the Covenant, wherein is sakīnah"* become very clear. The sign of his kingship is the vice-regency, through which the servant becomes the vicegerent of The Merciful ﷻ. With the attribute of Majesty, He inspires the self to be rebellious; with the attribute of Honor, He inspires the self to be pious. For as our Lord said:

فَأَلْهَمَهَا فُجُورَهَا وَتَقْوَاهَا

Then He inspired the self its rebellion and piety.[41]

He did not entrust the self to a close angel, nor did He entrust it to a prophet or messenger. There is a big difference between a nation whose *sakīnah*, their love and their hearts, are open to the enemies of Allāh ﷻ and a nation whose *sakīnah* is for their Lord and in His presence through the intercession of the Master of the sons of Adam, Owner of the beatific presence, the splendid image and the breeze of beauty. He is the Master of masters, the Owner of intercession and the Intercessor on behalf of the nation: our master Muḥammad ﷺ and his inheritors, the

---

[40] While this particular wording is not authenticated to the Prophet ﷺ, the meaning is true, and there are many ahadith to this effect.
[41] Sūratu 'sh-Shams [The Sun], 91:8.

saints—his companions and assistants in purifying the nation from the desecration of Satan.

The Ark of the Muhammadan Nation

If Allāh ﷻ made Ṭālūt king for the Children of Israel, surely He is sending in every age an inheritor of His Prophet ﷺ who is carrying the banner of the beloved Musṭafā ﷺ, inscribing the praise of Allāh ﷻ upon the hearts of his followers and guiding them to the presence of the All-Knowing King. The same goes for the rest of the saints, each according to his or her level. If the Children of Israel found the Torah in the Ark of the Covenant, Allāh ﷻ put in the Ark of this Muḥammadan nation the whole tablet of the Holy Qur'an. If in the Ark of the Children of Israel they found the images of their prophets, in the Ark of the Muḥammadan nation—the Ark of our hearts—there are only seclusions in which there is no one but Allāh ﷻ.

This is why seclusion is obligatory for every disciple by the order of his master, in order for this secret to manifest in him. He will then become one who is carrying the ark of the heart with all its Muḥammadan contents of Lordly, angelic and beatific majesty. Through seclusion, this hadith of the Prophet ﷺ manifests:

يقول الله : ما وسعني أرضي ولا سمائي ولكن وسعني قلب عبدي المؤمن

> Allāh, the Exalted, said, "Neither heavens nor earth contained Me, but the heart of My believing servant contained Me."[42]

What we conclude, then, is that in the same way in which Ṭālūt was granted kingship through his possession of Allāh's Knowledge, which He taught him in abundance, the soul of man is able to receive the ark of Lordly knowledge and become a knower of the science of hearts through the knowledge of Allāh ﷻ

[42] Al-Ghazālī mentioned it in his *Revival of the Religious Sciences.*

and godly power. Such a person will be granted the vicegerency and the seat of power. He will be entrusted with inheritance of truly human character. He will not be complacent with this treacherous, scheming material world. He will migrate from it and prepare himself to fight Jālūt, representing the evil-commanding ego, which asserts control the body with the aid of devils and sinister thoughts.

If such power can be given to the human soul, what kind of power is given to the inheritor of Muḥammad ﷺ, the Sulṭān of Saints, the Reliever and Owner of the Age? He is given a power from the secret of the Perfect Man, the one whom Allāh ﷻ has perfected in all the attributes He bestowed upon him. He is the master of the Two Universes, master of Men and Jinn. He is Muḥammad ﷺ, the Messenger of Allāh .

Then understand—O servant who is humbled by his Lord—that if not for your shaykh who delivered you to the Muḥammadan Presence, you would be nothing. You are everything with your shaykh and nothing without him. Therefore, you have to see things as the shaykh sees them. You have to do what he asks of you, because the shaykh is always in the presence of the Prophet ﷺ, receiving from him, and the Prophet ﷺ is always in the presence of The Knower of the Unseen, ʿAlimu 'l-Ghayb.

Know that whoever wants to receive more must commit to *aṭ-ṭarīqah*, the Sufi Path, to follow a perfect guide and thus to hold fast to the truth. By doing this he will achieve the Godly Gnosticism, *sakīnah* will enter his heart, and he will finally know true peace and contentment.

The Kings of the Heart Demolish All Its Idols

When the saint Abū Yazīd was asked about Gnosticism, he said that the Quran said:

قَالَتْ إِنَّ الْمُلُوكَ إِذَا دَخَلُوا قَرْيَةً أَفْسَدُوهَا وَجَعَلُوا أَعِزَّةَ أَهْلِهَا أَذِلَّةً وَكَذَلِكَ يَفْعَلُونَ

She said: "Verily! Kings, when they enter a town (country), they despoil it, and make the most honorable amongst its people low. And thus they do."[43]

One meaning for this verse is that when the saints—who are the kings of the spiritual realm—enter into the hearts of their followers, they deposit their secrets in there. These cause the follower to reach to the presence of the Prophet ﷺ, and after that to reach to the presence of the True One ﷻ. The saints will make the honored statues in their heart humiliated. These statues—the satanic images that are stored in the mud of the egos of the sons of Adam, mixed with the blood that flows in their veins—are glorified by their egos, but the saints will topple them.

Allāh ﷻ said of these saints:

أَلا إِنَّ أَوْلِيَاء اللّهِ لاَ خَوْفٌ عَلَيْهِمْ وَلاَ هُمْ يَحْزَنُونَ

No doubt! Verily, the friends of Allāh (saints), no fear shall come upon them nor shall they grieve.[44]

This means that, in their war against the devils entrenched in the hearts of their followers, the saints have no fear because they are supported by the True One ﷻ, al-Ḥaqq. They are strong through Allāh ﷻ. That is why they have no fear as they even enter into the bloodstream of the disciple. They hunt down the devils in their bodies and throw them out humiliated and defeated. These saints are powerful; they are experts in the games and schemes of devils. This is the reason they order the disciple to enter into seclusion, to cast out from him the confusions of the material world and cut the attachment of his ego to the material pleasures and the whisperings of devils. Blessed are those who are ordered by their shaykh to enter into seclusion at least once in their lifetime, because this will allow them to attain the greatest blessing: peace, tranquility and contentment.

---

[43] Sūratu 'n-Naml [The Ant], 27:3,4.

[44] Sūrah Yūnus [Jonah], 10:62.

Praise be to Allāh, the Lord of the Worlds, for every state, the number of the breaths of created beings. And ﷺ.

*****

The seclusion will make you see after you had been blind, since Allāh ﷻ said:

وَمَن كَانَ فِي هَـٰذِهِ أَعْمَىٰ فَهُوَ فِي الآخِرَةِ أَعْمَىٰ وَأَضَلُّ سَبِيلاً

And whoever is blind in this world, will be blind in the Hereafter, and more astray from the Path.[45]

If you are drowning in the pleasures of this world, you will be prevented from seeing the lights of the Hereafter. The Hereafter here means witnessing the enlightening power to which you will have access by staying connected to your shaykh.

Rābiṭah, the connection between your heart and the heart of your shaykh, is one of the most important tools that you are given. It will connect you to the wire of your shaykh. It is the electrical charge or the magnetic force through which you will receive the spiritual emanations. For some it is like a common phone line through which they can hear voices. For the more advanced followers, it becomes a fiber-optic line through which they are able to receive the image of all things around them, allowing them to see using the binoculars of the shaykh.

In this station, these tools will have great importance: observing, meditating, seeing with true vision and reflecting. Through them, you will be able to observe things, to meditate upon them, to reflect upon their wisdom and penetrate their realities.

Understanding this, the servant should give great importance to these five secrets:

- الرابطة *ar-rābiṭah,* Connection
- المراقبة *al-murāqabah,* Observation
- التأمل *at-ta'amul,* Meditation

[45] Sūratu 'l-Isrā [The Night Journey], 17:72.

- التفكر *at-tafakkur*, Reflection
- التبصُر *at-tabaṣṣur*, True vision

In all these practices, you must always be observing and in the company of your shaykh until the lights of these realities uncover themselves to you from the Ocean of the Realities of the Divine Presence. These realities are stored in the Treasurehouses of the Secrets of the absolute He-ness, which is safeguarded in the Essence of the Reality of Allāh's Greatest Name. Through this Name, you will be able to open the storehouses of the heavens and the earth and you will be able to rise in ascension to the presence of the True One ﷻ.

Blessed are those who have taken initiation with a perfect shaykh, because they have tied themselves to him and he is tied to the Messenger of Allāh ﷺ, who is the secret of the secrets related to the realities of created beings and the intricate Godly meanings. These meanings were deposited in the Oceans of the Essence. *Sayyīdinā* Muḥammad ﷺ receives from:

فهوَ يتَلَقّى مِن سِر الحقيقَة الكُنهية المخفِيَّة في سِر هو الله والله هو الله وبذاتِ السِّر الذي هوَ أنتَ وأنتَ هوَ

"the Secret of the Reality of the very Essence which is hidden in the Secret of *Huwa Allāh w'Allāh u Huwa Allāh* (He is Allāh and Allāh is He, Allāh), and from the Essence of the secret, which is: *wa bi-Dhāt as-sirr alladhī Hūwa Anta wa Anta Hūwa* (He is You and You are He)."

Understand, if you are from the people of unveiling and vision! The people of unveiling and vision are able to open the hidden vault of *Bismillah.* Its locks are their trust in Allāh ﷻ; its keys are *Lā ḥawla wa lā quwwata illa billāh* (there is neither ability nor power, except through Allāh). Only through Allāh's Strength and Power are they able to enter through special entryways, which open for them through the intercession of the Messenger ﷺ.

There, they will be given what no eye has ever seen, what no ear has ever heard and what no heart has ever conceived. They will then enter into the Ocean of the Names through:

بعَظيم قديم كَريم مَكنون مخزون هذهِ البُحوراً ويتعَرَّفون بمعرِفة خاصة إلى أنواع أجناس رُقوم نُقوش أنوار العِزة للهاً فَبعَزيز إعزاز عِزَّت الله يجولون بقُدرَة مقدار اقتِدار تحَمُلِهم لتَجلِّيات سِعة بِساط رحمة اللهاً فتُفتَح لهم بوارِق صواعِق عَجيج وهيج بهيج رهيج أنوار الذات التي تُبهِر الأنظاراً فتَصعَق الحقائق على بابِها كما صعِق موسى عندما تجَلى ربُهُ للجَبَل. فتُدرِك هُناكَ سِرَّ الوِحدانية الأزَلية المُترَبِطة بالأَحدية المُطلقة وبالهيكلِيات العُلويَّة والرُوحانيّات التي هي أملاك عَرش اللهاً أي ملائكة العَرش وبالاملاك الروحانيين المُديرين للكَواكِب والأفلاك

"The greatness, antiquity, generosity, hidden content, stored content of these oceans; where they will learn from Allāh's special knowledge about the kinds, types, numbers, engravings, lights of Allāh's Might; with the honor and empowerment of Allāh's Power, they will roam with power according to the quantity and their ability to carry the manifestation of the vast abundance of Allāh's Mercy. While there, the shining, flashing, thunderous, weeping, blazing, splendorous, dazzling lights of the Essence will open for them, stunning the vision. They will will become thunderstruck by the realities at that door, just as Prophet Moses ﷺ was thunderstruck when his Lord manifested His Attributes on the mountain. At that time, you will understand the secret of Eternal

> Oneness, which is related to the Absolute Uniqueness, to the heavenly and spiritual structures that are the angels of the Throne of Allāh and the angels that manage the planets and the orbits.

Because of the burning love for God these angels possess, their yearning and moaning will be poured into the heart of that *walī* (saint) who will be standing at the threshold, dumbfounded by these views, thunderstruck by these manifestations and astonished by this knowledge. There, he will experience the absolute oblivion of everything other than Allāh ﷻ.

This is the state I was in, O reader; these are the drawings and words that were cast upon me on the Night of Ascension, Tuesday, 26th of Rajab, 1426. I received it from the lights of these realities, which overtook my thinking and my mind. It then entered into my heart, only to come out through my pen, writing what I felt and what I witnessed with the eye of the heart.

O my Lord! Praise and gratitude to You! O my master, Messenger of Allāh ﷺ! To you belongs the favor and greatness because you are the beloved of Allāh and the owner of these secrets! O my shaykh! To you goes all the credit for your accompanying me in order for these realities to descend onto the heart of this servant who is poor before Allāh ﷻ! I hope that Allāh ﷻ gives us long life and will grant us to meet "the owner of this time" Muḥammad al-Mahdī ﷺ, and to send us a king who will lead us to fight in Allāh's Way the evil of our egos and the devils of this world.

Muḥammad ﷺ is a Mercy to all creation. In this hadith, found in Bukhārī narrated by Abū Hurayrah, he said:

> "Oh Messenger of Allāh, ask Allāh to curse the polytheists. He said, I was only sent as a mercy, I was not sent as a punishment."

Let those who reflect and meditate upon this hadith recognize how much mercy and compassion the Prophet ﷺ

showed while guiding the servants of Allāh to the Straight Path, the path of guidance leading them to their Lord. In this *ḥadīth qudsī*, Allāh ﷻ said:

بلغنا أن الله تعالى يقول: يا ابن آدم، خلقتك وتعبد غيري، وأذكرك وتنساني، وأدعوك وتفر مني، إن هذا لأظلم ظلم في الأرض. يا اِبنَ آدمَ خَلَقتُكَ لِلعِبَادةَ فَلا تَلعَب وَقسَمتُ لَكَ رِزقُكَ فَلا تَتعَب فإن طلبتني وجدتني. وإن فُتّني فُتك... وفاتك الخير كلّه.

> "Oh son of Adam, I created you and you worship another (your own ego), and I remember you and you forget Me, and I call you to My Presence and you run away from Me. This is truly a tremendous injustice. O son of Adam, I created you for My worship, so do not play around; I have guaranteed your sustenance, so do not tire yourself after it. If you seek Me, you will find Me. If you found Me, you found everything; but if you lost Me you lost everything; and I am of more benefit to you than anything else."

Our Lord is our refuge, His door is our Prophet ﷺ and the road to Him is our shaykh. Let us then show good manners with the *mashaykh*. Let us learn from their knowledge; let us learn the lessons of their teachings and let us not be stubborn in holding onto our opinion and our will. We have to be humble, because it will deliver us to the realities I mentioned. We have to leave the worldly pleasures, because if the hearts of the servants—and especially the scholars—become inclined towards this worldly life and its people, Allāh ﷻ will take from them the springs of wisdom and He will extinguish the lamps of guidance in their hearts. Greed for the material world will cause wisdom to leave the hearts of scholars and servants. Once wisdom is gone, humility will go with it.

Abase One's Self and Be Raised by the Lord

True humility flows in the bloodstream of the body, and as it flows it opens for you the gates of the heavens and the earths from the knowledge of the secrets of the secret of created beings, because as it is stated in this hadith:

من تواضَعَ لله رفعَه

> "Whoever humbles himself to Allāh, Allāh will raise his station."

Knowing the secrets will cause you to reflect further about the creation of the heavens and the earths, as Allāh ﷻ said in His Holy Book:

الَّذِينَ يَذْكُرُونَ اللّهَ قِيَاماً وَقُعُوداً وَعَلَىَ جُنُوبِهِمْ وَيَتَفَكَّرُونَ فِي خَلْقِ السَّمَاوَاتِ وَالأَرْضِ رَبَّنَا مَا خَلَقْتَ هَذا بَاطِلاً سُبْحَانَكَ فَقِنَا عَذَابَ النَّارِ

Those who remember Allāh (always, and in prayers) standing, sitting, and lying down on their sides, and think deeply about the creation of the heavens and the earth, (saying): "Our Lord! You have not created (all) this without purpose, glory to You! (Exalted be You above all that they associate with You as partners). Give us salvation from the torment of the Fire."[46]

Humbleness is what brings you to the Presence of the True One ﷻ, al-Ḥaqq, where you will see nothing but Allāh's remembrance. When you remember Him, He will open for you the reality that there is nothing worthy of worship besides Him. Therefore, you have to submit with humility in your prayer; you have to reflect, to meditate, to see with real vision and to observe. As *Sayyīdinā* Muʿadh ibn Jabal ؓ said while advising his son:

---

[46] Sūrat Āli ʿImrān [The Family of ʿImrān], 3:191.

"My son, when you pray, pray the prayer of a dying man who does not think he will pray again. Know my son that the believer dies between two rewards, one he sent ahead and the other he left behind."

This is why, O reader of these lines, you need to have piety in secret and in the open. You must follow the *sunnah* in word and deed. You must turn away from creation in your going and your coming. You have to be pleased with your Lord both when you possess little and when you possess much, and you have to turn to Allāh during times of ease and when hardship comes.

Know that the best of deeds is leaving hidden disobedience, because if a person leaves hidden disobedience it will be easier for him to leave open disobedience. When a person's hidden, inner self is better than his outer self, that is a favor. When the hidden and outer self are equal, that is justice. When the hidden is worse than the outer, that is injustice and oppression. Beware of oppression, because it takes you far away from humbleness.

وعن عروة بن الزبير رضي الله عنهما قال: رأيت عمر بن الخطاب رضي الله عنه على عاتقه قربة ماء فقلت: يا أمير المؤمنين، لا ينبغى لك هذا، فقال: لما أتاني الوفود سامعين مطيعين، دخلت نفسي نخوة؛ فأردت أن أكسرها.

'Urwah ibn az-Zubayr ؓ said:

I saw 'Umar ibn al-Khaṭṭāb carrying upon his shoulder a water container. I said, 'O Prince of the believers, this is something which does not befit you.' He said to me: 'When the delegations came to me listening and obeying, my ego felt some self-gratification, so I decided to break it."

This is *Sayyīdinā* 'Umar ibn al-Khaṭṭāb ؓ teaching us how to be humble by breaking the ego. When these delegations came to him in obedience, wanting to hear his opinion and listen to his words calling them to Islam, he felt some joy, and so did his ego. He immediately became fearful of his Lord, because he sensed that self-gratification and pride had entered his heart, and he knew that whoever allows pride and self-gratification to enter his heart will become farther from realities and Divine Knowledge. He will be thrown out from the presence of The True One ﷻ al-Ḥaqq.

The same happens when the self-projected delegations of self-gratification and pride enter the heart of the servant who is trying to come closer to Allāh ﷻ, through much prayers, meditation and worship during the early hours before dawn. The self projects itself to the servant in the image of a pious worshiper. This will cause him to forget his Lord and follow his desires. He will become complacent and content with his ego, the same way that Adam ؑ felt towards the devil, and this is the hidden danger. When pleasure enters into worship, know it is due to the whispers of Satan in the heart. So, run far away from it.

If you manage to escape from such worship, you will enter into the bottomless oceans of *Sayyīdinā* Muḥammad ﷺ that combine the light of the Essence and the secret which flows from the rest of the Names and Attributes. These oceans will carry you, then dip you, and then drown you in the oceans of Uniqueness. It will then lift you out of the mud of Oneness. This is what happened to *Sayyīdinā* Bilāl when he was being tortured. He was at the Station of Witnessing, the Station of the Gnostics, calling, "*Āḥad! Āḥad!* One! One!" After that these oceans open for you their hidden vaults, they will plunge you into the core of the Ocean of Oneness, until you can no longer hear, no longer see, no longer feel anything except your Lord, your Prophet and your shaykh, who is the life of your soul and his soul, the secret of your reality and his reality, the collective accumulation of Gnostic knowledge. All this comes from breaking the ego with humbleness, as *Sayyīdinā* 'Umar ibn al-Khaṭṭāb ؓ did.

By humbling yourself to the shaykh, your patience will increase, because he is always making you taste the bitterness of this world in order to prevent you from indulging in its pleasures. He does this because he wants you to receive instead the pleasures of the Hereafter and the delights of the heavens, which Allāh ﷻ promised to His pious and truthful servants. Therefore, be patient when the shaykh ignores you and turns the cold shoulder to you for a long time, because knowledge grows roots in you only through his displeasure with you and his repulsion from you. If you do not taste the bitterness of learning during your youth, you will drink from the cup of ignorance for the remainder of your life.

As Imam Shāfi'ī said:

ومن فاتَه التعَليم وقتَ شبابِه   فكبِّر عليهِ أربعاً لوفاتِه

Wa man fātahu 't-t'alīm waqta shabābih fa-kabbir 'alayi arba'īn li-wafātihi

The one who misses learning during his youth

Then make four *takbīrs* on him at his funeral (confirming his death).

Pride: the Worst Satanic Trait

The true life of man is learning, righteousness, piety, piousness, humility, patience, meditation, observation, reflection, connection and humility before your Lord. If you devote yourself to the pursuit of other things, you will fall in the trap of Satan, and you will lose any value you had. You will lose the favor your Lord granted to you.

Sayyīdinā 'Alī ؓ said:

"يا ابنَ آدَمْ إنْ رأيتَ رَبَّكَ يُتابع نِعمة عليكَ وأنتَ تَعصيه فاحذره
واعلَم أن أفضَل الزُهدْ إخفاءُ الزُهدا لأنَ إفشاؤه يعلِمُك الغُرور
بالنفس"

"Oh son of Adam! If you see that your Lord is continuing to send you His favor while you are disobedient to Him, then beware of Him; and know that the best asceticism is to hide you are an ascetic, because showing it will teach your ego to be proud of itself."

So, beware of pride. It will destroy you and throw you far away from the Divine Presence. Each of us overlooks his or her own mistakes and considers them to be small missteps, so much so that some of us think that we have no faults. We also overlook our bad manners to the point that we think we have none. If some faults become apparent that we cannot hide, we will minimize them and consider them too insignificant to mention. On the other hand, when we look at other peoples' faults we blow them out of all proportion!

An example of this is found in the Qur'anic story of the two brothers:

وَكَانَ لَهُ ثَمَرٌ فَقَالَ لِصَاحِبِهِ وَهُوَ يُحَاوِرُهُ أَنَا أَكْثَرُ مِنكَ مَالاً وَأَعَزُّ نَفَراً

And he had property (or fruit) and he said to his companion, in the course of mutual talk: "I am more than you in wealth and stronger in respect of men."[47]

أَبَداً وَدَخَلَ جَنَّتَهُ وَهُوَ ظَالِمٌ لِّنَفْسِهِ قَالَ مَا أَظُنُّ أَن تَبِيدَ هَذِهِ

[47] Sūratu 'l-Kahf [The Cave], 18:34.

And he went into his garden while in a state (of pride and disbelief) unjust to himself. He said: "I think not that this will ever perish."[48]

وَمَا أَظُنُّ السَّاعَةَ قَائِمَةً وَلَئِن رُّدِدتُّ إِلَى رَبِّي لَأَجِدَنَّ خَيْراً مِّنْهَا مُنقَلَباً

"And I think not the Hour will ever come, and if indeed I am brought back to my Lord, (on the Day of Resurrection), I surely shall find better than this when I return to Him."[49]

قَالَ لَهُ صَاحِبُهُ وَهُوَ يُحَاوِرُهُ أَكَفَرْتَ بِالَّذِي خَلَقَكَ مِن تُرَابٍ ثُمَّ مِن نُّطْفَةٍ ثُمَّ سَوَّاكَ رَجُلاً

His companion said to him, during the talk with him: "Do you disbelieve in Him Who created you out of dust (i.e. your father, Adam), then out a drop of seed, then fashioned you into a man."[50]

The same is true for us. It is not permissible for you to look down at your friend or to belittle him. A sign of true friendship is that you do not only show respect to your friend, but even to a friend of a friend—especially in his absence. In his presence, everyone will praise the other but in his absence everyone cuts down the other.

The man with highest esteem is the man who sees no value in himself, and the man with the most regard is the man who gives no regard to himself.

The Prophet used one of his Comanions to teach us. He said that person will never enter Paradiese. The other Companions were wondering why is he prevented from entering pradise. He is praying with the Prophet, staying with him. But he stands on the street and talks with his friends. He praises those

[48] Sūratu 'l-Kahf [The Cave], 18:35.
[49] Sūratu 'l-Kahf [The Cave], 18:36.
[50] Sūratu 'l-Kahf [The Cave], 18:37.

who pass by, but as soon as he is gone he cuts him down, and gossips about him. That was *ghībā* or if it is not true, *namīmah.*

Do not listen to the one who spread false rumors about you. Do not fight with him, because Allāh ﷻ will collect your right from him. Whoever speaks badly about others to you, will speak badly of you to others; and whoever delivers to your ears false rumors about others will spread false rumors about you to others. So, be careful O servant of God! Do not follow your whims and protect yourself from backbiting and from spreading false rumors.

Allāh ﷻ said in His Book:

أَيُحِبُّ أَحَدُكُمْ أَن يَأْكُلَ لَحْمَ أَخِيهِ مَيْتاً فَكَرِهْتُمُوهُ وَاتَّقُوا اللهَ إِنَّ اللهَ تَوَّابٌ رَّحِيمٌ

Would any of you like to eat the raw flesh of his dead brother? You would surely hate to do so, so beware of Allāh, Allāh is forgiving merciful.[51]

Servants are molded with faults, but you can avoid making mistakes through obedience to Allāh ﷻ, by following the Messenger ﷺ and by accompanying the perfect shaykh. Do not be of the stupid ones, who insist on making mistakes because they are molded with faults. They are stubborn and they do not accept advice. So, teach yourself to accept advice from the shaykhs.

Levels of Discipleship

There are three levels of discipleship:

In the first level, the disciple is like an annual crop, you can only harvest his fruits once a year. This is the level of beginners, *mubtadiʿyyīn,* where the shaykh plants the seeds in the heart of the student, and the seeds grow through Allāh's remembrance until the shaykh harvests them.

---

[51] Sūratu 'l-Ḥujurāt [The Private Apartments] 49:12.

In the second level, the level of students who are ready, *mustaʿidīn,* the shaykh plants a small tree in the student's heart. When the tree grows with Allāh's remembrance, the shaykh is able to harvest it many times throughout the student's life.

If the student persists and progresses, he will reach the third level, the level of a true disciple, *murīd,* in the highest spiritual path, which is the Naqshbandī Way. Here, the shaykh plants the Tree of Knowledge in the heart of his student. With this tree, the student is able to feed, to benefit and to teach an entire nation. Such a disciple becomes like an ocean torrent overflowing with knowledge, teaching those who follow him, guiding them to the Straight Path and bringing them first to know the shaykh, then to know the Prophet ﷺ and then to know Allāh ﷻ–an unceasing harvest of fruits.

Part Two

The Commentaries

Being a daily association during the holy month of Ramadan in which the Shaykh presents and explains the notes written during his seclusion.

ONE

Authentic Seclusion

When I went to visit my shaykh in Cyprus, it never occurred to me that he would order me into seclusion. Yet, when I arrived there, he said, "I am sending you to seclusion." He wanted to see my reaction. I had not prepared my affairs to go into seclusion, to be away from my family, my country and the affairs of my day-to-day life for forty days. When you know you are going into seclusion, you may take steps to prepare for it ahead of time. But this was an order, and I could not ignore it. When the order of the shaykh comes, though he makes it easy, it is very hard. It is not something that it is going to be simple.

When you ask your shaykh for something and he gives you permission, it is easy for you because it is coming through your will. Thus, your ego will not fight against it. However, when the shaykh orders you to do something, when he asks you to do something, then your ego is going to fight against it and against you. That is because your ego cannot accept the will of another over it. When you try to do something that someone else has asked you to do against the ego's will, it will declare war on you and marshal all the armies available to it through Satanic means to stop you from completing what you have been told to do.

When the order comes, especially from the Prophet ﷺ, by order of the Prophet ﷺ to Grandshaykh, from Grandshaykh to Mawlana Shaykh without you asking, it is very difficult. That seclusion that comes from the order of the Prophet ﷺ comes from Allāh ﷻ. That means there is something special you must go through, something difficult. So, when Mawlana Shaykh ordered, and when he said, "By order of Grandshaykh and by order of the Prophet ﷺ," I knew there was no way it was going to be easy. I surrendered and said, "As you like."

People say they want to make seclusion, to worship in solitude for forty days. They think it is easy.

وَتَحْسَبُونَهُ هَيِّنًا وَهُوَ عِندَ اللَّهِ عَظِيمٌ

...and ye thought it to be a light matter, while it was most serious in the sight of Allāh.[52]

I tried to get extra blood-pressure medicine, because I did not have enough for the whole time I would be gone. I had only enough for twenty days, not for three months. *SubḥānAllāh !* Glory be to Allāh, by Mawlana's order, I entered seclusion and my blood pressure dropped without any medicine. In fifty days, I did not have to take medicine even once. In fact, I brought back all of the medicine I took with me to Cyprus. That shows that, from the very first day, I was under the power of the shaykh.

I asked if I could read *tafsīr*, interpretation of the Holy Qur'an. Mawlana told me to read the Qur'an only. He said interpretations would come to my heart, and he told me to write then down as they came.

"As you are reading," he said, "the lights from these words and verses will come, bringing inspiration. As soon as this comes, you write it."

I was not prepared for that either. An author writes from the knowledge he has learned. However, I had to obey the order of Mawlana, and I resolved to do what he had instructed. After eight days of seclusion, when I was reading the Holy Qur'an, inspiration began to come to my heart and I began writing without even knowing what I was transcribing. It ended up being one hundred pages long.

Seclusion is a Test from the Shaykh

تَحْسَبُونَهُ هَيِّنًا وَهُوَ عِندَ اللَّهِ عَظِيمٌ

[52] Sūratu 'n-Nūr [The Light], 24:15.

and ye thought it to be a light matter, while it was most serious in the sight of Allāh.[53]

As we have said, this is true of seclusion, too. Some people think seclusion is so easy and simple, but when it is done by order of the shaykh, it is huge and heavy. When the shaykh orders complete disconnection from the people around you, your family, your country, from everything that you are in contact with, it is not easy. It is very difficult, but with that difficulty you will be able to polish your heart. He will polish your heart until the heart becomes like a mirror. When it becomes like a mirror, it reflects all the knowledge inside it. You cannot learn or acquire this heavenly knowledge without a polished heart. You need a mirror, a very polished one, so you can see everyone. Without that mirror you will not receive that reflection. When your heart becomes clean through different duties and *awrād* (recitations) the shaykh gives to you, this reflection of knowledge reaches your heart.

From the beginning, this was a seclusion of *aḍdād* (اضداد—opposition). All the desires and gossips of the self appear in order to make you run out from the place of seclusion. All kinds of wild thoughts come to you in the shapes of different untamed animals. They do not let you sleep. They do not let you eat. These negative thoughts do not just come and go. They attack you relentlessly. They lock you in mortal combat saying, "It's either you or me. You live or I live." The ego cannot accept to submit anyone but itself. That is why Iblīs could not accept to bow to Adam ﷺ, because he could not accept Adam ﷺ; he accepts only himself. So, these thoughts try to make you run away. Thoughts assail you and make you crazy.

Inna khalwat al-aḍdād—the seclusion of opposition cuts you off from *dunyā* (the world), family, children, country and money by order of the shaykh, so that you can be busy in *dhikrullāh,* reading the Holy Qur'an and making *ṣalawāt*, praising the Prophet

[53] Sūratu 'n-Nūr [The Light], 24:15.

ﷺ. When the shaykh orders, everything comes against his order. It must be that way. They do not let you feel at ease. They want you to run away, because if you run away you lose. The saints want you to run away, to show you how unprepared you are. They want you to see your mistakes, to see that you are not ready by yourself. If someone tells you, you will not accept this, so they test you a little bit.

However, with the *barakah* (blessing) of the shaykhs, you do not run away. This is because there is permission for your seclusion, because they want you to kill that desire of the self, that evil-commanding ego that makes itself a tyrant on the throne of your heart. Your heart is the place where all these beautiful inspirations come and the self is appointing itself to be a tyrant on you, using your heart as its place to sit. That is why *awrād* are important to polish that, to take that away and throw it away.

Through the experiences of inspiration and witnessing that your guide or master sends to you in seclusion you can understand things far better than in "real" life. When you are not secluded you are immersed in the worldly *dunyā* life. We say that this is the real life but in reality this life has no reality. It is going to an end. Every day that passes, means one day of the life of the world gone; one day less. Every hour that goes we are one hour less; every second that goes we are one second less. Every breath we breathe in and out is less from the days that we are going to live on earth.

So in seclusion this situation is completely different because through the guidance of your teacher who is constantly observing you with his spiritual vision, you will be inspired. He is trying to keep you on the track, like a railway train, it must not come off the track. If it comes off the track the whole train with all its passengers will derail and crash. The whole goal of the seclusion is to show you the reality of the eternal life, *ākhirah*.

Such seclusions are not only for *dhikr* and Qur'an and *ṣalawāt*. Their purpose is nothing less than the destruction of the ego that orders you to do wrong (*an-nafs la-ammāratan bi 's-sūw*), the overthrow of that tyrant that is sitting cross-legged on the throne of your heart.

Reclaiming the Throne of the Heart

The throne of the heart is bigger than the Throne of Sabā, Sheba. The throne of Sabā was enormous, and it was set with different kinds of diamonds and gems. A bird came to *Sayyīdinā* Sulaymān ﷺ saying, "I saw a lady worshipping the sun with her people and her throne is so huge." The throne of the self that is in your heart is also huge, but instead of being decorated with diamonds like the Throne of Sabā, it is decorated by Shaytan with *ḥiqd* (hatred) and *ḥasad* (jealousy). That is because you have surrendered the throne of your heart to your base desires. *Ḥubb ad-dunyā,* the love of worldly thing, is your biggest enemy. It prevents you from reaching that way of Gnosticism. It allows Shaytan to desecrate your throne and cover it with all kinds of sins, both hidden and overt.

The hidden sins are those that the Prophet ﷺ described when he said:

قال رسول الله : أخوف ما أخاف على أمتي الشرك الخفي

> "That is what I fear most for my nation, *ash-shirk al-khafī* (hidden idolatry)."

He feared the hidden *shirk,* which means associating someone with Allāh ﷻ.

We say, "No, we do not associate anything or anyone with Allāh ﷻ."

But we are wrong. The Christians associate Jesus ﷺ with Allāh ﷻ. We Muslims do not. We say, "*Allāh lā sharīka lah.* Allāh has no partner." But in reality we are associating partners with Him without even knowing it. We are associating our egos with Allāh ﷻ!. We say, "Me, me! I am here! I am stronger than you! You are nothing! I am better than you!" That is the problem: *ananīyā* (selfishness). That is what makes everyone fight with everyone else. That hidden *shirk*, unbelief is what distracts you away from reflecting and thinking about your Lord. Instead you are reflecting and thinking about yourself.

When we say do *murāqabah* (meditation), what do we mean? *Murāqabah* means to reflect on Allāh's creation. But how long are we able to truly reflect? Let us be truthful. After one minute or two, your reflection shifts to yourself. Even when we enter prayer, saying *"Allāhu akbar,"* our thoughts quickly turn away from Him and to ourselves. We should be reflecting on Allāh ﷻ, on His creation. We should be imagining ourselves between His Hands. Yet, in reality, we are thinking about how much money we have; what business we have to attend to; what meeting we have to go to next. Every kind of worldly matter comes to you when you are praying. That is associating yourself with Allāh ﷻ. That is worshipping yourself instead of worshipping Allāh ﷻ.

This hidden *shirk* is difficult to eliminate. That is the role of seclusion. It teaches you not to associate yourself with your Lord. That is why *awlīyā* spend most of their time in seclusion; they are always secluding themselves somewhere.

The Trials of Seclusion

When Grandshaykh was in seclusion—a seclusion lasting five years–a snake appeared and coiled itself around him for forty days. The serpent was facing his head, and Grandshaykh knew that it would bite him if he showed the slightest hint of fear. He said, "I never thought, 'I am afraid of that snake.' When I stood, it stood with me. When I slept, it slept with me. When I prayed, it prayed with me, until forty days had passed."

That is a real seclusion, and it is not easy. And Grandshaykh did this not once, but twice.

Just as the Indian Ocean tsunami left people with no family, with no parents, no children, no spouse, so too was I feeling as though this storm had ripped my family away from me. In that small room, I was completely cut off. I was locked inside, and could not leave except to make ablution. It was like being locked in a prison cell.

When you are in seclusion, you come to know what people feel when they are thrown into solitary confinement. They show you how these people are suffering, and you experience their suffering and you have to make *duā*ʿ for every one of them. With the enormous power of Mawlana Shaykh, you see every one of those who are oppressed. You see those who are innocent and wrongly incarcerated, not those who are killers. In some countries, they oppress their citizens by throwing them into solitary confinement. These innocent ones appear to you in seclusion, and you see how they are suffering after being taken away from their children, their wives, their mothers and fathers. They do not give them food. They kick them and abuse them. They put their fingers in acid and pour it on their chests. Can you imagine how these innocent ones suffer? *Alḥamdulillāh,* we are spared from this.

The only solace that the shaykhs give you is to look at the holy books, to read the Qur'an and the *Dalā'il al-Khayrāt* and to perform the desired *awrād*. That is what you have in front of you. That is what reminds you that you are in seclusion, in the Divine Presence. Thus, you become like one who has died.

They order you to do many recitations: at least 10,000 "Allāh," 3,000 *ṣalawāt*, then three *juz* from the Qur'an. They order you to recite "*ḥasbunallāh*" 1,000 times, "*lā ilāha illa-Llāh*" 1,000 times, "*qul hūw Allāhu āḥad*" 1,000 times, "*istaghfirullāh*" 500 times, "*SubḥānAllāh wa bi-ḥamdihi SubḥānAllāh il-ʿaẓīm istaghfirullāh*" 100 times, *Bismillāhi 'r-Raḥmāni 'r-Raḥīm dhālika taqdīru 'l-ʿazīzi 'l-ʿalīm* 100 times,"*subūḥun qudūsun rabbunā wa rabbu 'l-malā'ikati wa 'r-rūḥ*" 100 times, "*anta al-qādir wa anā ʿabdik al-ʿajiz*" 100 times, "*tawakaltu ʿalā Allāh* " 100 times and "*Allāhu akbar*" 100 times.

You finish all of these, and it is still only the middle of the day.

Then you recite the *duā‘ ismu 'l-jalāla* of ‘Abd al-Qādir Jilānī of then the *duā‘* of Muḥīydīn ibn ‘Arabī. Then there is nothing to do except reciting from Qur'an and *awrād.* You read 15 *juz* of the Qur'an and recite 50,000 or even 100,000 *ṣalawāt.* This completes the day, and all the while you are being assailed by bad thoughts.

That is how you have to pass your day: in the recitation of these *awrād* and in what there is permission to speak about. This is your only solace, and so you keep reading until *maghrib* comes. At that time, you remember that you are in seclusion with Allāh ﷻ and with His *ḥabīb,* our Prophet Muḥammad ﷺ.

That is your goal: to be near to the Prophet ﷺ, to be with the *awlīyāullāh,* to be with Grandshaykh and to be with Mawlana Shaykh Nāẓim. So, you make *murāqabah,* for as he said, "Keep your *rābiṭah* with me, lest you fall down. Keep *murābiṭah* and *murāqabah,* then it will be easier on you."

Before I entered my seclusion, Mawlana told me that we are living in a time in which there is too much darkness in the world. He said, "This is one of the most difficult times in the history of this planet," and he warned me that this would make my seclusion one of the most difficult. And so it was.

Afterwards, he told me, "If I was not supporting you and watching over you during your seclusion, by permission of Grandshaykh and by permission of the Prophet ﷺ, you would have died." He was sending that power to protect and support me.

Mawlana warned me that bad thoughts would assail me during my seclusion. He warned me of this saying, "All kinds of gossips are going to jump on your heart from every side."

Mawlana's title is Ḥaqqānī Rabbānī al-‘Adil, meaning the truthful, lordly and just. Therefore I was asking Allāh ﷻ for the justice of Mawlana Shaykh and the truth that he carries to finish my seclusion with as few problems as possible, because he had warned me how difficult it would be.

I was asking, "O Allāh, *farrij ʿannī*! Relieve me from the fight of the self against me and grant me the power to control the devil of the self, the part of the ego that is dressed with satanic power that rebels against You. Take the reins of my horse against the self, by means of the Lordly Power (*al-quwwāt ar-rabbānīyyat al-kāminah*), which is planted deep inside the secret of the secrets of the heart. Open up to me Your Lordly Power, the lordly power, O Allāh, and give me heavenly support and allow that secret power to rise and bloom within my heart accompanied by all the signs of the heavenly and prophetic lights, *al-quwwāt ar-rabbānīyyat al-kāminat al-mulhimah*. Grant me that secret power that is inspired by those Muḥammadan lights, empowered by the secret of the secret of heavenly knowledge, which has been revealed especially to some of Your righteous servants and saints:

فَوَجَدَا عَبْداً مِّنْ عِبَادِنَا آتَيْنَاهُ رَحْمَةً مِنْ عِندِنَا وَعَلَّمْنَاهُ مِن لَّدُنَّا عِلْماً

They found a servant from amongst our servant whom we have given a mercy from Our presence and whom we taught knowledge from Our Divine Presence.[54]

وَاتَّقُواْ اللّهَ وَيُعَلِّمُكُمُ اللّهُ وَاللّهُ بِكُلِّ شَيْءٍ عَلِيمٌ

And be aware of Allāh and Allāh will teach you, and Allāh is all knowing of everything.[55]

At that time, *munājāt* was coming, and those secrets that I asked for were being opened to me. Mawlana was trying to dip me into that ocean of sacred knowledge—by his power, not by mine—in order that I might extract some of its secrets, which he already possesses.

[54] Sūratu 'l-Kahf [The Cave], 18:65.
[55] Sūratu 'l-Baqara [The Heifer],2:282.

TWO

Praying for a King

At the beginning of my seclusion, Mawlana said, "During the last third of the night, around two o'clock in the morning, I want you to be awake. I want you to be in my presence, to be in the presence of Grandshaykh and in the presence of the Prophet ﷺ, and I want you to ask Allāh ﷻ to send a king to save the whole world from the possession of evil-doers and from the hands of Shaytan and to take away all the different kinds of satanic powers that have afflicted the hearts of humanity."

He said, "*nājī rabbak.* Supplicate to your Lord, with the company of Grandshaykh Sulṭān al-Awlīyā, *maʿīyatihi,* and with my company, coming spiritually to the Presence of the Prophet ﷺ, asking on behalf of everyone for Allāh ﷻ to send a king, to send heavenly support, to send someone, *mālikan ẓāhiran,* not only a hidden king, but a king to be seen and to control everything in his hand, guiding people towards their destinies. That is why I am sending you into seclusion. That is the importance of what you are doing."

The spiritual meaning of this was clear: You have to ask Allāh ﷻ to send a king to every individual living on Earth, without distinction, *li yaṭrud,* to oust the tyrant that has usurped the thrones of their hearts. He has to govern the hearts of the people, to control them and take them towards the different levels of servanthood to *maqām al-ʿubudīyyah,* the level of absolute servanthood, of worship to Allāh ﷻ.

Reflecting on Allah's Creation

أَلَا لِلَّهِ الدِّينُ الْخَالِصُ وَالَّذِينَ اتَّخَذُوا مِن دُونِهِ أَوْلِيَاء مَا نَعْبُدُهُمْ إِلَّا لِيُقَرِّبُونَا إِلَى اللَّهِ زُلْفَى إِنَّ اللَّهَ يَحْكُمُ بَيْنَهُمْ فِي مَا هُمْ فِيهِ يَخْتَلِفُونَ إِنَّ اللَّهَ لَا يَهْدِي مَنْ هُوَ كَاذِبٌ كَفَّارٌ

Is it not to Allāh that sincere devotion is due? But those who take for protectors other than Allāh (say): "We only serve them in order that they may bring us nearer to Allāh ." Truly Allāh will judge between them in that wherein they differ. But Allāh guides not such as are false and ungrateful.[56]

So, when you meditate and reflect, as the Prophet ﷺ said to his Companions:

تفكروا في مخلوقات الله، ولا تفكروا في ذات الله

"Do not reflect on Allāh's [Essence], reflect on His creation."

No one can reflect on His Lord, for He is a Hidden Treasure. But we can reflect on the people around us. That is the meaning of reflection, to separate in every person the two different levels of the self, *an-nafs al-ammārah* (the evil-commanding self) and *an-nafs al-muṭma'innah* (the peaceful self, which commands good). When you separate them, you can differentiate and you can understand.

You think that everything that takes place is of no consequence, but to Allāh ﷻ it is something great. You assume that things that are insignificant are not important, but to Him everything is important, even small things.

وَكُلٌّ فِي فَلَكٍ يَسْبَحُونَ

[56] Sūratu 'z-Zumar [The Groups], 39:3.

Everything is swimming in its orbit.[57]

This whole universe is a void. In Arabic, we say *faḍā.* It is space, coming from the root of the word that means "it is empty," a vacuum. It is *mawjūd wa ghayr mawjūd*—it is there, but at the same time, not there. You see it there because of what is in it—stars, galaxies and planets. But at the same time, it is not there because it is void. At any moment, Allāh ﷻ can change it and everything will disappear.

ٱللَّهُ ٱلَّذِي رَفَعَ ٱلسَّمَاوَاتِ بِغَيْرِ عَمَدٍ تَرَوْنَهَا

Allāh is He Who raised the heavens without any pillars that ye can see.[58]

Allāh ﷻ created the heavens without pillars. How are the heavens and earth standing in a void with no support? Allāh ﷻ is putting all these galaxies in a void, *faḍā.* It does not exist. Something that does not exist has something that exists in it. When His Will, *irādah,* comes, He destroys everything that He caused to exist in one blow. Everything goes.

We see from this why it is not easy to understand the sort of knowledge that Allāh ﷻ gives to *awlīyāullāh* (saints of Allāh) from the secrets of the Holy Qur'an. It is not as though we take the Holy Qur'an, and we read it, and the verse means this and that. That is what a storyteller does, reads and passes on to the next page. But to those who can see, every word of the Holy Qur'an contains endless meanings.

When you look outside in the daytime, you cannot see anything in space. When there is no sun, you can see countless small stars, so you know there is something there.

When *ma'rifatullāh,* Allāh's Light, comes to the heart of the believer, everything disappears, and there is nothing visible except the Divine Presence. Everything else is exposed as false

---

[57] Sūrah YāSīn, 36:40.

[58] Sūratu 'r-Ra'd [Thunder], 13:2.

and unimportant. When *ma'rifatullāh*, gnosis, comes to the heart of the believer, that light is what is important: the light of knowing the secrets of this universe.

There are six forces that pull in six different directions, and Allāh ﷻ created the universe in six days. So, there are six different levels to everything that is created, and there are six powers that are required continuously to maintain it all.

As Allāh ﷻ said in the Holy Qur'an:

إِنَّ اللَّهَ يُمْسِكُ السَّمَاوَاتِ وَالْأَرْضَ أَن تَزُولَا وَلَئِن زَالَتَا إِنْ أَمْسَكَهُمَا مِنْ أَحَدٍ مِّن بَعْدِهِ إِنَّهُ كَانَ حَلِيمًا غَفُورًا

It is Allāh Who sustains the heavens and the earth, lest they cease (to function): and if they should fail, there is none—not one—can sustain them thereafter. Verily He is Most Forbearing, Oft-Forgiving.[59]

Allāh ﷻ is holding the heavens and earth together so as not to perish, not to disappear. If He did not hold it all together, it would disappear—everything. It would not simply collapse (*an tazūla)*; it would cease to be. If it disappears, no one can bring it back.

This is what the commentators have explained, that the universe is held together by these six powers. But in reality, it is not just the universe as a whole, but each individual atom that is being held in existence by these forces. Every atom is a universe unto itself, and Allāh ﷻ is holding each atom together with these six different forces.

Look at the Periodic Table. Hydrogen has one proton and one electron; helium has two protons and two electrons, and so forth. Allāh ﷻ holds each of these electrons in place in such a way as to maintain the stability of the atom as whole. Though each atom is moving, Allāh ﷻ is holding it together.

[59] Sūratu 'l-Fāṭir [The Originator], 35:41.

Think about the Qur'anic verse "It is something light, but in Allāh's Presence it is most serious" in light of this. The creation of stars, planets and galaxies is great indeed.

لَخَلْقُ السَّمَاوَاتِ وَالْأَرْضِ أَكْبَرُ مِنْ خَلْقِ النَّاسِ وَلَكِنَّ أَكْثَرَ النَّاسِ لَا يَعْلَمُونَ

Assuredly the creation of the heavens and the earth is a greater (matter) than the creation of men: Yet most men understand not.[60]

To Allāh ﷻ, the creation of the heavens and the earth is far greater a task than the creation of a human being. Even today, scientists cannot understand the creation of a human being. Allāh ﷻ says the creation of the universe is greater, but we are blind. Today's scientists say that a human being's creation is greater than everything. We cannot see the greatness that He has brought by His Power of *qudrah* to create this entire universe. We think there is a star here, a star there, constellations, and astronomical objects, but Allāh ﷻ shows us that the creation of this is greater than the creation of a human being.

Accountability to the Creator

When we look at these stars and reflect on them, we must wonder, what kind of creation is there? When Allāh ﷻ says the creation of heavens and earth is greater than the creation of human beings, it means we are nothing. Yet, we persist in thinking that we are everything. We do not give importance or value to what Allāh ﷻ has given to us because we think it is easy for Him. In fact, what He created, He accounts for—even small things.

لَقَدْ أَحْصَاهُمْ وَعَدَّهُمْ عَدًّا

---

60 Sūrah Ghāfir [The Forgiver of Sin], 40:57.

Laqad aḥṣāhum wa ʿaddahum ʿaddā

He does take an account of them (all), and hath numbered them (all) exactly.[61]

This means that Allāh ﷻ keeps an account of everything that He has created, that He is still creating and that He will create. He has counted everything—not only counted them, but counted them one by one (*ʿaddahum ʿaddā*). Consider this. Does Allāh ﷻ need to count? Why did He say *aḥṣāhum wa ʿaddahum ʿaddā*? He counted them, He knew the total count, and yet He counted them again? He knows what is going to be created from *baḥru 'l-qudrah,* everything that is going to be created from the Ocean of His Power. *Aḥṣāhum* means He knew about it all, and what He knew about it from the past, the present and into the future is all under His count. It has been counted one by one. Allāh ﷻ does not need to count, so why did He say, "count them one by one?"

Allāh ﷻ has assigned special angels for that count, angels that He created just for this purpose. Their job is to count. No one knows their number, because their number has to be huge in order that to count everything, one by one. How many are there on this one small planet we call Earth? Its radius is 20,000 kilometers. Its diameter is 40,000 kilometers. It is a small planet, but on it there are not just billions of living organisms and non-living entities, but trillions, quadrillions or zillions. Maybe even 10 to the power of 1,000,000,000,000. How can you count all the bacterium and viruses? How can you count all the leaves on all the trees? And this is on Earth alone. What about the rest of this galaxy we inhabit, with its billions of stars?

Allāh ﷻ said, *aḥṣāhum*. He surrounded them. They are under His observation and *ʿaddahum,* He counted them. So angels withut number, meaning we cannot comprehend their number,

[61] Sūrah Maryam, 19:94.

have been created to count everything. It means, "O My servant! Anything you do is counted."

فَمَن يَعْمَلْ مِثْقَالَ ذَرَّةٍ خَيْرًا يَرَهُ

Faman ya'mal mithqāla dharratin khayrin yarah.

If anyone does an atom of good He will see goodness.[62]

That includes the smallest thing you can imagine, so do not underestimate even the smallest order of your Lord. Even the smallest order from what Allāh ﷻ ordered us to do, from what His Prophet ﷺ ordered us to do and from what our *shuyūkh* ordered us to do is important. It might be small in our eyes, but it is great in theirs, as we have seen from the aforementioned Qur'anic verse.

The Value of Seclusion

If people knew the value of seclusion, they would ask the Angel of Death to give them just one day in it before he took their souls. If we knew its worth we would give all our wealth just to spend one day in seclusion. We would sacrifice everything in this world for it, even part with the rest of our lives, just to be granted one day of it, one day sitting and meditating on nothing but the creation of Allāh ﷻ.

I realized this during my seclusion, when I was reading Surat al-Ḥadīd. In it, Allāh ﷻ said:

اعْلَمُوا أَنَّمَا الْحَيَاةُ الدُّنْيَا لَعِبٌ وَلَهْوٌ وَزِينَةٌ وَتَفَاخُرٌ بَيْنَكُمْ وَتَكَاثُرٌ فِي الْأَمْوَالِ وَالْأَوْلَادِ كَمَثَلِ غَيْثٍ أَعْجَبَ الْكُفَّارَ نَبَاتُهُ ثُمَّ يَهِيجُ فَتَرَاهُ مُصْفَرًّا ثُمَّ يَكُونُ حُطَامًا وَفِي الْآخِرَةِ عَذَابٌ شَدِيدٌ وَمَغْفِرَةٌ مِّنَ اللَّهِ وَرِضْوَانٌ وَمَا الْحَيَاةُ الدُّنْيَا إِلَّا مَتَاعُ الْغُرُورِ سَابِقُوا إِلَى مَغْفِرَةٍ مِّن رَّبِّكُمْ وَجَنَّةٍ عَرْضُهَا

[62] Sūratu 'l-l-Zalzala [The Earthquake], 99:7.

كَعَرْضِ السَّمَاء وَالْأَرْضِ أُعِدَّتْ لِلَّذِينَ آمَنُوا بِاللَّهِ وَرُسُلِهِ ذَلِكَ فَضْلُ اللَّهِ يُؤْتِيهِ مَن يَشَاء وَاللَّهُ ذُو الْفَضْلِ الْعَظِيمِ

Know ye (all), that the life of this world is but play and amusement, pomp and mutual boasting and multiplying, (in rivalry) among yourselves, riches and children. Here is a similitude: How rain and the growth which it brings forth, delight (the hearts of) the tillers; soon it withers; you wilt see it grow yellow; then it becomes dry and crumbles away. But in the Hereafter is a Penalty severe (for the devotees of wrong). And Forgiveness from Allāh and (His) Good Pleasure (for the devotees of Allāh). And what is the life of this world, but goods and chattels of deception?[63]

Be ye foremost (in seeking) Forgiveness from your Lord, and a Garden (of Bliss), the width whereof is as the width of heaven and earth, prepared for those who believe in Allāh and His apostles: that is the Grace of Allāh, which He bestows on whom he pleases: and Allāh is the Lord of Grace abounding.[64]

Indeed, they shall have besides a generous reward, those who believe in Allāh ﷻ and his messengers. Nor can any misfortune befall them, if He so wills. That is easy for Allāh ﷻ. So, if the shaykh orders you into seclusion, you must be happy that he gave you not just one day, but many. Because if Allāh ﷻ gives you one day, you will say, "O Allāh, send me back! I will do better." If one would give everything in this *dunyā* for one day in seclusion, think how much forty days, one year or even five years must be worth.

[63] Sūratu'l-Ḥadīd [Iron], 57:20.
[64] Sūratu'l-Ḥadīd [Iron], 57:21.

THREE

Dangers of Seclusion

Know that there are three different dangers that assail the seeker in seclusion. They may attack all at once, or separately. They are:

Boredom (*al-malal*)

In the course of your everyday life, you may feel bored and may say to yourself, "I am bored. I want to go see a movie. I want to go to a restaurant. I want to go visit my friend." The same thing happens in seclusion, though in seclusion boredom is much more acute. In seclusion, you may say to yourself, "I am bored with reading the Qur'an, with making *ṣalawāt*, with doing *dhikr*."

You become bored with your Lord, but not with Shaytan. That is one of the main bad character attributes. Students at study, people at work, even people engaged in worship and the remembrance of Allāh ﷻ may get bored and begin wishing they were somewhere else or doing something different.

Boredom is born of the feeling that someone or something is forbidding you from being with your self—with your ego—because if you are left alone with your ego, you can do whatever it wants and go wherever it wants to go. But when you try to be with your Lord, away from everyone else, then your ego rebels and your self comes against you. That is because the self wants to be busy with other servants (*al-ʿibād*), not with the Lord of the servants (*rabb al-ʿibād*). The ego wants you to be busy with other people, to speak with everyone. It gets bored when instead you spend your time reading the Holy Qur'an, doing *dhikr*. Instead of wanting to continue in this worship, it becomes impatient. By assailing you with boredom, the ego tries to prevent you being secluded with your Lord.

By entering into seclusion with your Lord, you aim to reach the station of proximity to the Diving Presence, penetrating the levels of sacred knowledge and secrets that have been hidden between the mind and the soul. These are the secrets that are contained between the earthly and the heavenly worlds. The ego, with the power of the mind, tries to hide all the secrets that were given to the soul on the Day of Promises

قال النبي صلى الله عليه وسلم: الأرواح جنود مجندة، ما تعارف منها ائتلف، وما تنافر منها اختلف

> *Al-arwāḥu junūdan mujannadah. Mā t'arafa minhā atalaf wa mā tanāfara minhā 'khtalaf.*
>
> Spirits are like conscripted soldiers; those whom they recognize, they get along with, and with those whom they do not recognize they will clash.[65]

That is why when you begin taking those steps that lead to the uncovering these hidden secrets the ego assails you with boredom. It wants to keep you busy with the things of this world, so that you may remain ignorant of what is hidden between the mind and the soul. Boredom will prevent you from reaching these lights and knowledge.

That is why when you try to make *dhikrullāh,* the remembrance of Allāh ﷻ, boredom assails you. When you are occupied with the things of this world, *dunyā* and Shaytan, then you are not bored. But you become bored with Allāh ﷻ. That is why, after spending just a few minutes reciting "Allāh, Allāh," we stop and say, "That is enough." You may recite it 1,500 times, then stop and say, "Today, there is no need to do 50,000."

In this way, boredom tries to throw you into the mud of *shirk* and *dunyā,* chasing you away from Allāh's Divine Presence. That is why, in seclusion, you find yourself constantly struggling with boredom—particularly when you are reciting the Holy

[65] Saḥīḥ al-Bukhārī.

Qur'an or making *dhikr*. That is to chase you from the Divine Presence.

Worry (*al-qalak*)

To worry is, in this sense, to fear a mistake. You feel that you did something wrong, and your conscience makes you feel bad for it. And that leads directly to the third danger of seclusion, the feeling of failure.

Failure (*al-ifāk*)

When you feel that you have already failed, continued effort begins to seem pointless.

This is the way of the world today. People are bored, and their boredom casts them into an ocean of worry and they sink down into the black pit of failure. If they fail in school, they give up studying and turn to drugs and alcohol. We say, "That is what happens to unbelievers," but in truth believers are also afflicted by these same problems.

Those who decide they have already failed as Muslims then decide there is no longer any need for them to pray or fast. Instead, they may go to a psychatrist who will put them on antidepressants. The ego is constantly playing tricks with believers. They may say their five prayers, but their ego will tell them, "That is enough, go to the mall now."

That is why you must seek to follow the way of the *awlīyā*, lest failure keep you at the lowest level. Instead of being a failure, be a beginner. Listen to the shaykh, sit in his circle, but do not worry about doing more than that. Then you will not be a failure. However, if you do not achieve more than that, neither will you progress. But even this may make you worry and lead to fears of failure.

When you see that you are not progressing, worry comes and your conscience makes you feel guilty of the mistakes you have made and your lack of effort. If you are not patient and persistent enough to lift yourself up out of this pit, you fall deeper and deeper into it. The only real remedy is to challenge yourself.

You cannot say, "I leave it to Allāh ﷻ and His Prophet ﷺ," and make no effort. They are watching you to see if you surrender to these fears or fight back. If you are not patient and persistent enough to do what is necessary to extricate yourself from this murk of despair, you sink deeper and deeper into *dunyā*. You will say, "I am fed up with *ṭarīqah*. I will go back to what I was before."

That is why you see many people leave *ṭarīqah*. They spend many years, but they do not achieve anything, and so they give up. Some may have even gone into seclusion—not once, but several times—and, yet, they saw nothing. That is because they did not do it in the right way. They are lost like a ship in a blinding storm, turning and turning, but never finding the correct course.

Once, in the 1980s, I left Tripoli aboard a cargo ship headed for Antakya. Normally, it would only take us three hours to travel from Tripoli to Syria, but a storm overtook us, and the ship lost its way. We were turning and turning, but never arriving at our port. I thought we would never make it back ashore, but Allāh ﷻ saved us.

For some people, it is the same with *ṭarīqah*. They may enter seclusion, but they come out unchanged because they did not achieve what must be achieved. That is why you must not give in to failure; you must always strive your hardest.

Grandshaykh used to say, "*Ṭarīqah* is three nails that you hammer into your forehead." What did he mean by "three nails"? He meant three principles. The first is this: If your shaykh tells you, "Come, take this cup and empty the ocean," you must try to do it. Of course you cannot empty the ocean with a cup, but you must try, because that is your assignment. It means that when you receive an order from your shaykh, you must listen and obey (*Asmaʿū wa atīʿū*). Today, there are many people listening, but no one obeys.

The second principle is that, if the shaykhs tell you, "Take this broken shovel and dig through the seven earths to acquire your trust," you must not only do it, but you must keep on digging until you reach it. If you stop, you fail.

The third principle is to be like an ant that overcomes all obstacles. If they tell you, "Your provision is in the west," then you leave the east and move west until you reach it. You must not say, "I cannot. There are mountains and oceans in the way." It may be that they give you the power to cross mountains and walk on oceans. Do not listen to your ego, which will tell you why you cannot do what the shaykhs have instructed. If you do, you will fail.

Overcoming the Three Dangers

The way to overcome each of these three dangers is by facing them with consistency (*muthamara*). That is how you succeed.

In this struggle, you must know that your enemy is trying to cast you into depression: *inna ʿaduwaka yurīd an yunkirūka bi 't-tajammud.* Your dire foe is trying to constrict you (*tajammud*) and disintegrate you (*tafākuk*). It will try to make you believe that you can do nothing for your *ākhirah*; that you are a failure. As soon as you give into these doubts, it will plunge you into the desires of *dunyā*. It will come at you from every side, tempting you with these things in order to make you its slave. And when you become its slave, it will never let go of you. *Dunyā* is the ruler of whoever seeks it. If you give in to these temptations, it will become your king and you will become its subject. But *dunyā* is the servant of whoever leaves it behind, so turn your back on this world and make it your subject.

For it is said:

Ad-dunyā ṭālibatun wa maṭlūbah

This world is sought and it seeks.

It means that *dunyā* wants something from people, even as they seek it.

Faman ṭalabahā rafaḍathu

Whoever seeks it, it rejects.

Dunyā makes the one who runs after it its slave.

Amman rafaḍahā ṭalabathu

Whoever rejects it, it seeks out.

For this reason, the Prophet ﷺ refused *dunyā,* and when Jabal Uḥud came to him and said, "I will turn myself into gold, and you may take whatever you want." He said, "No, it is not our way."

Ad-dunyā is the bridge for *ākhirah*:

Ad-dunyā jisr al-ākhirah f'aburūha wa lā tāmurūhā

This world is a bridge so pass over it and do not build on it.

So, leave *dunyā* and forget it, and remember *ākhirah* and do not forget it. Remain mindful of the life that is to come. Keep the *ākhirah* in your heart and leave *dunyā* out.

Wa lā tākhudh min ad-dunyā mā yamnaʿuka min an taṣil ila 'l-ākhirah.

And do not take from this world what prevents you from connecting with the hereafter.

If Allāh ﷻ gives to you because you are running from *dunyā,* do not alter your course and begin running after it. Let *dunyā* throw wealth to you. Forget it, and remember *ākhirah.*

Khudh min ad-dunyā ma yaṣiluka al-ākhirah

Take from this life what makes you reach the hereafter. As *Sayyīdinā* ʿAlī said:

كما قال سيدُنا علي: اعمل لدُنياكَ كأنكَ تَعيشُ أبداً واعمَل

لآخرَتِك كأنكَ تموتُ غداً ثُمَ زادَ على قدرِ مقدارِكَ فيها.

> "Work for your worldly life as if you will live forever, and work for the Hereafter as you will die tomorrow; then he added: in proportion to the length of time you will stay in each."

That is what the Prophet ﷺ explained to the Sahaba when he took them to Jabal Uḥud. It was *ishrāq* (sunrise) time, and he said to them, "Whoever can catch his shadow, I will give this *jubbah,* mantle." They knew they could not catch their shadows, but they listened and obeyed. They ran towards Jabal Uḥud, and when they finally reached the mountain their shadows were cast on the mountain. Then he said, "Run towards me." They ran towards the Prophet ﷺ. Then he said, "Look. Your shadow is running behind you to catch you. So it is with *dunyā*. If you run after this worldly life you never catch it, but if you run away from it this life runs after you."

Thus it is said tht *dunyā* is a corpse and those who seek it are like dogs that scavenge—like hyenas. We are like hyenas, with our ego's wild characteristics. You cannot find anyone with a transparent (*shafāfiyah*) ego. They are always wild for everything. They are wild with their children, with their wives, with their relatives.

Yet, none of us is going to take anything with us to *ākhirah* except your deeds (*'amal*). If your actions are in the way of Allāh ﷻ and the Prophet ﷺ, you will win. If *actions* are for Shaytan and one's desires, he will throw you in the mud and garbage. You will be covered with a foul, stinky smell—the stench of *dunyā*. It is an evil smell, such that if Allāh ﷻ would allow it to be exposed , the stench would destroy whole mountain ranges.

Failure makes you forget the hereafter and immerse yourself in this worldly life. It makes you forget to thank Allāh ﷻ for the most important thing: that He created you and made you His servant. Failure makes you forget that Allāh created you and that He made you to be part of the Ummah of the Prophet ﷺ. That is why it is necessary for you to recite *"shukr alḥamdulillāh"* 500 times, because you are of that Ummah and because you are of the Golden Chain that leads from *Sayyīdinā* Muḥammad ﷺ to *Sayyīdinā* Abū Bakr ؓ all the way to *Sayyīdinā* Shaykh Sharafuddin to Shaykh 'Abd Allah and to Shaykh Nāẓim. You have to give thanks 500 times that Allāh ﷻ did not make you part of other nations. It is a great honor and great favor to be created from the Ummah of *Sayyīdinā* Muḥammad ﷺ. When you perform this recitation 500 times, meditating on it, veils will part. As you say, "*Alḥamdulillāh*," you will see the reality of being from the Ummah of the Prophet ﷺ, the reality of *Sayyīdinā* Ja'far ؓ, of *Sayyīdinā* Salmān ؓ, of *Sayyīdinā* ShāhShāh Naqshband. You will see the reality of all these *awlīyā*, the levels of each shaykh up to your own shaykh, and they will take you to the level of *mushāhadah*, witnessing, and enlightenment. That is why it is important to be constant in the thanking of Allāh ﷻ, saying, "*Alḥamdulillāh, yā Rabbī.* You created us from the Ummah of Prophet Muḥammad ﷺ."

This is why Sayyīdinā 'Alī ؓ said:
an-ni'am muṣilatan bi 'sh-shukr.
Favor is connected to thankfulness.

When you get a blessing (*ni'amah*), that *ni'amah* is connected to thankfulness. You have to say *alḥamdulillāh* and say, "Thank you, O Allāh ." When you thank Allāh ﷻ, He gives more, according to the verse:

وَإِذْ تَأَذَّنَ رَبُّكُمْ لَئِن شَكَرْتُمْ لأَزِيدَنَّكُمْ

Wa idh tadhhana Rabbakum la'in shakartum la-azīdanakum

And remember! Your Lord caused to be declared (publicly): "If ye are grateful, I will add more (favors) unto you."[66]

If you want your time in *dunyā* to be good, you must be thankful. But we forget and are heedless. But Sayyīdinā 'Alī ؓ said that all favors are connected to thankfulness, and increase in favors is connected to thankfulness —and Allāh ﷻ will continue to increase and will not cut His servant off until he ceases to be thankful:

Wa qilla min ni'am shukrihā. Wa man shakr astawjab al-mazīd.

---

[66] Sūrah Ibrāhīm, [Abraham], 14:7.

The one who thanks for favors is deserving of increase.

O servant of Allāh, you have to thank Him for He is your Lord. And if you thank Him, He will give you more.

Fa da'īmān al-mazīdu marbūṭan bi 'sh-shukr.

Increase is always is tied to thanks.

Do not let boredom and failure make you forget to thank Allāh ﷻ for His favors, for it is said that whoever is not content with Allāh ﷻ, Allāh ﷻ will cause that person to be in need of His servants. It is also said that whoever is content with Allāh ﷻ, Allāh ﷻ will make other people to be in need of him. So, always be content with Allāh ﷻ and empower yourself with Allāh ﷻ. Fight failure, worry and boredom with that power that Allāh ﷻ gives you.

Prerequisites of the Authentic Seclusion

There are some people who do not think they need the shaykh's permission to enter into seclusion. They make up their mind to do so without being ordered. Even non-Muslims are going into their own seclusions today. They say they are going to meditate. But that is not correct. There are conditions for seclusion: You must be a Muslim, you must be a Sufi and you must be following the Islamic Law (*Sharīʿah*).

You cannot play with *Sharīʿah* as many people do today and still claim that you are a Sufi. There is no *Taṣawwuf* without *Sharīʿah*, and there is no *Sharīʿah* without *Taṣawwuf*. Following the *Sharīʿah* is vital to winning the war (*mudamirrah*) between Good and Evil (*bayn al-khayri wa 'sh-shar*).

While there is no way, in the end, for Evil to overcome Good, battles are won and lost. To win, you must have a strategy, for you cannot wage war without a strategy. That strategy is outlined in the *Shariʿah*.

Seclusion Requires a Perfect Shaykh

You also must be under the guidance of an authentic shaykh.

The ego is able to retain its control over you unless you are under the guidance of a real shaykh. It cannot be a normal shaykh, such as you find are imams in mosques holding a variety of scholarly views. Rather, it must be a *shaykhun kāmil,* a complete and perfect shaykh. There are only 124,000 of these *awlīyāullāh* in the world at any given time.

Whoever has no shaykh, Shaytan is his shaykh. You must take refuge with a strong shaykh who, like a victorious lion, fears nothing and will not let anyone attack his children.

With a shaykh like that, with the *baraka* of Mawlana Shaykh, we hope to be safe from the attacks of the ego that can come at any time. Good tidings, then, to those who have taken initiation from a perfect and complete shaykh because they have been connected with one who is connected with the Prophet ﷺ and the Prophet ﷺ is connected with the Secret of Secrets, the most hidden oceans of realities of creation.

FOUR

War Against the Ego

It is important, both in seclusion and in reflection, to fight the four enemies of the self. As we have said, these are the *nafs*, the self; *dunyā*, worldly life; *hawā*, base desires; and, Shaytan. You have to fight these four enemies, because their constant aim is to control you completely. *Fafham in kunta zakīyyah*: So, understand, if you are clever. You have to understand how to fight these four enemies. If *Sayyīdinā* Adam ﷺ ate from the Tree when Shaytan whispered in his ear, what hope can we have to resist these foes?

Adam ﷺ was a prophet of Allāh . Yet, Shaytan came and whispered a little bit and what did he do? He went and ate from the Tree. Why did he eat from the Tree? Because Satan promised him whispering:

فَوَسْوَسَ إِلَيْهِ الشَّيْطَانُ قَالَ يَا آدَمُ هَلْ أَدُلُّكَ عَلَى شَجَرَةِ الْخُلْدِ وَمُلْكٍ لَّا يَبْلَى

"O Adam! shall I lead you to the Tree of Life and to a kingdom that never decays?"[67]

The Tree of Life and an eternal kingdom: these are things the self likes. Every one of us would like to live forever and to rule over a kingdom that never disappears. *Sayyīdinā* Sulaymān ﷺ was the richest one on earth. He asked.

قَالَ رَبِّ اغْفِرْ لِي وَهَبْ لِي مُلْكًا لَّا يَنبَغِي لِأَحَدٍ مِّنْ بَعْدِي إِنَّكَ أَنتَ الْوَهَّابُ

---

[67] Sūrah Ṭā.Hā, 20:120.

> *He said, "O my Lord! Forgive me, and grant me a kingdom which, (it may be), suits not another after me: for You art the Grantor of Bounties (without measure)."*[68]

He was asking for a kingdom the likes of which would never be seen again. Yet, where is his kingdom today? Allāh ﷻ gave it to him, but it is gone. Allāh ﷻ said in the Holy Qur'an, "He asked me for such a kingdom, and I gave it to him. But now it is gone." There is nothing that can last forever except Allāh ﷻ. He alone is eternal.

What about us? We are not even like *Sayyīdinā* Sulaymān ؑ, and he was a prophet, favored by his Lord. So then do we want to be like Qārūn, of whom the Qur'an says:

$$فَخَرَجَ عَلَى قَوْمِهِ فِي زِينَتِهِ قَالَ الَّذِينَ يُرِيدُونَ الْحَيَاةَ الدُّنْيَا يَا لَيْتَ لَنَا مِثْلَ مَا أُوتِيَ قَارُونُ إِنَّهُ لَذُو حَظٍّ عَظِيمٍ$$

> *So he [Qārūn] went forth among his people in the (pride of his worldly) glitter. Said those whose aim is the Life of this World: "Oh that we had the like of what Qārūn has got, for he is truly a lord of mighty good fortune!"*[69]

They said, "If only we had the like of Qārūn!" But what happened to Qārūn in the end?

$$فَخَسَفْنَا بِهِ وَبِدَارِهِ الْأَرْضَ فَمَا كَانَ لَهُ مِن فِئَةٍ يَنصُرُونَهُ مِن دُونِ اللَّهِ وَمَا كَانَ مِنَ الْمُنتَصِرِينَ$$

> *Then We caused the earth to swallow up him and his house; and he had not (the least little) party to help him against Allāh, nor could he defend himself.*[70]

---

[68] Sūrah Ṣād, 38:35.
[69] Sūratu 'l-Qaṣaṣ [The Stories], 28:79.
[70] Sūratu 'l-Qaṣaṣ [The Stories], 28:81.

Khasafa ʿalayhi 'l-arḍ. The earth swallowed him.[71] Look at today's kings and presidents. What do they take with them when they leave this world? They die, and they take nothing. In the end the earth swallows everyone.

Sayyīdinā Adam ﷺ listened to Iblīs and was fooled into thinking he would granted immortality and an eternal kingdom, and thus he was cast down. But he repented. That is what is important.

Allah Wants Us to Repent

Allāh ﷻ knows we are weak, but he wants us to repent. Anytime you repent, Allāh ﷻ forgives you. The Companions used

---

[71] Qarun was doubtless of the people of Moses; but he acted insolently towards them: such were the treasures We had bestowed on him that their very keys would have been a burden to a body of strong men, behold, his people said to him: "Exult not, for Allah loveth not those who exult (in riches). But seek, with the (wealth) which Allah has bestowed on thee, the Home of the Hereafter, nor forget thy portion in this world: but do you good, as Allah has been good to thee, and seek not (occasions for) mischief in the land: for Allah loves not those who do mischief." He said: "This has been given to me because of a certain knowledge that I have." Did he not know that Allah had destroyed, before him, (whole) generations, which were superior to him in strength and greater in the amount (of riches) they had collected? But the wicked are not called (immediately) to account for their sins. So, he went forth among his people in the (pride of his wordly) glitter. Said those whose aim is the Life of this World: "Oh that we had the like of what Qarun has got, for he is truly a lord of mighty good fortune!" But those who had been granted (true) knowledge said: "Alas for you! The reward of Allah (in the Hereafter) is best for those who believe and work righteousness: but this none shall attain, save those who steadfastly persevere (in good)." Then We caused the earth to swallow up him and his house; and he had not (the least little) party to help him against Allah, nor could he defend himself. And those who had envied his position the day before began to say on the morrow: "Ah! It is indeed Allah Who enlarges the provision or restricts it, to any of His servants He pleases! Had it not been that Allah was gracious to us, He could have caused the earth to swallow us up! Ah! Those who reject Allah will assuredly never prosper." That Home of the Hereafter We shall give to those who intend not high-handedness or mischief on earth: and the end is (best) for the righteous. (Sūratu 'l-Qaṣaṣ [The Stories], 28:79-83)

to come to the Prophet ﷺ when they did something with which the Prophet ﷺ was displeased. What did Allāh ﷻ say to the Prophet ﷺ?

خُذْ مِنْ أَمْوَالِهِمْ صَدَقَةً تُطَهِّرُهُمْ وَتُزَكِّيهِم بِهَا وَصَلِّ عَلَيْهِمْ إِنَّ صَلاَتَكَ سَكَنٌ لَّهُمْ وَاللهُ سَمِيعٌ عَلِيمٌ

Of their goods, take alms, that so you mightest purify and sanctify them; and pray on their behalf. Verily your prayers are a source of tranquility for them: And Allāh is One Who heareth and knoweth.[72]

They came to the Prophet ﷺ after they committed a major wrong. In fact this verse was revealed concerning three Companions who disobeyed the order to go in the Way of Allāh . After the Prophet ﷺ returned to Madina, they came to him seeking forgiveness. Allāh ﷻ told him, "Never mind, they are coming to repent. Take their *ṣadaqa* to clean them and then pray for them. Your *salāt* is going to be a source of tranquility for them." And what did the Prophet ﷺ do? He took one third of their wealth. For those three that Allāh ﷻ was referring to in this verse, he took not one tenth or one fifth, but one third of their wealth! Today, they come and say, "We did something wrong" and they make *ṣadaqa* of $5 or $10. The Prophet said to those three ﷺ, "How much wealth do you have?" Then he took a third of it in order to cleanse them.

The strongest attachment human beings have to *dunyā* is their longing for a kingdom that never perishes. That means attachment to wealth, and specifically money. The Prophet ﷺ broke that attachment, by taking a third of their wealth.

Then Allāh ordered him: صَلِّ عَلَيْهِمْ —*"then pray on them."* It means, "Give them your prayers." إِنَّ صَلاَتَكَ سَكَنٌ لَّهُمْ—*"Surely your*

[72] Sūratu 't-Tawbah [Repentance], 9:103.

prayer is going to be a source of tranquility for them." [73]They will feel at ease, at peace, they will be forgiven. Are we looking for that peace today? No, no one cares. We hear, but we are not acting as adviced. It goes in one ear and out the other. There are a few that listen and obey, but only a few.

Distractions of *Dunya*

When you are in *dunyā*, Shaytan and his minions come to you with all their marshaled forces to make sure you to continue chasing this world's attractions, *dunyā*, like a dog running after a bone, never stopping by day or by night. All of your *hamm* (concern) is for *dunyā*. There is nothing else between your two eyes. They keep you so busy with the world, *dunyā*, that you cannot fulfill your prayers, nor you can do your assigned recitations, *awrād*, nor can you do anything that you are assigned by the shaykh. Your only concern is running after that bone. They decorate this *dunyā* with ornaments to distract you from your true goal:

زُيِّنَ لِلنَّاسِ حُبُّ الشَّهَوَاتِ مِنَ النِّسَاء وَالْبَنِينَ وَالْقَنَاطِيرِ الْمُقَنطَرَةِ مِنَ الذَّهَبِ وَالْفِضَّةِ وَالْخَيْلِ الْمُسَوَّمَةِ وَالأَنْعَامِ وَالْحَرْثِ ذَلِكَ مَتَاعُ الْحَيَاةِ الدُّنْيَا وَاللّهُ عِندَهُ حُسْنُ الْمَآبِ

Fair in the eyes of men is the love of things they covet: Women and sons; Heaped-up hoards of gold and silver; horses branded (for blood and excellence); and (wealth of) cattle and well-tilled land. Such are the possessions of this world's life; but in nearness to Allāh is the best of the goals (To return to).[74]

Think about the commercials you see on television. They make everything beautiful in order to attract your eyes. That is what Shaytan is doing—Shaytan, and the minions of Shaytan.

[73] Sūratu 't-Tawbah [Repentance], 9:103.
[74] Sūrat Āli 'Imrān [The Family of 'Imrān], 3:14.

How do they catch your eye? With *ḥubb ash-shahawāt,* the love of every sort of base desire. Shaytan tantalizes you with every kind of low desire. Nowhere is this more evident than in Las Vegas, which Shaytan and his friends have decorated with all kinds of attractions, putting men and women in front of you in sexually suggestive or explicit ways. *"Fair in the eyes of men is the love of things they covet."* That verse refers to loving all kinds of desires, but especially the desire for women. Shaytan and his followers know this. The videos they show on television always feature women, rarely men.

In this verse, Allāh ﷻ mentioned children, He mentioned gold and silver, and He also mentioned horses. Even today, horses are the most expensive objects of desire, more valuable even than diamonds. There are horses sold for $20 million or more today. There are horses that are more expensive than houses. The rich of the world—particularly the princes and other wealthy people of the Gulf—purchase these horses and keep them. Why? It is yet another proof of the continuing relevance of the Holy Qur'an, whose passages are as true today as they have ever been.

Declare War on Your Enemy

We see from this that we have an enemy. We must declare war on him. However, we must know that our enemy is not going to take that lightly. Rather, he is going to respond with all his forces against us. If you bomb him, he retaliates with ten bombs. If you fight him with something, he fights you with something a hundred times stronger. So, if you declare war against the attractions of Shaytan, when you declare war against him and his followers, they are going to declare war against you.

That is why *khalwah,* seclusion, is important. In seclusion, you can focus all your energy on fighting Shaytan and winning this war. But imagine how much you are going to suffer from Iblīs and his supporters! He is going to bombard you with every weapon imaginable.

In the stories of the saints of old, snakes used to come to them during their *khalwah*. So, I was always looking for a snake. I did not see one, but I was constantly hearing a sound in the wall, like the rattle of viper. I could not sleep because of this sound. I would turn my head, listening, but I did not want to move. However, after a while, it would go away. When I stopped paying attention to it, it faded away.

Once, a *walī* was asked, "Are you doing your *dhikr*, reciting 'Allāh, Allāh ?'"

"Why?" he replied. "Have I forgotten Him? Why would I need to remember Him if I am with him in every moment of my life? How could I forget Him?"

When we concentrate on our *awrād*, when we keep our focus on the shaykh and—through him—on the Prophet ﷺ—then nothing can faze us. This is how we prevail in the war against Shaytan.

Shaytan Does not Accept Defeat

Understand that your enemy does not accept *hazīma* (defeat). Understand that you must kill him, or he will kill you. Either you die or they die. You must choose. This is important, because when you realize that you are going to die if you lose, you will fight to the end with all your might. You will not pause or relent, because you know that you will be destroyed if you do.

This was the attitude I adopted during my seclusion. Right from day one, I decided that there was no other alternative. It was total war, a fight to the death. It was not a war of guns and bombs, but a war of thoughts and inspirations. Victory came from always being in *m'aīyyat ash-shaykh*, in the presence of my shaykh.

If you are in the company of the shaykh in every moment, you are safe. If for a blink of an eye you lose that connection, your enemy will defeat you. Remember, he is the one who said:

قَالَ رَبِّ بِمَآ أَغْوَيْتَنِي لأُزَيِّنَنَّ لَهُمْ فِي الأَرْضِ وَلأُغْوِيَنَّهُمْ أَجْمَعِينَ إِلاَّ عِبَادَكَ مِنْهُمُ الْمُخْلَصِينَ

(Iblīs) said: "O my Lord! Because You hast put me in the wrong, I will make (wrong) fair-seeming to them on the earth, and I will put them all in the wrong, Except Your servants among them, sincere and purified (by Your Grace)."[75]

And Allāh ﷻ said:

إِنَّ عِبَادِي لَيْسَ لَكَ عَلَيْهِمْ سُلْطَانٌ إِلاَّ مَنِ اتَّبَعَكَ مِنَ الْغَاوِينَ

For over My servants no authority shall you have, except such as put themselves in the wrong and follow you.[76]

Note that he is accepting Allāh ﷻ. He is speaking with Him. He said, "I am going to misguide them, but not those who are sincere to You." Look at the negotiation. Iblīs is doing his job—the job Allāh ﷻ assigned him to do. He sacrificed himself for the sake of the Ummah, and He is cursed, and he accepted that curse, and on Judgment Day he is going to say, "Give me my reward."

When you go deep into any verse of Quran, your mind will be shattered into dust.

How did Allāh ﷻ answer him? He said, "*You have no control over My sincere servants.*"

Why is Allāh ﷻ negotiating with Iblīs? This is from the Holy Qur'an. Allāh ﷻ cursed him, and he is cursed. But he did what he had to do by Allāh's *irāda* (Will). Allāh ﷻ willed Iblīs not to obey Him. Allāh ﷻ ordered him to make *sajdah*, but Allāh's Will was for him not to make *sajdah. Irādah wa amr. Amrun wa irāda,* Will and order, order and will. Understand, if you are clever.

---

[75] Sūratu 'l-Ḥijr [The Stony Tracts], 15:39, 40.
[76] Sūratu 'l-Ḥijr [The Stony Tracts], 15:42.

So, Iblīs was ordered to make *sajdah.* He did not. All of the angels did, but not him. Allāh ﷻ wanted him to take responsibility for testing human beings, to find out their qualities: are they are good or not. Thus, if you declare war against Iblīs, know that it is going to be a destructive war—an atomic war—and it is going to be either you or him. If you win, he will certainly continue to come against you until Judgment Day, but his power will be diminished. He will cry.

One day, Grandshaykh told me the story of his seclusion with Mawlana Shaykh Nāẓim. They were alone together for one year in Madinat al-munawarrah, facing the Dome of the Prophet ﷺ. Mawlana Grandshaykh brought two big plywood boards and covered the two windows of their room. They had no light, day or night. They used their watches to determine when it was time for prayer.

Mawlana Shaykh Nāẓim later told me that, during that whole year, Mawlana Grandshaykh was making *duāʿ*, invocation, for two hours each morning without stopping. He would begin at 1:30 or 2:00 in the morning, and each day he would recite a different *duāʿ* than the day before. Supplications were coming out of his heart like water from a fountain, and the energy of these prayers would shake the room. Grandshaykh said, "When I was making *duāʿ*, I was holding Allāh's Throne and asking for power for the Ummah of the Prophet ﷺ." When that *tajallī* comes on you in seclusion, you will feel you are flying and no one can stop you. It is like a laser with which you can move mountains.

Grandshaykh told me that, as *maghrib* time approached at the end of that year—for seclusions always end by *maghrib*—there came the sound of wailing from outside the door. He could hear a voice crying, and thousands of others crying behind that one.

"I was in the room with Shaykh Nāẓim, and I was hearing those lamentations. And the one that was crying was wailing, 'Those two are lost from our control forever!'"

Grandshaykh immediately realized that the one so lamenting was none other than Shaytan, and those wailing behind him were his minions.

"I opened the door quickly, wanting to catch him by his neck," Grandshaykh recalled. "But as soon as I made a move, they stopped me—for they knew that I was going to finish them! They stopped me. He will remain free until Judgment Day. It is his job, and he will be paid for it. However, he knew that we were beyond his control."

How to Win the War Against Shaytan

Allāh ﷻ has already shown us the outlines of that strategy by revealing to us the *Sharīʿah*. He has told us what is good and what is bad, and He has commanded us to pursue the former and avoid the latter. He has taught us the ways of piety and their methods. He has given us 500 obligations (*mā'mūrāt*) that we must follow, and He has shown us 800 forbiddens (*manhīyāt*) that we must avoid. He has informed us that our egos will try to use these 800 forbidden things against us to ensnare and enslave us, and He has revealed that our defense against these weapons of the ego lies in our performance of the 500 obligations.

It is for this reason that Allāh ﷻ inspired the self with the knowledge of Good and Evil, saying:

قَدْ أَفْلَحَ مَن زَكَّاهَا

Truly he succeeds that purifies it.[77]

The one who succeeds is the one who does good, and the one who fails is the one who does evil.

Allāh ﷻ also said:

وَنَفْسٍ وَمَا سَوَّاهَا فَأَلْهَمَهَا فُجُورَهَا وَتَقْوَاهَا

And its enlightenment as to its wrong and its right.[78])

[77] Sūratu 'sh-Shams [The Sun], 91:9.

As we have mentioned, you must come up with a strategy for combating devils if you are to survive in seclusion. If you succeed, you will master the strategy required to combat the lower self.

قال رسول الله صلى الله عليه وسلم : الحرب خدعة (و في رواية

أبو يعلى "الحرب خداع")

The Prophet ﷺ said, "War is strategy."[79]

This is true of the greatest war, the war against our egos. It is not only strategy, but stratagems—tricks. Either you must trick your ego, or your ego will trick you.

You must know that you declared war on your ego when you first took initiation with the shaykh. At the same time, it declared war on you. A constant battle has been going on ever since. It is a war based on trickery and deceit.

Your ego comes to you and makes you feel happy for being so pious, for doing your *awrād* and performing your prayers. It leads you believe you are someone important. You must guard against that.

I know one shaykh, may Allāh ﷻ bless him, who sometimes stops when he is in the middle of making *dhikr*. I asked him why he stops. He said, "That is when I feel happiness, doing *dhikr*. That is where my ego is tricking me. I feel like I am proud of what my ego is telling me."

Some people are happy and satisfied with what they achieved. That is wrong. That is why in the Naqshbandī Way, the shaykhs do not take the veils off their students until the very end. However, other *ṭarīqats* remove the veil from the eyes of their followers and they immediately begin to see. That is when the ego tricks you. It says, "Oh! Now you can see. Now you are something!"

---

[78] Sūratu 'sh-Shams [The Sun], 91:8.

[79] al-Bazzār, related by al-Ḥasan ibn ʿAlī ibn Abī Ṭālib.

There are 70,000 veils between you and the Prophet ﷺ. The shayks of the Naqshbandīyyah begin removing the thin veils from the side of the Prophet ﷺ first until all that is left is the last thick veil on the side of the student. Once permission comes to remove that veil, the student immediately finds himself in the presence of the Prophet ﷺ. The other *ṭarīqahs* reverse this process. They begin by first removing this thick veil on the side of the student, then strip away the successive layers between the student and the Prophet ﷺ. The danger with this method is that the student will become satisfied prematurely, before reaching the presence of the Prophet ﷺ. Even in the Naqshbandī *ṭarīqah*, the student may reach a level where they can experience true sight. When they do, Shaytan comes to trick them through their ego, and they may become satisfied with their station.

Seclusion Requires Support of the Shaykh

Until you experience this yourself, you can never fully understand and appreciate the experiences of those who have completed seclusions. You may read what Grandshaykh related about Mawlana Shaykh Nāẓim's seclusion, but you cannot really understand it until you yourself become an expert. It is the same as medicine. You may hear about a medical procedure, but you cannot truly understand it until you become a doctor—and to become a doctor, you must first complete a residency. That is to say, you must practice. Until you enter seclusion yourself, until you taste its difficulties, you will never be able to understand what the shaykh is describing when he speaks about what his own seclusion.

This is true of *ṭarīqah* in general. You cannot understand The Way until you are in it. Those who are not in *ṭarīqah* do not understand, nor can they understand, that it is primarily a path of difficulties. The shaykh does not send you candy. He does not give you what you like. He gives you difficulties in order to test you and train you.

If you try to perform seclusion without permission from the shaykh, or if you do so after asking the shaykh for permission instead of being ordered to do so by him, all you are really doing is meditating.

Seclusion is not meditation. Sometimes, when you meditate, you feel happy. In seclusion, you do not feel happy. You feel as though you are under constant attack. They bombard you. They throw all kinds of difficulties at you. Nor is seclusion like prayer, for even while praying you may still feel some pleasure from your worship. In seclusion, they want to cheat you. That is why they send all sorts of whisperings to your heart—bad thoughts and gossip.

These come mostly during the day, from *ishrāq,* sun-up to *maghrib,* sundown. From *maghrib* to *ishrāq,* you feel more peaceful, and fewer bad thoughts come to your mind. During the day, however, when you are busy with all kinds of *awrād,* the *shayāṭīn min al-jinn wa'l-ins,* devils from Jinn and mankind will attack you and try to stop you. At night, there is some respite from these attacks, which is why Allāh ﷻ ordered the Prophet ﷺ to pray and recite the Holy Qur'an for half the night or more, for one's personal devils are jailed and chained at night.

For this reason, it is easier to perform *murāqabah* at night. During the day, it is better to read and do *awrād.* That is why Mawlana Shaykh Nāẓim told me to begin *duāʿ* at 2 a.m.

In seclusion, every day brings new attacks, new barrages of bad thoughts and gossips, new difficulties and new problems. These whisperings of Shaytan attack the heart from every angle, with thoughts of family and children, with thoughts of health and wealth—even with wrong thoughts about religion, the Prophet ﷺ and Allāh ﷻ. Shaytan throws every kind of weapon at the heart.

While this onslaught is occurring, the *awlīyā* are watching. They look at you to see how you are reacting. Mawlana told me, "I am monitoring you day and night."

You feel them watching you, checking in on you. Sometimes, you even see them. A shadow may pass through the room, or you may smell a pleasant scent. These are the *awlīyā* coming and going. You can feel them, but hide as much as possible they try to of their presence.

The attacks waged by Shaytan and his armies against you in seclusion are like a tempest upon the sea. It is like a storm with terrible winds and huge waves, like Hurricane Katrina that drowned the city of New Orleans. It sweeps everything in front of it. It is like the raging ocean that destroyed Pharaoh and his army.

The ego is a coward. That is why it enlists the armies of Shaytan to attack you with all sorts of dirty, worldly thoughts and all the devils fighting under his banner.

Because it is a coward, it does not come at us directly in our daily lives. There is no need, because we are already immersed in *dunyā,* already covered with its stench. Our ego says, "This one is already smelly. Everyone is already running away from him or her."

In seclusion, however, we try to cleanse ourselves of that stench. We begin to polish our hearts and so remove that taint of worldly life that in the Allāh's Eyes does not amount to the weight of one mosquito's wing. When the ego sees this, it tries to drown us with the stench of all the wild and evil animal characters at its command.

Importance of Pacing

While it is important not to relent in this spiritual combat, it is also necessary to pace yourself. You cannot fight incessantly. It will kill you. You have to give yourself a little treat.

In my case, Mawlana instructed me to make tea immediately after praying the *sunnat al-wuḍū* upon waking up. This was my candy. When you drink tea, it makes you to wake up quickly and gives the self some happiness because you did something for it. So, when too many bad thoughts assail you, drink tea quickly. They will diminish, and you will feel more at ease.

FIVE

The Staff of Musa

What was this staff, this stick that gave Mūsā ﷺ the power to cause the sea to rise up and drown Pharaoh and his followers? Nothing was able to stand before that staff. When Pharaoh called his magicians to challenge Mūsā ﷺ, they came with all sorts of magic tricks. They came with snakes and illusions. But their staffs and wands were just wooden sticks, and Mūsā's staff overcame them all.

It is related in the Holy Qur'an that Allāh ﷻ asked Mūsā ﷺ about his staff, saying:

وَمَا تِلْكَ بِيَمِينِكَ يَا مُوسَى

And what is that in your right hand, O Moses?[80]

قَالَ هِيَ عَصَايَ أَتَوَكَّأُ عَلَيْهَا وَأَهُشُّ بِهَا عَلَى غَنَمِي وَلِيَ فِيهَا مَآرِبُ أُخْرَى

He said, "It is my rod: on it I lean; with it I beat down fodder for my flocks; and in it I find other uses."[81]

He said, "On it I lean." Can you lean on anything other than Allāh ﷻ? You cannot. When you lean on something, you surrender to it and ask it for support. What else is there to surrender to and ask for support other than Allāh ﷻ? There is nothing. So, what was this stick that Mūsā ﷺ was using to herd his sheep and beat down their fodder? It was a stick that he knew was never going to break—the stick that everyone on Earth must lean on if they do not want to fall: *lā ilāha illa-Llāh Muḥammadun rasūlullāh.* It is the staff of *maqām at-tawḥīd*. There is nothing to lean

---

80 Sūrah ṬāḤā 20:17.

81 Sūrah ṬāḤā 20:18.

on except the intercession of the Prophet ﷺ and *maghfiratullāh*, Allāh's forgiveness.

There is nothing else to lean on but that. Can you lean on a wooden stick? No, because it and everything else is bound to perish . The only thing that does not disappear and does not perish is *lā ilāha illa-Llāh Muḥammadun rasūlullāh*.

This, then, was the staff of Mūsā ؑ, the staff of *lā ilāha illa-Llāh Muḥammadun rasūlullāh*. With it, he herded his flock of sheep. What does that mean?

It means that he was teaching his people *lā ilāha illa-Llāh Muḥammadun rasūlullāh*, telling them that the Prophet Muḥammad ﷺ was coming after him. Indeed, all of the prophets informed their followers that *Sayyīdinā* Muḥammad ﷺ was coming.

That staff was standing firm, like the letter *alif*, in *istiqāmah*, the station of standing forth. The *alif* is always standing, as the *alif* in Allāh . That letter and the staff of Mūsā ؑ both signify one and the same thing. They both indicate *maqām at-tawḥīd: lā ilāha illa-Llāh Muḥammadun rasūlullāh*—the Station of Oneness, realization of the reality of "there is no god except Allāh ."

This is one of the things that were revealed to me in my seclusion, as were the meanings of the other letters in the Holy Name.

Secret Meanings of the Letters of the Holy Name

When we look at the Holy Divine Name, Allāh, which encompasses all the Beautiful Divine Names and Attributes, we see it is composed of four letters: *alif*, two *lāms* and *hāh*.

alif is always indicating the truth. Everyone is in need for the *alif*, for it is related to *ākhirah*. Islam begins with *alif*, *īmān* (faith) begins with *alif* and *iḥsān* (spiritual excellence) begins with *alif*. The first chapter of the Holy Qur'an, Surat al-Fātiḥah, begins with *alif*: "*Alḥamdulillāh*." Surat al-Baqara, the second chapter of the Qur'an, also begins with *alif*: "*alif lām mīm*." If you want to ask for anything, you begin with *ismillāh,* the Name of Allāh," which also begins with *alif.*

Alif is the only letter that has nothing before it. It is the beginning and, as such, indicates the Absolute Divine Essence (*adh-dhāt al-buḥt*). It is a term that has no explanation in English. The Divine Essence has no description. Allāh ﷻ described His Essence by saying "Allāh," and all of the other Beautiful Divine Attributes and Names manifest within that one Name.

In the two *lāms,* all secrets have been placed. They are like two wings, and in between these two wings, everything is found. The two *lāms* represent the *Maqām al-mulk,* the Station of Worldly Dominion and the *Maqām al-malakūt,* the Station of Heavenly Dominion. Simultaneosly, these correspond to the Station of the Mind (*mulk*) and the Station of the Spirit (*rūḥ*). Both of these words—*mulk* and *malakūt*—contain the letter *lām.* At the same time, *Mulk* is whatever surrounds you in this physical universe, while *malakūt* is heavenly. Between the two *lāms* is secreted the knowledge of these two kingdoms and that secret and that knowledge relate to "There is no god but Allāh ."

The *hāh* is everything that is going to appear from that hidden treasure, the whole creation emanating from the *Hūwīyyat al-muṭlaq,* the Absolute Unknown Divine Identity, and *adh-dhāt al-buḥt,* the Absolute Divine Essence, as represented by the letter *hāh.* All are wrapped up by the letter *hāh.* The *hāḥ* wraps up the two *lāms* of "Allāh " and points to the illuminating Godly power: *ad-dāllah 'alā al-qudrat an-nūrānīyyā al-ilāhīyyah.* This illuminated power is heavenly and Lordly and indicates the Oneness of Allāh ﷻ everywhere.

Between *alif* representing *ākhirah,* the Afterlife and the Divine Presence and *hāh,* representing Hūwa, the Hidden Divine Identity, that is, between the Beginning and End, exists the treasury of the two divine kingdoms: the worldly dominion and the heavenly dominion. In these two kingdoms, which represent what is other than Allāh, *mā siwā 'Llāh,* the Beautiful Divine Names reveals themselves, making their Divine Impressions.

Lā ilāha illa-Llāh represents the Divine Reality, *and Muḥammadun rasūlullāh,* represents the creation, *mā siwā 'Llāh,* whatever is other than Allāh . *Lā ilāha ill 'Llāh* describes the Creator. *Muḥammadun rasūlullāh* is a description of creation. *Muḥammad* is *rasūlullāh,* the prophet and messenger of Allāh, to all creation, thus the two *lām*s of the Divine Name "Allāh ", representing the kingdoms of this life and the afterlife, are a grant from Allāh to His Chosen Messenger.

Hāh is the first letter of the Divine Name *Hūwa,* and at the same time it is the last letter of the Divine Name *Allāh* . Thus in saying:

قُلْ هُوَ اللَّهُ أَحَدٌ

Qul Hūwa Allāh Āḥad—*Say: He is* Allāh, *the Unique!*[82]

"Hūwa Allāh" in the Chapter of Sincerity, the letter *hāh* contains within its two appearances these two Divine Names. Thus we find two *hāhs* enclose the two Names: Hūwa Allāh.

This is further alluded to by the verse:

هُوَ الْأَوَّلُ وَالْآخِرُ

Hūwa 'l-āwwalu wa 'l-ākhiru

He is the First and the Last.[83]

Sūratu 'l-Ikhlāṣ stands as a witness to the fact that of the Prophet ﷺ being clothed with the Divine Attributes, the First and the Last, and this is the reason why he ﷺ said:

فأورثني علم الأولين والآخرين

He bequeathed to me knowledge of *al-Āwwalīn wa 'l-Ākhirīn* – the Firsts and the Lasts.

---

[82] Sūratu'l-Ikhlāṣ [Absolute Oneness], 112:1.

[83] Sūratu'l-Ḥadīd [Iron], 57:3.

These are the *tajallīyāt* or disclosures of the Divine Reality to him ﷺ. Between *alif* of Allāh, representing *ākhirah* and the *hāh* of Hūwa, representing the Hidden Divine Essence, that is, between the Beginning and End, the treasury encompassing all the Beautiful Divine Names reveals itself.

Everything related to *ākhirah* must begin with *alif*. If you remove the *alif* from the Name Allāh, what is left remaining? *Lām lām hāh,* which is read *lillāh. Lillāh* means "for the sake of Allāh", or "What is owned by Allāh " or "what belongs to Allāh ."

So that first letter shows you the meaning of the name Allāh. If you take it away it shows you *mā siwā 'Llāh,* whatever is other than Allāh, i.e. the creation. Without Him it cannot be. *Alif* refers to Allāh. If you take *alif* away, it becomes *lillāh,* all that is other than Him.

If you now remove the first *lām,* what is left? *Lām hāh, lahu. Lahu* means "Everything is for Him." You don't own yourself, or anything, but He owns all.

What then is left if you take away the final *lām*? *Hāh.* It represents *Hū*. Back to *Hū*. Whatever you knew you still are back to where you were—you know nothing, He is completely unknown.

If you take the first letter, *alif,* which belongs to *ākhirah* it becomes *lillāh.* And if you take away the first *lām,* which is *lām al-mulk,* representing the Earthly Kingdom, it become *lahu.* If you remove the final *lām,* which is *lām al-malakūt,* representing the Heavenly Kingdom, what is left? *Hū*. That means there is nothing except Him. What lies between *alif,* the first and *hāh,* the last, between the Beginning and End, are the kingdoms of *dunyā* and *ākhirah.*

If we turn around now, we see that all of the powers and secrets of the last three letters *lām, lām, hāh,* are pouring into the first letter, *alif,* before which is nothing. It is the beginning, signifying the beginning of creation. There is "nothing" before the *alif,* but from that unknowable impenetrable void emerges all these secrets. This *alif* will witness for you and point you toward the level of Divine Uniqueness, *āḥadiyya*: *Qul Hūw 'Allāhu Āḥad—Say: He is Allāh, the Unique.*

The Name that encompasses all the Divine manifestations and knowledges is "Allāh ." The Prophet ﷺ mentioned 99 other Divine Names, but there are more—infinitely more. The name "Allāh " encompasses all of these and describes them all. This is the secret of the *Maqām at-tawḥīd,* the Station of Allāh's Uniqueness and Oneness.

So *Qul Hūw 'Allāhu Āḥad* means: "Tell them, O Muḥammad, that what you are describing is One and Only." *Āḥad*. He did not say *Wāḥid,* One. *Āḥad* is more compelling than *Wāḥid*. *Āḥad* is the Unique One, to Whom there is no resemblance whatsoever:

لَيْسَ كَمِثْلِهِ شَيْءٌ وَهُوَ السَّمِيعُ البَصِيرُ

Laysa ka-mithili shay wa Hūwa 's-Samīʿu 'l-Baṣīr.

there is nothing whatever like unto Him, and He is the One that hears and sees (all things). [84]

That word Allāh is the Name encompassing all the Beautiful Names. When it is revealed to the Prophet ﷺ it comes to Him with all its manifestations and with all the knowledge that it contains. These infinite descriptions of infinite Names are produced and gifted to Prophet Muḥammad ﷺ and he is clothed with each and every one of them. Allāh clothed him with these manifestations, revealing the importance of *Qul Hūw 'Allāhu Āḥad.* "I am the One with no partner," He is telling Muḥammad ﷺ. Now when Allāh is telling him is He not showing him as well? Did He not take him up on ascension? Every verse of Qur'an is a dress, is a *tajallī* and it is a light from Allāh's Ancient Words. And this entire dress, Allāh's Divine Words, were dressed on the Prophet ﷺ on the Night of Power.

---

[84] Sūratu 'sh-Shūra [Mutual Consultation] 42:11.

All of this is contained between the *alif* with its *istiqāmah,* its standing upright—a reminder that everything stands in need of the *alif.* Justas every number needs the number 1, so every word needs the letter *alif.* It is the first letter of the alphabet. Thus to make a word you need an *alif.* That is because it is the first letter of "Allāh ." Without it, there is no alphabet. You need *alif* to keep your life upright. If you bring the *alif* up, as it is in the *Ism al-Jalālah,* Allāh, your life will be upright. And man is the only creature which stands completely upright, just as *alif* is the only such letter of the alphabet and the number one, 1, is the only such number among all numbers. It is this nature of uprightness which differentiates humankind from the other creatures.

This knowledge is of all kinds: heavenly, worldly and universal. It is the knowledge of animate and inanimate things, the knowledge of those which are silent and those which speak. It is the knowledge of rocks and mountains, plants and animals, human beings, jinn and angels. It is the knowledge of the Universe (*kawnīyyah*), the Earth (*dunyāwīyya*) and the Heavens (*samāwīyyah*). It is also the knowledge of the *ṣawāmit*—the silence of the cosmos that surrounds us.

There are angels that hold together the structure of the universe. They are silent, the knowledge of them is silent and you cannot understand it except through silence. This silence is a language for those that are silent, and its hearing does not come except through *murāqabah* and *rābiṭah.* Some of the angels carry messages in this silent language and some of the *awlīyā* can understand that language and hear those messages. It is like a sort of telepathy, completely without sound. These are *aṣ-ṣawāmit,* the silent ones.

The *an-nawāṭiq,* those that speak with each other, also share a knowledge.

All of this, as we have said, is between the two *lāms* of the Holy Name. All of this is hidden between the mind and the soul. If you have developed a strong connection with your shaykh, you can penetrate these levels of knowledge that are hidden within you.

However, the ego wants to keep you locked in the prison of worldly pleasures. It wants to prevent you from ascending through the stations of *ma'rifah,* and to display the Godly lights that will shine forth from you as you ascend to the level of tasting. The ego tries to keep you down and prevent the opening of these lights of knowledge in your heart that will allow you to make that ascent.

That is why knowledge of *awlīyā* is utterly different from knowledge of ordinary people. This kind of knowledge will astonish the mind because it is the door to the Secret of the Secret of the Secret of the Divine Essence. If you remain outside, it is impossible to reach the Essence, just as the jinn are able to approach Paradise and snatch some of its fruits like one who steals apples hanging over an orchard fence but are unable to enter within.

The *awlīyā* can reach the Secret of the Essence. They can learn from the manifestations of the Beautiful Names and Attributes. That is what is meant by *Sirr as-sirr adh-dhāt alladhī Anta 'Llah.* That is the Hidden Essence—*Hūwa 'Llah, Hūwa Anta 'Llah*—"You, the Most Hidden Unknown Essence, are Allāh ."

These doors are only opened for the people of remembrance (*Āhl adh-dhikr*). You do not have to enter them. Some people are happy to stay in a modest house. Others want to live in a palace. The people of *dhikr* go to palaces. They are asking to reach the Divine Presence. Whoever does not ask does not reach there.

إذا ذكرني في ملأ ذكرته في ملأ خير منهم

> Allāh ﷻ said in a hadith *qudsī,* "If you remember Me in a gathering, I will remember you in a better one."

It is a holy hadith of the Prophet ﷺ. In the Holy Qur'an, Allāh ﷻ also made special mention of those who remember Him standing, sitting or laying down—those who, in every moment of their lives –remember their Lord.

الَّذِينَ يَذْكُرُونَ اللّٰهَ قِيَامًا وَقُعُودًا وَعَلَىٰ جُنُوبِهِمْ

Men who celebrate the praises of Allāh, standing, sitting, and lying down on their sides.[85]

The Station of Oneness and the Station of Uniqueness

The Station of Oneness is *waḥdānīyyah,* and the Station of Oneness that begins with *Āḥadīyyah* is the level of *mushāḥadah,* witnessing. This was the level of *Sayyīdinā* Bilāl when he was being tortured by the idolators. At that time he was in the Station of Seeing and Witnessing the Divine Presence.

The Station of Uniqueness (*Maqām al-āḥadīyyah*) is the Station of Witnessing (*Maqām al-mushāḥadah*): *An yushāhidu mā lā tushāhidu*—I am witnessing what you are not witnessing. Anyone who endures difficulty and cries out for the sake of Allāh ﷻ, glorifying the Lord and praising the Prophet ﷺ, will be on the right track. That person will have reached the Station of Witnessing.

Sayyīdinā Bilāl was witnessing in the Divine Presence, and he was dressed with these robes (*khila*ʿ) and medallions (*khila*ʿ *al-anwār*), which are the manifestations of the Names and Attributes that are coming from the Beautiful Name of Dhu 'l-Jalāl wa 'l-Kamāl, the Majestic and Beautiful Perfection of the Lord. When you endure boredom and the other challenges that come with seclusion patiently, you will be dressed in the same way.

Allāh ﷻ does not give to everyone directly, but gives through the Prophet ﷺ because people would not be able to carry His gifts otherwise. Only the Prophet ﷺ can carry these

[85] Sūrat Āli 'Imrān [The Family of 'Imrān], 3:191.

manifestations. When he is dressed with them, they are sent to his Companions, and from them, to the entire *Ummah*.

The Prophet's name in heaven is Āḥmad.

وَإِذْ قَالَ عِيسَى ابْنُ مَرْيَمَ يَا بَنِي إِسْرَائِيلَ إِنِّي رَسُولُ اللهِ إِلَيْكُم مُّصَدِّقًا لِّمَا

بَيْنَ يَدَيَّ مِنَ التَّوْرَاةِ وَمُبَشِّرًا بِرَسُولٍ يَأْتِي مِن بَعْدِي اسْمُهُ أَحْمَدُ فَلَمَّا

جَاءهُم بِالْبَيِّنَاتِ قَالُوا هَذَا سِحْرٌ مُّبِينٌ

And remember, Jesus, the son of Mary, said: "O Children of Israel! I am the apostle of Allāh (sent) to you, confirming the Law (which came) before me, and giving Glad Tidings of an Messenger to come after me, whose name shall be Āḥmad." But when he came to them with Clear Signs, they said, "This is evident sorcery!"[86]

Because his name is Āḥmad, Allāh ﷻ is dressing him with these different manifestations and he is taking these gifts and distributing them. He gave such a gift to *Sayyīdinā* Bilāl ؓ when he was being tortured.

> *Fa-ahdāhā ila Sayyīdinā Bilāl fī maqām al-āḥadīyyah, bi 'n-nūr al-khāṣ aṣ-ṣāfi bi ṣafā jamāl unsi ishrāqihi.*
>
> The Prophet ﷺ was gifting Bilāl ؓ in this Station of Uniqueness with those special lights—the pure and beautiful lights of intimacy and familiarity of the Lordly illuminations of his secret dawn.

These lights bestow a fresh, clean beauty, such as you see when you watch the dawn transform the dark night into a beautiful and radiant morn. That is what the Prophet ﷺ was giving to *Sayyīdinā* Bilāl ؓ.

The ego is only interested in the pleasures of *dunyā*. It seeks excess of wealth and beauty, desiring only the ornaments of

[86] Sūratu 'ṣ-Ṣaff [The Ranks], 61:6.

the material world. However, if you struggle against your ego and confront it head on, the Prophet ﷺ will bestow such gifts on you.

They asked a *walī* named 'Umar, "Where is that *walī*, 'Umar?" He said, "There is no more *walī* 'Umar. He died. He is gone. He is there. He is not here anymore. He is not in *dunyā* anymore, but in his Lord's Presence. He cannot see anymore. He can only sees the Divine Presence. He sees only his Lord."

Allah's Generosity and Majesty

Jalīlan kalīman, majestic generosity, is one of the characteristics expressed by the Holy Name "The Majestic" (*al-Jalāl*). The power of this majestic generosity extends to the other Names and Attributes, including "The Merciful" (*ar-Raḥmān*) and "The Compassionate" (*ar-Raḥīm*). *Ar-Raḥmān* and *ar-Raḥīm* have been dressed with the majestic power of the Name that encompasses all Names: "Allāh ." That is why Allāh's Mercy (*Raḥmān*) and Compassion (*Raḥīm*) are endless in their giving. There is no limit to them. They are giving and never stopping, praise be to Allāh ﷻ!

Whatever you take, Allāh ﷻ gives, for He is *ar-Raḥmān ir-Raḥīm*. However, if someone else fills your container, then there will be no place for what Allāh ﷻ is giving you. If your container is filled with the delicious tastes of this worldly life (*ladhāt ad-dunyā*), there will be no room for His Divine gifts.

Awlīyāullāh understand that Allāh's giving is endless, so they are always taking and giving to their followers so that they can fill up their containers with these heavenly gifts. Both *murshid,* the guiding teacher, and *murīd,* the seeking student, are in need of each other. It is obvious that the student needs the shaykh, but the converse is also true. If there is no student, what is the purpose of the shaykh? The importance of the shaykh lies in his ability to guide his students. If there are no students, to whom does he give what Allāh ﷻ bestows on him? Even *Sayyīdinā* Muḥammad ﷺ needed his Ummah. Without his Ummah, to whom is he Prophet

ﷺ? Allāh ﷻ made the Ummah to be in need of the Prophet ﷺ, and He made the Prophet ﷺ to be in need of the Ummah.

That is why the shaykh likes to be with his students. He does not like to be away from them, because he needs to be with them. He needs to empty his heart to them, because Allāh ﷻ is constantly filling it up through His Endless Majestic Divine Generosity. That is why Shaykh ʿAbd Allah and Mawlana Shaykh Nāẓim would give talks (*suḥbah*) that lasted three hours. People would get tired and leave, but other people would come—and still the *suḥbah* continues. They were trying to empty their containers in order to receive more.

If the cup is full, you cannot receive more. Of course, there is a limit to how much you can consume. If you eat a lot of honey, it loses its sweetness. It is the same with everything, except for Divine Knowledge (*maʿrifah*). Whatever you consume of that, still you need and desire more. That is why *awlīyāullāh* eat what is revealed to them, digest it and give it to their students, not unlike the mother bird with her chicks. Then *awlīyāullāh* take more.

SIX

The Prophet is the Centerpoint of Creation

Allāh ﷻ raised the Prophet ﷺ to the *maqām qāba qawsayni aw adnā*, the Station of Two Bow's Length or Nearer. He made him to see the secrets of secrets (*sirr al-asrār*) and the unseen lights (*anwār al-ilāhīyyah*). Allāh ﷻ made *Sayyīdinā* Muḥammad ﷺ to see these Lordly lights and caused him to enter into them, because they denote the circle of all creation and the Prophet ﷺ is the center of that circle. He is like the Sun, taking and giving. He takes from his Lord and he becomes like the source of light (*iḍā'a*), just as the Sun produces light through enormous atomic reactions. In the same way, the Prophet ﷺ is the source of light and reflects it through the Moon.

No one can reach the Sun. One cannot even look at it. If you look at it, it will blind you. But you can look at the Moon and see the light of the Sun reflected on it. Similarly, no one can approach the Prophet ﷺ, but you can approach the *awlīyā*. They are like transformers. Electricity is transmitted through high voltage lines at 250,000 volts. That is too powerful for the appliances in your house. Before the electricity reaches your house, it passes through a transformer that modifies its intensity to make it safe and usable. *Awlīyā* do the same thing with the light of the Prophet ﷺ.

Allāh ﷻ gave the Prophet ﷺ the knowledge of the smallest details. In a newspaper there are headlines. But under the headlines are the details. Allāh ﷻ gave the Prophet ﷺ not only the headlines, but all of the details as well—every detail of knowledge. He knows everything about everyone.

These two Names, *ar-Raḥmān* and *ar-Raḥīm* are both a healing (*shifah*) and a blessing (*baraka*). So, anyone who calls on his Lord by these two Names will be cured of any sickness. That is why it is good to say, "*Yā Raḥmān, yā Raḥīm.*" If you do, Allāh ﷻ

will cleanse you. *Raḥmān* relates to the favors of this world, while *Raḥīm* relates to the favors of the next.

رَبَّنَا آتِنَا فِي الدُّنْيَا حَسَنَةً وَفِي الآخِرَةِ حَسَنَةً وَقِنَا عَذَابَ النَّارِ

Rabbanā ātinā fi 'd-dunyā ḥasanatan wa fi'l-ākhirati ḥasanatan wa qinā ʿadhāb an-nār.

Our Lord! Give us good in this world and good in the Hereafter, and defend us from the torment of the Fire![87]

Allāh gives from the secret of *Raḥmān* in this life and from the secret of *Raḥīm* in the next life.

The *awlīyāullāh* pray, "O Allāh, through the secret of these two Names, send us a king that we may fight in the way of Allāh ."

What do they want to fight? They want to fight the ego; to fight arrogance; to fight pride and and to fight the other ruinous traits of the self.

The Children of Israel and Talut

In the same way, the Children of Israel asked their prophet to send them a king to fight against the tyranny that was oppressing them.

وَقَالَ لَهُمْ نَبِيُّهُمْ إِنَّ اللّهَ قَدْ بَعَثَ لَكُمْ طَالُوتَ مَلِكاً قَالُوَاْ أَنَّى يَكُونُ لَهُ الْمُلْكُ عَلَيْنَا وَنَحْنُ أَحَقُّ بِالْمُلْكِ مِنْهُ وَلَمْ يُؤْتَ سَعَةً مِّنَ الْمَالِ قَالَ إِنَّ اللّهَ اصْطَفَاهُ عَلَيْكُمْ وَزَادَهُ بَسْطَةً فِي الْعِلْمِ وَالْجِسْمِ وَاللّهُ يُؤْتِي مُلْكَهُ مَن يَشَاءُ وَاللّهُ وَاسِعٌ عَلِيمٌ

Their Prophet said to them: "(Allāh) has appointed Ṭālūt as king over you." They said: "How can he exercise authority over us when we are better fitted than he to exercise authority, and

[87] Sūratu 'l-Baqara [The Heifer],2:201.

he is not even gifted with wealth in abundance?" He said: "(Allāh) has Chosen him above you, and has gifted him abundantly with knowledge and bodily strength: Allāh Grants His authority to whom He pleases. Allāh cares for all, and He knows all things."[88]

Their prophet said, "Allāh has chosen Ṭālūt to be your king," but they did not accept him. Their prophet said, "Allāh chose him because he surpasses you in knowledge and in bodily strength."

He was *ʿalimun bi ūmūri dunyāhum wa ākhiratahum.* Allāh ﷻ made him knowledgeable in the affairs of their *dunyā* and *ākhirah.* It means that he was a true guide for his people, like a true Shaykh that guides his students in both *dunyā* and *ākhirah.* Allāh ﷻ gave Ṭālūt the knowledge and wisdom to do both for his people. He made him an *ʿalim* and gave him that power and those secrets.

This sort of knowledge is that special knowledge referred to in the Holy Qur'an:

فَوَجَدَا عَبْدًا مِّنْ عِبَادِنَا آتَيْنَاهُ رَحْمَةً مِنْ عِندِنَا وَعَلَّمْنَاهُ مِن لَّدُنَّا عِلْمًا

...they found one of our servants that We taught him from our heavenly knowledge.[89]

قُل رَّبِّ زِدْنِي عِلْمًا

Qul Rabbī zidnī ʿilman.

Say, "O my Lord! advance me in knowledge."[90]

This is not normal knowledge (*ʿilm*), but Divinely-revealed knowledge, as in:

---

[88] Sūratu 'l-Baqara [The Heifer],2:247.
[89] Sūratu 'l-Kahf [The Cave], 18:65.
[90] Sūrah ṬāḤā 20:114.

واتقوا الله ويعلمكم الله

w 'attaqullāh wa yu'alimakumullāh

Observe your duty to Allāh. Allāh is teaching you.[91]

There are three relevant verses here, look:

"O Allāh increase my knowledge" and *"we taught him from our heavenly knowledge"* and *"be pious and Allāh will teach you."*

Where does the *'ilm* come from in all three verses? In each case, it means that you are asking it from the heavens. You are not asking this knowledge from *dunyā*. Allāh ﷻ said:

سَنُرِيهِمْ آيَاتِنَا فِي الْآفَاقِ وَفِي أَنفُسِهِمْ حَتَّى يَتَبَيَّنَ لَهُمْ أَنَّهُ الْحَقُّ أَوَلَمْ يَكْفِ بِرَبِّكَ أَنَّهُ عَلَى كُلِّ شَيْءٍ شَهِيدٌ

Soon will We show them our Signs in the (furthest) regions (of the earth), and in their own souls, until it becomes manifest to them that this is the Truth. Is it not enough that your Lord doth witness all things?[92]

We must seek that heavenly knowledge. The knowledge of this world is going to end with it, but heavenly knowledge will remain.

Where is that heavenly knowledge today? In most mosques, they are not teaching that *'ilm* anymore. It is hidden now. *'Ilm al-ḥaqā'iq, 'ilm al-adhwāq* is hidden now. There is only the knowledge of papers: *Wa hunā yātī min qibl as-samā.* You must ask for that heavenly *'ilm*: "O Allāh, give us knowledge from the hidden knowledge." If you do, do you think that Allāh ﷻ will not put that hidden knowledge on your tongue? He will, as long as you are pious and sincere.

---

[91] Sūratu 'l-Baqara [The Heifer],2:282.

[92] Sūrah Fuṣṣilat [Explained in Detail], 41:53.

Sincerity is not just praying your prayers. The one who is truly sincere never acts inappropriately to others. That means that you must not hate, you must not get jealous, you must not create confusion (*fitnah*). To be truly sincere, you must not be arrogant (*aẓamah*). These characteristics must be molded inside you if you are to receive that kind of knowledge. You do not give a diamond to children, because they do not know its value. Do not say, "O Allāh, clean me." He will clean you when He sees that you are patient and steadfast on the Way.

Allāh ﷻ gave Ṭālūt "superiority in body and knowledge" (*basṭatan fi 'l-ʿilmi wa 'l-jism*), but his people continued complaining and would not accept him. When their prophet said, "Ṭālūt is going to be king," they said, "How he is going to be king? We surpass him in wealth."

See how they quarreled with their prophet? In the same way, the ego quarrels with the divine light in the heart. The ego always argues with your divine aspect. That is why we always feel like we are being torn by some inner struggle, to the point that we no longer know what is correct and what is not. This is a result of that constant stuggle between the ego and the heart.

Ark of the Covenant

The Ark of the Covenant was the sign of the kingship of Ṭālūt. Allāh ﷻ sent angels carrying this chest containing the relics of *Sayyīdinā* Mūsā ؑ and *Sayyīdinā* Hārūn ؑ. Those relics were peacefulness and tranquility.

The children of Israel wanted to see a sign. They said, "O our Lord! Show us a sign!" The sign that Allāh ﷻ gave them was the Ark of the Covenant:

وَقَالَ لَهُمْ نَبِيُّهُمْ إِنَّ آيَةَ مُلْكِهِ أَن يَأْتِيَكُمُ التَّابُوتُ فِيهِ سَكِينَةٌ مِّن رَّبِّكُمْ
وَبَقِيَّةٌ مِّمَّا تَرَكَ آلُ مُوسَى وَآلُ هَارُونَ تَحْمِلُهُ الْمَلَائِكَةُ إِنَّ فِي ذَٰلِكَ لَآيَةً لَّكُمْ
إِن كُنتُم مُّؤْمِنِينَ

And (further) their Prophet said to them: "A Sign of his authority is that there shall come to you the Ark of the covenant, with (an assurance) therein of security from your Lord, and the relics left by the family of Moses and the family of Aaron, carried by angels. In this is a symbol for you if ye indeed have faith."[93]

Their prophet told them the Ark contained *sakinatun min rabbikum*—peace from your Lord. What is that *sakīnah*? Why did Allāh ﷻ mention it? *Sakīnah* is not security, as it is often translated, it is tranquility.

The student finds the same sense of tranquility in his relationship with the shaykh. However, just as the Children of Israel also found in the Ark the relics of Mūsā ﷺ and Hārūn ﷺ, there is something else precious here, too. That is the first sight of the shaykh. As soon as your eyes fall on the face of the shaykh or you meet his eyes, you are instantly attracted and say, "Oh! I found him." Then you take *baya*ʿ and receive that tranquility.

[93] Sūratu 'l-Baqara [The Heifer],2:248.

SEVEN

Three Levels of Tranquility

It is said that there are three levels of tranquility, and each is related to the connection:

Tranquility of the Heart:

The Children of Israel looked inside the Ark and what they saw there brought peace to their hearts. Similarly, as you make your ascension under the guidance of the shaykh—through what he gave you of *awrād, rābiṭah* and *murāqabah*—your vision clears and you find tranquility because you perceive that you are approaching the presence of the Prophet ﷺ.

What is that tranquility? It is the breath of knowledge (*rīḥ al-ʿilm*). When tranquility comes, you begin to breathe in from the breeze of knowledge. That is why we say *nafs al-muṭma'inna.* When peacefulness comes, that means *taqwā* comes:

واتقوا الله ويعلمكم الله

w 'attaqullāh wa yuʿalimakumullāh

Observe your duty to Allāh and Allāh will teach you.[94]

It is like the *rīḥ al-ʿilm,* the breeze of knowledge, which is the pleasant breeze that comes in the morning bearing the scent of dew on the leaves of the leaves of the trees. When that fragrance comes, you feel refreshed. That is also known as *rīḥ aṣ-ṣibā* the fragrant breeze of youth. That is a heavenly power, and when it emanates, and you inhale it, it rejuvenates your whole system. That is why *awlīyā* are always physically strong as well as knowledgeable in matters both of *dunyā* and matters of *ākhirah,* because Allāh ﷻ gave them everything.

---

[94] Sūratu 'l-Baqara [The Heifer],2:282.

Where does the dew that is carried by this breeze come from? It is from the atmosphere. It is precipitation that accumulates and becomes a drop on a leaf. In the same way, when you open your heart, the dewdrops of the Holy Names *ar-Raḥmān*, the Beneficent and *ar-Raḥīm*, the Most Merciful, begin to drip onto your heart, and when they drip onto your heart it gives you *rīḥan sākinan ṭayyibah*—a sweet and peaceful breeze that opens to you all kinds of inner knowledge. You then become like one who has just brushed his teeth with a delightful toothpaste and carries its sweet scent on his breath. In the same way, when a pious person opens his mouth, the breath of that heavenly dew will emerge. This speech is what attracts followers to the shaykh. That is the breath of knowledge, and that breath is tranquil and sweet. It emerges from the mouth of the knower because he is able to share the Divine Knowledge that Allāh ﷻ granted him.

However the sound of his speech is like thunder to the enemy of Allāh making him flee. That is why Shaytan cannot stay in the presence of the shaykh. Shaytan or Iblīs are afraid of the sound of the true gnostic and must flee from it. Even the ego must run away. The shaykh's tongue has this power because it is busy with constant remembrance of Allāh ﷻ, as is his heart.

Allāh's Mercy:

There are two parts of this secret, one of which was given to the Prophet ﷺ, the other which was inherited by *awlīyā*. This secret derives from Allāh's Subtle, Kind and Gentle Mercy (*luṭf*).

Because of His Love and His good pleasure with His dedicated servants, Allāh will pour that knowledge upon the heart of whoever has dedicated his life to gnosis, *maʿrifatullāh*. Allāh ﷻ will pour that on his tongue, from the subtleness of the word of the truthful one, *aṣ-ṣādiq*. God will put that knowledge on his tongue and in his heart, and the truthful one will share that information with his students. Whatever Allāh ﷻ pours into his heart, he gives his students. Allāh ﷻ gives him the heavenly knowledge and wisdom that he needs to the guide people. With this knowledge and wisdom, shaykhs can gaze at the the Preserved Tablets (*lawḥ al-maḥfūẓ*), and see what your covenant (*'aḥd*) was on the Day of Promises and direct you to keeping that.

Sometimes keeping the order of the shaykh, as he directs, according to what he observes of the divine destiny on the Preserved Tablets is hard on the *murīd* because he is combating his ego. When a seekter receives initiation, *baya'*, he must know that he is now entering the arena of real combat. Those battles that take place in *dunyā* between gathered armies are nothing compared to the battle between a person and his or her ego. That is why we always surrender to our ego, all of us—even the *walī*. The saint is not sinless, (*ma'ṣūm*) like the prophets. However, the *walī* does not err with bad intention, but mistakes take place, nonetheless.

We, on the other hand, are not erring with good intentions. We make mistakes because of our bad intentions, because our ego dictates to us what to do.

> The true gnostic, the knower of Divine Knowledge and the follower of Allāh's Way will find the lights and secrets of that knowledge manifest upon him because he purified himself. He will be adorned with Allāh's Names and Attributes. This is the second level of tranquility.

Tranquility of the Prophets

How did *Sayyīdinā* Jibrīl ﷺ, (*al-malik 'alā qulūbi 'l-anbīyā*), the King of the Angels, who reveals Divine revelations to the hearts of the prophets and messengers, pour knowledge and revelation into the hearts of the prophets? *ma' tarwīḥ al-asrār wa kashf as-sarā'ir*, Thus, Jibrīl ﷺ revealed to them the secrets that Allāh ﷻ wanted them to know, according to their levels and *kashf as-sarā'ir*, unveiling to them the secrets of the hearts of the Ummah, and he knows the heart of everyone that follows them, believer and unbeliever what they want.

There is Community of the Call (*Ummat ad-daʿwah*) and the Community Which Responded to the Call (*Ummat al-ijābah*). You are from the prophet's Ummah, whether you accept his message (*daʿwah*) or not.

كما يلقي الملك الوحي علي قلوب الانبيأ مع ترويح السرار و كشف السراءر الكامنة بالمتلبدة بالظلوم الشرك الخفي فيطهرها و يخرجها

Kamā yulqī al-malika 'l-waḥīy ʿalā qulūb al-anbīyā maʿ tarwīḥi 'l-asrār wa kashf as-sarā'ira 'l-kāmina bi 'l-mutalabidhat bil ẓulūmi 'sh-shirki'l-khafī fa yuṭahiruhā wa yukharijuhā.

"Allāh ﷻ shows them what is in the hearts of everyone. He will give them the secrets and open for them all that is hidden in you. He will reveal to them your personality, all that you do in your life—the blueprints, as it were—even the cloudy secrets that are buried inside the deepest part of the heart—the hidden idolatry (*ash-shirk al-khafī*)."

The prophets are able to see these most minute details in each of us, so that they can clean and purify their Ummah.

That is why the intercession (*shafaʿ*) of the Prophet ﷺ is for the big sinners of the Ummah. He knows what is concealed deep within the inner self, what is covered by the clouds of the heart. He is able to bring it out and discard it, throwing away that hidden *shirk*.

Tranquility of the Prophets' Inheritors

Just as *Sayyīdinā* Jibrīl ﷺ revealed these things to the prophets, their inheritors among the *awlīyā* are also able to see what is concealed inside their followers. That is why you cannot hide what it is in your heart.

One *walī* went to Mecca, and as he approached the Kaʿaba, he did not see anyone making *ṭawāf*. There were only wild animals. That is because he was able to perceive with his eyes the wild character of those pilgrims circumambulating the Kaʿaba.

When the *walī* is looking at you, you have to hide yourself. That is why it is better not to look at the eyes of the *walī*, because if you are looking it might put you in a bad position. Look down instead and say to him, "I know you are looking in my heart, and that I am sinful, and it is your duty to clean me. I am helpless and have no power." If you do that, he must cleanse you. What else can he do?

> Such is the power that was revealed to the Prophet ﷺ and to those who inherited that secret from him.

What is this light that came first to the heart of the Prophet ﷺ? It is something that collects the power of light, power and spirit. *Nūrun* means Allāh ﷻ is the light of heavens and earth. He gave to the Prophet ﷺ knowledge of all His creation, because all creation is created from the light of the Prophet ﷺ. Moreover, He gave the Prophet ﷺ power from the ocean of power (*baḥr al-qudrah*) and from the secret of the statement "I was a prophet when Adam ﷺ was between water and clay."

> That secret is a source of tranquility, similar to the peace and satisfaction that the husband finds with his wife or that one finds in his home.

The one who is fearful of his own wrongdoing will run to the Prophet ﷺ and to those guides (*ʿarif*) who are the followers of the Prophet ﷺ, regretting his misdeeds and filled with awe at the greatness and power of Allāh ﷻ. When you reach this level of awareness of Allāh's Majesty, you know that you are nothing, and so you run to the Prophet ﷺ and those guides that are his inheritors.

By the *baraka* of the Prophet ﷺ we have the Golden Chain that we can run to and grab hold of. Where else is there to go? To scholars wearing jeans to Jummah and giving lectures? No, you must find a real *walī*, someone who can lead you on the difficult spiritual journey towards the Divine Presence. Then you will find the ocean of tranquility.

The one who is sad will find solace and entertainment—not the modern distractions that are favored by the people of *dunyā*, but real solace and entertainment from Allāh's Mercy. That is what you need. In Allāh's presence, there is no hate and jealousy. There is no hate and envy. There, all are happy with what Allāh ﷻ gives them saying, "What reason do I have to complain? He saved me from hellfire."

Such is the peace that Allāh ﷻ gives to His sad servants that find no solace except in the ocean of tranquility that He gave to the prophets and they gave to *awlīyāullāh*. They are dipped in the ocean of *'ishq*, the endless ocean of Divine Love. The seeker's thirst cannot be quenched and his self cannot be cured because he is always worried and cannot find peace until they dip him into that ocean of tranquility and send it to his heart in *dunyā*, that mercy from the Holy Names *ar-Raḥmān* and *ar-Raḥīm*. When that mercy is thrown into his heart, at that moment finds tranquility. For, as it is said in the Holy Qur'an:

فَأَنزَلَ اللَّهُ سَكِينَتَهُ عَلَىٰ رَسُولِهِ وَعَلَى الْمُؤْمِنِينَ وَأَلْزَمَهُمْ كَلِمَةَ التَّقْوَىٰ

وَكَانُوا أَحَقَّ بِهَا وَأَهْلَهَا وَكَانَ اللَّهُ بِكُلِّ شَيْءٍ عَلِيمًا

Fa anzala'Llāhu sakīnatahu 'alā rasūlihi wa 'alā'l-muminīna wa alzamahum kalimatat-taqwā wa kānū aḥaqq bihā wa āhlahā wa kāna'Llāhu bi-kulli shayin 'alīma.

Then Allāh sent down His peace of reassurance upon His messenger and upon the believers and imposed on them the word of self restraint, for they were worthy of it and meet for it. And Allāh is Aware of all things. [95]

[95] Sūratu 'l-Fatḥ [Victory], 48:26.

"I descend and send My Tranquility, Peace and Security on the Prophet and on the believers, and cast down the unbelievers and raise up the believers."

That is the external meaning, but there is also a deeper spiritual meaning. Allāh ﷻ will send His tranquility and spirit (*rūḥ*) and bring the ego down and foil its strategy, and He will raise you up and dispel your sadness with solace and entertainment.

First, you must taste the sadness of that burning love. The closer you are to the Divine Presence, the more that love will burn you, because the closer you come, the farther away you feel. You can experience this in *dunyā*. As Ramadan comes to an end, the last two days might feel as long as all the days of fasting that preceded them.

That is why they order seclusions, to make the *murīd* feel this eternal infatuation and taste the sadness that comes with it so that he may flee from his ego and the things it desires and feel the mercy that comes from the heart of the Prophet ﷺ. That tranquility does not come until you are prevented from reaching that which you aspire to. If your spouse leaves you and takes the children, you feel overwhelmed with sadness. Yet this is only a drop of the sadness that you experience in seclusion. Similarly, when someone you love dies, you miss him or her. But this longing is not even equal to a single drop of the sadness you taste in seclusion. In seclusion, you feel the sadness that comes from knowing that you are finished and condemned to the hellfire because of the way you have been living.

That is why the Prophet ﷺ said:

شفاعتي لاهل الكبائر من امتي.

shafaʿtī li āhl al-kabā'ir min ummatī

My intercession is for those who commit grave sins from my community.

That intercession is for everyone, but even if you attain it you know that you will be separated from the Prophet ﷺ in the life that is to come, and that is eternal sadness. However, if you follow your shaykh, running after him, then you will not feel that separation in the next life. You will be among the *anbīyā, ṣiddīqīn, shuhadā* and pious sincere people, *ṣāliḥīn*.

EIGHT

Ark of the Knowers

Just as the Children of Israel found tranquility in the Ark of the Covenant, so too can the believer find tranquility in himself. This tranquility becomes a bridge connecting the body and the heart. The heart is the ark of the self and, in it, the seeker can find this peace. However, the heart must first be cleansed.

The heart of the true knower, the true gnostic, contains Allāh's knowledge and tranquility and peace eminate from it. Through this peace and tranquility, he is able to understand the level of *īmān* and level of *iḥsān*. That is why Allāh ﷻ said that belief in His angels is part of *īmān*. It means that, just as the angels are bearing the Ark of the Covenant, so will the angels carry you to the *amānah* that Allāh ﷻ gave you on the Day of Promises.

In the Holy Qur'an, Allāh ﷻ said that He showed His trust to the heavens and the earth and gave it to them to carry, but they said it was too difficult a burden to bear. So, human beings took it and carried it. They took it as a gift from their Lord, but they did not understand the conditions of this gift—that they must follow His principles or be judged. You cannot take a trust and then spend it in your own way. You cannot squander it on your worldly desires. You are responsible for it and must give it back Allāh ﷻ told human beings that they could only spend this trust in the way that He ordered them to follow. He outlined the conditions and principles to which we must adhere.

The Ark that Allāh ﷻ gave to the people of Shemuel ؑ was a reminder to them of this trust. That is why the Ark of Moses ؑ is called the Ark of the Covenant. Allāh mentions the covenant where He said:

مِنَ الْمُؤْمِنِينَ رِجَالٌ صَدَقُوا مَا عَاهَدُوا اللَّهَ عَلَيْهِ فَمِنْهُم مَّن قَضَىٰ نَحْبَهُ

وَمِنْهُم مَّن يَنتَظِرُ وَمَا بَدَّلُوا تَبْدِيلًا

Among the Believers are men who have been true to their covenant with Allāh . of them some have completed their vow (to the extreme), and some (still) wait: but they have never changed (their determination) in the least.[96]

The *awlīyāullāh* are the inheritors of this Ark. They are small in number, but they have great power. There are only 124,000 of them, but they can do more than 6 billion because they have that Ark, they follow the principles and conditions of that trust.

Today, there are many people who claim superiority in knowledge, but they are like an empty drum that makes a lot of noise but contains nothing but air. The gnostic (*ʿarif billāhi*) is not a drum. When you hit him, he does not give a sound. That is because his heart is full. When you drum on him, he gives you meditation. He gives you what you need to hear. Sometimes it is very difficult on the ego to accept. Allāh ﷻ gave true superiority to the gnostics. He raised them because they kept their covenant, their trust.

"Men who have been true to their covenant with Allāh ."

The men Allāh ﷻ mentioned here are the gnostics, the knowers who kept the promise to Allāh ﷻ that they made on the Day of Promises. This verse reminds us that Allāh ﷻ took a promise from each of us on that day. The gnostics kept their promise. They kept their covenant with Allāh ﷻ. Some passed away. They followed the Sunnah of the Prophet ﷺ and passed to *ākhirah*.

The station of *iḥsān* is *maqām al-uns*—the station of intimacy with the Divine Presence. That is why the Prophet ﷺ said, "The time that I am most happy is when I am in prayer, because there I feel the intimacy of being between the hands of my Lord." The *maqām* of *iḥsān* is to worship Allāh ﷻ as if you see him.

---

[96] Sūratu 'l-Aḥzāb [The Confederates], 33:23.

That is the station of intimacy. There you are in complete infatuation (*ʿishq*) in the ocean of the Divine Presence.

One of the believers once asked *Sayyīdinā* Mūsā ﷺ for faith. He said, "O Mūsā, when you go to your Lord on Mount Sinai, ask your Lord to give me *īmān*."

"Why do you think you have no faith?" asked *Sayyīdinā* Mūsā ﷺ. "You believe in me."

But the man persisted, saying, "Ask what I am requesting."

That man was a believer who had reached a high level, yet he did not feel like he had faith. He knew that one who makes the profession of faith (*shahādah*), and prays and fasts will reach Paradise, but he also knew that such a one had not necessarily reached the *maqām al-iḥsān*. So, *Sayyīdinā* Mūsā ﷺ asked Allāh ﷻ to grant that believer faith. When he came back down the mountain, he found that man staring blankly—his eyes wide open. Allāh ﷻ said, "Leave him now. Even if you grind him to dust he will not feel anything."

What is faith? According to the hadith of Jibrīl ﷺ, it is "to believe in Allāh ﷻ,and His angels and His prophets and His books and in the Last Day and in Destiny, its good and its bad."

If you believe in the Last Day, in Judgment Day, how do you have time to work for *dunyā*? Yet, people who say they are believers are spending their days looking at the computer, reading the news and seeing how many people died in this or that war or disaster. Or they are buying and selling stocks or, even worse, playing games on the computer. That is the worst thing.

You have to believe in the hereafter and the heavenly judgment (*yawm al-ākhirah*). That means you have to fight your ego and slay it. When you kill your ego, you will be resurrected in the intimacy and tranquility of the station of perfected character—*maqām al-iḥsān*. That is one of the meanings of the Last Day. In fact, there are three meanings of the last day: The day of resurrection, the day of death, and the day of "dying before you die" (*mūtū qabl an tamūtū*).

You cannot see your Lord in this world, in *dunyā*, but you can reach the level of the Divine Presence. In *ākhirah*, however, the reward is not only Paradise, but also to see Allāh ﷻ. Very few will achieve this reward, the sight of their Lord in Paradise. It is reserved for those in the Assembly of truth, (*maqʿad aṣ-ṣidq*) who are in the company of the prophets, the trustyworthy ones, the martyrs and the *ṣāliḥīn*. It is for the prophets, *nabīyyūn,* and the veracious saints, *ṣiddīqūn,* for those who kept their covenant and the martyrs who fought and struggled against their egos—those who sacrificed their very selves, in love to God, *shahīd fī ḥubbillāh*. It means those who left this life, *dunyā,* and asked instead for the hereafter, *ākhirah*. It is for those who, though they are still living, care nothing for their lives. That is what it is to be a martyr in Allāh's Love. That is the greater jihad, for the Prophet ﷺ said:

قدمتم خير مقدم وقدمتم من الجهاد الأصغر الى الجهاد الأكبر

مجاهدة العبد هواه.

> The Prophet came back from one of his campaigns
>
> saying: "You have come forth in the best way of coming forth: you have come from the smaller jihād to the greater jihād." They said: "And what is the greater jihād?" He replied: "The striving (*mujāhadat*) of Allāh's servants against their idle desires."[97]

When you fight against your ego, you reach the level of the Divine Presence. There you feel surrounded by that Presence, for you have achieved the station of intimacy. You become a different person at that time. Then the ark will be opened for you.

[97] Al-Khaṭṭābī in his *Ṭārīkh,* Īmām Ghazālī in his *Iḥyā'* and al-ʿIrāqī said that Bayhaqī related it on the authority of Jābir.

The ark is not important. What is important is what it contains. Even though angels are carrying it, the chest itself is not important. When you reach the level of intimacy, what is inside that chest is what is important.

According to the Holy Qur'an, the Ark of the Covenant contained what was left of what *Sayyīdinā* Mūsā ﷺ and *Sayyīdinā* Hārūn ﷺ had—*baqīyyah*—what remains. The significance of this is that you cannot inherit from a prophet completely. You are standing at the feet of that prophet, and you are only going to receive what he wants you to inherit.

What was left inside the Ark of the Covenant? The staff of *Sayyīdinā* Mūsā ﷺ. That stick was inside there.

The Snake that Devours Untruth

When Mūsā ﷺ came to the first meeting with His Lord, in darkness of the windswept Sinai night, manifesting Himself in the form of the Burning Bush, Allāh ﷻ said to Mūsā ﷺ:

فَأَلْقَاهَا فَإِذَا هِيَ حَيَّةٌ تَسْعَى قَالَ خُذْهَا وَلَا تَخَفْ

Fa alqāhā fa idhā hīya ḥayatan tas'a. Qāla khudh-hā wa lā takhaf.

He threw it, and behold! it was a snake, moving rapidly. Said He: "Take hold of it, and fear not.[98]

When Mūsā ﷺ threw the staff, it became a slithering snake and he was afraid. But Allāh ﷻ said, "Do not be afraid. Take hold of it."

The snake is the most terrifying animal. It is poisonous and eats everything. It is deadly. So, too, was the staff of Mūsā ﷺ deadly to anyone who came against him. And so it was when Pharoah's magicians challenged *Sayyīdinā* Mūsā ﷺ. His staff consumed all of their snakes. Allāh ﷻ says, "they came with great magic" (*siḥrun 'aẓīm*). That means the most powerful of all magics.

[98] Sūrah ṬāḤā 20:20-21.

Yet, what happened? Allāh ﷻ told Mūsā ﵇, "Throw that stick." When reality comes, all illusions are destroyed.

It is the same with us. All of our lives are illusions. Physics proves that what we perceive is not reality. For example, we may see a star sparkling in the sky, but that star may have been extinguished eons ago. Yet, the light that it emitted millions of years ago is only now reaching us. It is an illusion. Allāh ﷻ is showing His Greatness to these physicists. He is showing them that what they think is something is really nothing. He has revealed to them that this entire universe is emptiness. That is why some systems of belief, such as Hinduism and Buddhism, urge the seeker to strive for complete emptiness. The universe may be a void, but Allāh ﷻ put whatever you need in that void. For Allāh ﷻ, that is no problem. He can put the nothing into something and the something into nothing. That is why what we see is an illusion.

So, too, with those serpents that were conjured by Pharoah's magicians. They were illusions, but powerful ones. Everyone was overwhelmed by that magic and thought Mūsā ﵇ was finished. Even Mūsā ﵇ was afraid, but Allāh ﷻ told him not fear. He told Mūsā ﵇, you are going to overcome them, because theirs is the magic of Shaytan.

Shaytan's magic is everywhere in the world today. He is tricking us with MTV, "Music Television." What we need is "Mercy Television." We need Divine TV. Instead, we are losing ourselves in more illusions. Allāh ﷻ wants to dispel those illusions. That is why He gave Mūsā's staff the power to overcome Shaytan's magic.

The staff of Mūsā was sent to destroy illusions:

وَقُلْ جَاءَ الْحَقُّ وَزَهَقَ الْبَاطِلُ إِنَّ الْبَاطِلَ كَانَ زَهُوقًا

And say: "Truth has (now) arrived, and Falsehood perished: for Falsehood is (by its nature) bound to perish."[99]

Our *dunyā* is false (*bāṭil*). It is only going to last a short time. You are going to live 65, 70, 80 or 100 years at the most, but even that short life is a struggle. Reality is higher, because it is true and eternal.

وَجَاء السَّحَرَةُ فِرْعَوْنَ قَالْوَاْ إِنَّ لَنَا لأَجْرًا إِن كُنَّا نَحْنُ الْغَالِبِينَ قَالَ نَعَمْ وَإَنَّكُمْ لَمِنَ الْمُقَرَّبِينَ قَالُواْ يَا مُوسَى إِمَّا أَن تُلْقِيَ وَإِمَّا أَن نَّكُونَ نَحْنُ الْمُلْقِينَ قَالَ أَلْقُوْاْ فَلَمَّا أَلْقَوْاْ سَحَرُواْ أَعْيُنَ النَّاسِ وَاسْتَرْهَبُوهُمْ وَجَاءوا بِسِحْرٍ عَظِيمٍ وَأَوْحَيْنَا إِلَى مُوسَى أَنْ أَلْقِ عَصَاكَ فَإِذَا هِيَ تَلْقَفُ مَا يَأْفِكُونَ فَغُلِبُواْ هُنَالِكَ وَانقَلَبُواْ صَاغِرِينَ

And the sorcerers came unto Pharaoh [and] said: "Verily, we ought to have a great reward if it is we who prevail." Answered [Pharaoh]: "Yes; and, verily, you shall be among those who are near unto me." They said: "O Moses! Either you shalt throw [your staff first], or we shall [be the first to] throw." He answered: "You throw [first]." And when they threw down [their staffs], they cast a spell upon the people's eyes, and struck them with awe, and produced mighty sorcery.

And [then] We inspired Moses, "Throw down your staff!" - and lo! it swallowed up all their deceptions; And thus were they vanquished there and then, and became utterly humiliated.[100]

What happened to Pharoah's magicians when that reality came through Mūsā's staff?

They fell down prostrate:

وَأُلْقِيَ السَّحَرَةُ سَاجِدِينَ

[99] Sūratu 'l-Isrā [The Night Journey], 17:810.
[100] Sūratu 'l-'Arāf [The Heights], 7:113-119.

But the sorcerers fell down prostrate in adoration.[101]

They recognized that they were wrong and believed in Allāh ﷻ, the Lord of Mūsā ﷺ and Hārūn ﷺ. Only the pious and sincere will surrender to their Lord. Thus, the magicians followed Mūsā ﷺ and the rest ran away.

When *ḥaqq* comes, it destroys all *bāṭil*. *Ḥaqq* is coming soon, and it will take everything that is wrong from this world. The staff of Mūsā, it is *ʿasā dhikrullāh,* the staff of God's remembrance. It is a snake that opens its mouth and consumes all the illusions and tricks of the Pharoahnic self (*ṣiffāt al-firaʿawnī*). That is *lā ilāha illa-Llāh Muḥammadun Rasūlullāh,* and that is given to Ummat an-Nabī.

See how much mercy Allāh ﷻ bestowed on this Ummah? He also has for you the ark, and He will open for you its secrets when you enter into the Divine Presence. Allāh ﷻ will give all these treasures to you if you throw away the bad characteristics of the Pharoahnic self, and your heart will begin to shake, wanting more and more. When that love comes into your heart, you cannot contain it. It will explode and jump to the level of intimacy. So, do not be left out of the Divine Presence, or you will be crying after that intimacy, peace and tranquility.

[101] Sūratu 'l-ʿArāf [The Heights], 7:120.

NINE

Purification of the Heart and the Three Levels of the Self

The Prophet ﷺ said:

اَلاَ وَاِنَّ فِي الْجَسَدِ مُضْغَةً اِذَا صَلَحَتْ صَلَحَ الْجَسَدُ كُلُّهُ وَاِذَا فَسَدَتْ فَسَدَ الْجَسَدُ كُلُّهُ اَلاَ وَهِيَ الْقَلْبُ

> There is in the body a small flesh, if it is clean and pure the whole body will be clean and pure and if it is not, and it is contaminated, then the whole body will be contaminated, and that is the heart.[102]

For the heart must be purified so that it can be sincere in its love for Allāh ﷻ if that tranquility is to come. How is the heart purified? Through *dhikrullāh*. Indeed, it is through the remembrance of Allāh ﷻ that tranquility comes to the heart, and it is through this remembrance that one reachs the level of the tranquil self (*nafs al-muṭma'inna*).

There are three levels of the self: the commanding self (*an-nafs al-ammāra*), the reproachful self (*an-nafs al-lawwāma*) and the tranquil self (*an-nafs al-muṭma'innah*). To reach the third level where one finds peace, you must have godfearingness (*taqwā*) and *dhikrullāh* in your heart.

They asked *Sayyīdinā* Muḥyīddīn ibn 'Arabī, "Why is it that we often see you not doing *dhikr*?" Of course he was doing *dhikr*, but to teach them he said, "Why do I have to do *dhikr*?" They replied, "To remember Allāh ." He said, "Who said I forgot Him? I am in the Divine Presence. I am sitting there with Him. I am in His Ocean. I have passed that level." His point was that you must never forget your Lord.

---

[102] Saḥīḥ Muslim, #4178.

When you do *dhikr*, peace and tranquility come to the heart and will it to be like the heart of the knowers in Allāh's Way. That is how the *awlīyā* became knowers in the Way of Allāh ﷻ. The heart of the true gnostic is the headquarters of knowledge and loyalty. This is the secret of what you must do to unlock that Divine Knowledge. This is the secret of the knowledge from which springs the understanding of the universe and creation. That knowledge is thrown into the heart of the *'arif billāh,* the knower of Allāh , the gnostic.

The first level in seclusion is to hear the recitation (*taṣbīḥ*) of the angels as chorus, all mixed together. The next level is to hear each of the angles independently. It is like the different types of radio. If you listen to analog radio, there is static—the waves are mixed up and distorted. But digital radio is clear, and accurate and precise. Thus, you are able to hear and differentiate different sounds at the same time.

If a Shaykh can hear the *tasbīḥ* of the angels, what about the hearts of his followers? He keeps it secret; he does not show he knows the heart. That is necessary to keep the follower following. Shaykhs are masters of diplomacy.

The Heart of the Believer is between the Two Fingers of the Lord

إن القلوب بيد الله بين أصبعين من أصابع الرحمن يقلبها كيف يشاء

> The Prophet ﷺ said, "The heart of the believer is between the two fingers of the Lord, and He turns it how he likes."

It is just like cooking: you turn the meat this way and that in the pan in order to cook it. When the heart of the believer is moving in *dhikrullāh,* Allāh ﷻ will move it upside down, and turn it in different ways in order to cook the love that is within His servant and bring it out.

That is why we say that *imtithālan li-amr ash-shaykh,* following the order of the shaykh will take you to presence of the Prophet ﷺ. He will introduce you and, if you follow the orders of *Sayyīdinā* an-Nabī it will take you to the presence of Allāh ﷻ. If you follow that order, it will give you the strength to reach that station in the heart that very few can reach. To achieve that, obeidience is important.

The two fingers the Prophet ﷺ referred to are not real fingers. They are metaphors for the two Divine Attributes of Majest (*Jalāl*) and Beauty (*Jamāl*). It is said that, if Allāh ﷻ allowed one *ḥūrī* (*ḥūr al-ʿayn*) to put one finger into this world, all of *dunyā* would faint from the beauty and scent of it. What about Allāh's Love? If Allāh ﷻ lets one drop of it fall upon you, you would faint.

That is why *Sayyīdinā* ʿAli ؓ asked them to pull his tooth while he was praying. Today, they use anesthesia, but all he needed was that love.

That heart when it opens what is inside the chest of *Sayyīdinā* Mūsā ؑ. When Allāh opens to you the secret of that stick it is between *ṣiffāt al-Jamāl wa 'l-Jalāl.* From the attribute of majesty he will inspire the ego with bad things. When you are in majestic situation you don't accept wrong. So that is why he put between Jalāl and Jamāl. So from Jalāl he will inspire the heart to avoid these bad things.

فَأَلْهَمَهَا فُجُورَهَا وَتَقْوَاهَا قَدْ أَفْلَحَ مَن زَكَّاهَا وَقَدْ خَابَ مَن دَسَّاهَا

Fa alhamahā fujurahā wa taqwāhā qad aflaḥa man zakāhā wa qad khāba man dassāhā.

By the soul and the proportion and order given to it and its inspiration as to its wrong and its right. Truly he succeeds who purifies it.[103]

---

[103] Sūratu 'l-ʿAlaq [The Clot], 96:7-10.

Allāh inspired the self, *fujūrahā*. Its rebellion. The bad things that it might do. Be careful. That is one. And *bi-ṣiffat al-ikrām*. The attribute of mercy and generosity and beauty, will inspire its *taqwā* and how to be obedient servant.

Allāh ﷻ did not leave that matter to any angels. Everything is by angels, except the matter of the heart, it is directly inspired with what is bad and what is good. That you cannot be rebellious and with His generosity and that goodness is what He wants from a good servant. No angels can intermediate for that. Only the Prophet brought that in the Holy Qur'an and the Sunnah of the Prophet.

Two Types of Believers

There are two groups in the Ummah. One finds its satisfaction in the Four Enemies—in *dunyā, hawā,* Shaytan and *nafs*—while the other finds satisfaction in Allāh ﷻ and His Prophet ﷺ. There is no way to balance these two groups. One group has been abased by its own low desires, while the other has been raised by Allāh ﷻ to unimaginable heights. One group is guided by Allāh's Way. The other group is ruled (*musalaṭun ʿalayhim*) by the Four Enemies.

> *W'alladhīna raḍū bi-Rabbihim wajadū 's-salāma wa 's-sakīnata fī unsi shafaʿati sayyidi waladi Ādam ṣāḥib al-ḥaḍarat al-Jamālīyyah wa 'ṣ-ṣūwar al-bahā'īyyah wa 'n-nasma 'l-Jamālīyyati 'llatī yātī min sayyid as-sādat wa ṣāḥib al-wasīlah wa shāfiʿī 'l-ummah Sayyīdinā Muḥammad wa warathātihi min al-awlīyā,*
>
> Those that are satisfied with their Lord find peace and tranquility in the intimacy of their nearness with the intercession of the master of the Children of Adam, the Owner of the Beautiful Presence and the Owner of Illuminating Images, the Breeze of Beauty that comes fromMaster of masters, the Owner of the Means of Approach to the Lord, the

Interecessor of the CommunityOur master Muḥammad and his inheritors among the saints.

His inheritors from the *awlīyā* are in that beautiful presence, which purifies them from the filth of Shaytan. Just as Allāh ﷻ sent Ṭālūt as a king to the Children of Israel, to raise them to a higher level, so too has He sent inheritors of the Prophet ﷺ. These inheritors are the true kings of the earth, fixing it like the mountain pegs. Allāh ﷻ put the mountains on the earth to balance it. In the same way, He has sent the prophets and their inheritors to serve as weights for balancing. With prophecy comes power. Who killed Jālūt? *Sayyīdinā* Dāwūd ؑ. So prophets kill the enemy. *Sayyīdinā* Muḥammad ﷺ killed the enemy.

Awlīyāullāh bring the prayers of the Ummah to the presence of the Prophet ﷺ. Then the Prophet ﷺ, with his intercession, burns everything They are like the tasteful ornaments with which Allāh ﷻ has decorated His Prophet ﷺ, and He continues to send them. Moreover, in every century, He sends to humanity a king of the saints (*Sulṭān al-Awlīyā*), and when that one departs this life, Allāh ﷻ sends another *Sulṭān al-Awlīyā* to take his place on the chair. Allāh ﷻ sends this king, and he gives assignments to each of the saints.

It is true even in our own time. He sent Shaykh ʿAbd Allāh al-Faizi ad-Dāghestānī who then passed that station that to *Sayyīdinā* Mawlana Shaykh Nāẓim. They carry the beautiful banner of the magnificent and lovely Prophet ﷺ—*liwā al-ḥamd*—the Banner of Praise. On Judgment Day, the Prophet ﷺ will be carrying that banner. In Saḥīḥ Bukhārī, a hadith relates that Allāh ﷻ will give him the power of *sajdah*, the power to pray in a way that no one prayed before: *s'al tuʿṭā*—Whatever he asks will be given. Never has such power of prayer been granted before. The Prophet ﷺ will use that power to remove a portion of his Ummah from Hell. Three times the Prophet will seek Allāh's Mercy for the Ummah, and each time Allāh will grant him to pull forth another portion of his Ummah from Hellfire. Today, that banner has been given to the head of his inheritors, the *Sulṭān al-Awlīyā*. By Allāh's Grace ,he is able to seal the hearts of his followers so that Shaytan cannot reach them.

Shaytan might come to us. We might even think that we are following Shaytan, but in reality that is sealed. The *Sulṭān al-Awlīyā* has blocked him. That saint is also able to do things on your behalf. He can change your imitation prayer to a real prayer. He can do *dhikr* on your behalf. This is because he has a duty to present you clean to the Prophet ﷺ. Allāh ﷻ gave him that power from the Prophet ﷺ. The Prophet ﷺ passed that power to him. With it, he is able to seal the hearts of his followers and take them to his presence and, from there, to the presence of the Absolute Knower, the *Malik al-ʿalām*, Allāh ﷻ Knower of all things. Moreover, Allāh ﷻ has given the *Sulṭān al-Awlīyā* the ablility to delegate a portion of these powers to the other 123,999 saints, so that each can guide his followers, each according to his level. *Alḥamdulillāh*, we were guided to Mawlana.

Seclusion unlocks the Six Secrets of the Heart

Entering into seclusion in a cave or room by order of the shaykh is a requirement (*wājib*) for every disciple, for every student and for every apprentice. The student cannot decide to enter seclusion himself. If he does, then his ego is sharing in that seclusion. The order must come from the top, because that is what the ego cannot accept. The ego knows that there is no way to subvert the *murīd* if he enters seclusion by order of the shaykh, because the ego knows that the shaykh will beat it with spiritual "sticks". When the *murīd* enters into seclusion by order of the shaykh, he will open for him a reality in which there is nothing but the remembrance of Allāh ﷻ. Then the secrets of the heart will be opened to him.

Know that the heart contains the secrets of the Six Realities:

- *Ḥaqīqat al-jadhbah, the Reality of Attraction,*

- *Ḥaqīqat al-fayḍ, the Reality of Divine outpouring,*
- *Ḥaqīqat at-tawajjuh, the Reality of Focusing on the heart,*
- *Ḥaqīqat at-tawassul, the Reality of Intercession,*
- *Ḥaqīqat aṭ-ṭayy, the Reality of Compressing time and space,*
- *Ḥaqīqat al-irshād, the Reality of Guidance.*

Just as the relics of *Sayyīdinā* Mūsā ﷺ and *Sayyīdinā* Hārūn ﷺ were secreted in the Ark of the Covenant, so are the secrets of these six realities contained in the heart of the believer. These six realities are given to every human being, but they cannot be accessed until the *murīd* enters into seclusion.

The *murīd* will be carrying these six realities, and whatever manifests from the Muḥammadan secrets (*asrāran Muḥammadīyyah*), the Lordly Divine secrets (*asrāran rabbānīyyah*), the heavenly secrets (*asrāran malakūtīyyah*), the secrets of Beauty (*asrāran jamalīyyah*). Five levels will open in the heart, then he will be under the hadith of the Prophet ﷺ:

ما وسعني سمائي ولا أرضي ولكن وسعني قلب عبدي المؤمن

> Allāh said, "Neither My heavens contain Me nor My earth. But the heart of My Believing Servant contains Me."[104]

Secrets of Talut and Powers of the Saints

These are the secrets that Allāh ﷻ gave to Ṭālūt when He made him king of the Children of Israel. Allāh ﷻ inspired his heart with this knowledge, and that is what He referred to in the Holy Qur'an when He said that He gave Ṭālūt "superiority of body and knowledge." Allāh ﷻ made him a knower—a true gnostic—and set him on the right course.

If the human soul is granted this lordly heart and the understanding of the Divine Presence, if it is dressed with the

---

[104] Al-Ghazālī mentioned it in his Revival of the Religious Sciences. It is similar to an Israelite tradition related by Aḥmad in *al-Zuhd* from Wahb ibn Munabbih.

lordly power of *"kun fa-yakūn,"* saying to a thing "be" and it is. Surely such a person will be a knower of the hearts of people (*'alimun fīmā 'ilm al-qulūb*). He will be able to look in the hearts of people and know what is hidden by the six secrets of each person—each one being different and none overlapping the other. He will be a gnostic and he will be able to understand the Lordly Power (*qudrat al-ilāhīyy*). Then he will be given the kingdom and he will have kingship over it.

There are *awlīyā* who are kings of countries, but the *awlīyā* see themselves as kings of hearts. They are not limited by boundaries. They can reach the hearts they rule over at any moment through their hearts. Such a saint is dressed with lordship and given a kingdom and the throne of sultanhood (*sarīr sulṭāna*). When you are given that, everyone becomes your subject and you can guide them through their hearts.

When *Sayyidinā* Mūsā hit the rock with his staff, twelve springs gushed forth—one for each of the Tribes of the Children of Israel (*aṣbāṭ*). *Ṣibṭ* means one who is coming from that line of descent back to *Sayyidinā* Nūḥ. *Sayyidinā* Mūsā was able to control each of these lineages, controlling himself and his followers. In the same way, the *walī* is able to control himself and his followers.

The saint is completely disconnected from *dunyā*. He will never look at or stay in this worldly life that is betraying and conspiring against us. He will be able to control that and he will be migrating from *dunyā* to *ākhirah*. He will leave that worldly life for the heavenly life and take his followers with him. At that moment, he declares war against Jālūt, who represents Satan and the ego. He declares the war against the enemy of Ṭālūt. Just as *Sayyidinā* Dāwūd killed Jālūt, the one traveling the Way of Allāh and following the Prophet will destroy all of your bad characteristics when he brings you to the presence of the Prophet

فَهَزَمُوهُم بِإِذْنِ اللّهِ وَقَتَلَ دَاوُدُ جَالُوتَ وَآتَاهُ اللّهُ الْمُلْكَ وَالْحِكْمَةَ وَعَلَّمَهُ مِمَّا يَشَاء وَلَوْلاَ دَفْعُ اللّهِ النَّاسَ بَعْضَهُمْ بِبَعْضٍ لَّفَسَدَتِ الأَرْضُ وَلَـكِنَّ اللّهَ ذُو فَضْلٍ عَلَى الْعَالَمِينَ

By Allāh 's will they routed them; and David slew Goliath; and Allāh gave him power and wisdom and taught him whatever (else) He willed. And did not Allāh Check one set of people by means of another, the earth would indeed be full of mischief: But Allāh is full of bounty to all the worlds.[105]

Jālūt symbolizes the self-commanding ego that goads you and conspires against you, controlling your body by the power of Shaytan, sending his whispers into your heart. That is the character of Jālūt. That is why the Children of Israel said, "We cannot take it anymore.There are too many tyrants."

You must have a king. If you do not have a king ruling over you, you will always be falling down. The Children of Israel were clever. They knew that they needed a king. We have to go to our Prophet ﷺ every night saying, "*Yā Sayyidī! Yā Rasūlullāh,* ask Allāh to send us a king!"

You have to know who your teacher is, the one who guides you to the presence of the Prophet ﷺ. If that power has been given to Ṭālūt, from the power the human soul carries within it from the manifestations of the different Holy Names and Attributes, what do you think has been given to the soul of the Prophet ﷺ? What do you think then of the soul of the inheritors of the Prophet ﷺ, the Sulṭān al-Awlīyā, the Owner of the Age (*ṣāḥib al-ʿAṣr*). If Ṭālūt understood the secret of the soul of his people, what do you think of the one who is given from the soul of the perfect human being, the soul of *Sayyīdinā* Muḥammad ﷺ?

That *walī* is far higher than Ṭālūt, for he is taking from *Sayyīdinā* Muḥammad ﷺ, the perfect soul. As a king, Ṭālūt was

[105] Sūratu 'l-Baqara [The Heifer],2:251.

taking from the soul of human beings. But *Sayyīdinā* Muḥammad ﷺ is the perfect soul. Such a saint is taking from the soul of he whose characteristics have been perfected by Allāh ﷻ. He is the master of the two universes, the heavens and the earth. Understand, o servant of Allāh !

This is what came to me during my seclusion: "O servant that is sitting and doing seclusion, understand how low you are, of such a base quality (*dhull*). You must humiliate yourself. Stay low, and do not raise your head. No one can raise his head. You have to keep your head down for the sake of your Lord, because Allāh ﷻ is Great! If not for your shaykh who brought you to this level and to the presence of the Prophet ﷺ, you would have been nothing. You are nothing. You are only something with your shaykh. It is for you to watch what the shaykh sees and do what the shaykh does. He is in the presence of the Prophet ﷺ, and the Prophet ﷺ is in the presence of Allāh ﷻ. He is taking from the heart of the Prophet ﷺ who is in presence of *'alām al-ghūyyūb*. He is giving those secrets to your heart."

You have to understand that, if you want to go higher, you have to take initiation from a perfect, completed Shaykh who is in the presence of *Sayyīdinā* Muḥammad ﷺ.

TEN

Necessity for a Guide

Whoever wants to increase his connections and his knowledge has to take initiation with a complete shaykh that is perfected in the Sufi Way and must follow his guidance. He has to hold on to truth and reality (*tamassuk bi 'l-ḥaqīqah*). He cannot hold on to illusions, but must hold onto the truth—and the truth is nothing but the Divine Presence and *Sayyīdinā* Muḥammad ﷺ.

This is not something you can do alone. You cannot figure out how to grasp hold of these truths by yourself. Look at what happened with *Sayyīdinā* Āḥmad al-Badawī. He was trying to reach a high station and he was asking Allāh ﷻ to open to His door to him. He was asking, and asking and asking. He never stopped asking. The lesson here is, you must not stop asking, and say, "I failed."

Finally a *walī* appeared to him and said, "I have your key. Do you want the key to that door?" But he was still holding on to his illusions, and the *walī* left. After six months, the saint returned and asked him again, "Do you want the key?" He said, "Of course I want it!" The saint told him, "I will give it to you, but it has a price. And that is that you must give me the illusions that you are still harboring in your heart." Then he looked into his eyes and through them extracted from his heart all his book-based knowledge, then in turn filled it, again through his eyes, with all of the knowledge for which he had been longing.

You need a guide. That is why *Sayyīdinā* Muḥammad ﷺ took Archangel Jibrīl ؑ as a guide. The archangel took him to the level of *qāba qawsayn*, then said, "Now you are on your own." Jibrīl ؑ took him to that level and from there the Prophet ﷺ proceeded. If the Prophet ﷺ took a guide, how can you say that you do not need one?

To hold onto truth is the bond between you and your shaykh. That is the connection. The *ḥaqīqah* is with that guide, the *ʿarif billāh* that shows you the way of that journey and takes you to reach the *maʿrifah al-ilāhīyyah.* It is said:

فَوَجَدَا عَبْداً مِّنْ عِبَادِنَا آتَيْنَاهُ رَحْمَةً مِنْ عِندِنَا وَعَلَّمْنَاهُ مِن لَّدُنَّا عِلْماً

They found a servant from amongst Our servants whom We have given a mercy from Our presence and whom We taught knowledge from Our Divine Presence[106]

وَاتَّقُواْ اللّهَ وَيُعَلِّمُكُمُ اللّهُ وَاللّهُ بِكُلِّ شَيْءٍ عَلِيمٌ

And be aware of Allāh and Allāh will teach you, and Allāh is all knowing of everything.[107]

Be sincere, and Allāh will teach you.

Unfortunately, we study for our own egos, not for Allāh ﷻ. The shaykh makes you sincere. He makes you sincere by grinding you. He wants you to experience difficulty.

Kings Despoil the Land

They asked Abayāzīd about heavenly knowledge (*maʿrifah*). He recited this verse:

قَالَتْ إِنَّ الْمُلُوكَ إِذَا دَخَلُوا قَرْيَةً أَفْسَدُوهَا وَجَعَلُوا أَعِزَّةَ أَهْلِهَا أَذِلَّةً وَكَذَلِكَ يَفْعَلُونَ

She said: "Kings, when they enter a country, despoil it, and make the noblest of its people its meanest thus do they behave.[108]

---

[106] Sūratu 'l-Kahf [The Cave], 18:6.
[107] Sūratu 'l-Baqara [The Heifer],2:282.
[108] Sūratu 'n-Naml [The Ant], 27:34.

When kings conquer a nation or a city, they take those people who were in positions of power and authority and they cast them down and humiliate them. They do not allow them to remain in their elevated positions. They destroy that nation or city.

Sayyīdinā Sulaymān ﷺ sent a message to the Queen of Sheba, Sabā: "Come to me submitting to Allāh's Will, and become a believer. Otherwise, I will come to you and destroy your kingdom."

He sent the letter with a hoopoe (*hudhud*). He sent him because he has a crown on his head, (*tāj*). He has superiority over other birds. He has power.

The hoopoe delivered that message to Sabā. When the queen read it, she consulted with her ministers and they told her, "We are powerful. You have no need to worry."

وَإِنِّي مُرْسِلَةٌ إِلَيْهِم بِهَدِيَّةٍ فَنَاظِرَةٌ بِمَ يَرْجِعُ الْمُرْسَلُونَ فَلَمَّا جَاء سُلَيْمَانَ قَالَ

أَتُمِدُّونَنِ بِمَالٍ فَمَا آتَانِيَ اللَّهُ خَيْرٌ مِّمَّا آتَاكُم بَلْ أَنتُم بِهَدِيَّتِكُمْ تَفْرَحُونَ

But lo! I am going to send a present unto them, and to see with what (answer) the messengers return. So when (the envoy) came unto Solomon, (the King) said: What! Would you help me with wealth? But that which Allāh has given me is better than that which He has given you. Nay it is you (and not I) who exult in your gift. [109]

She said, "Let us send a gift to Sulaymān. Let us bribe him."

So, she sent him some gifts, for even a king likes the things of this world.

But *Sayyīdinā* Sulaymān ﷺ rejected her gifts, saying, "What is this? I want you to become a Muslim. If you do not, I will come to you."

---

[109] Sūratu 'n-Naml [The Ant], 27:35,36.

She understood. She knew that when he entered her country, he would take all those who were in authority and cast them down.

قِيلَ لَهَا ادْخُلِي الصَّرْحَ فَلَمَّا رَأَتْهُ حَسِبَتْهُ لُجَّةً وَكَشَفَتْ عَن سَاقَيْهَا قَالَ إِنَّهُ صَرْحٌ مُّمَرَّدٌ مِّن قَوَارِيرَ قَالَتْ رَبِّ إِنِّي ظَلَمْتُ نَفْسِي وَأَسْلَمْتُ مَعَ سُلَيْمَانَ لِلَّهِ رَبِّ الْعَالَمِينَ

It was said unto her: Enter the hall. And when she saw it she deemed it a pool and bared her legs. (Solomon) said: Lo! it is a hall, made smooth, of glass. She said: "My Lord! Lo! I have wronged myself, and I surrender with Solomon unto Allāh, the Lord of the Worlds."[110]

So she understood, and she came to *Sayyīdinā* Sulaymān ﷺ. He had made for her a river of glass that she could step on. She thought it was a river and she took up her dress, showing her legs. He said, "There is no need to show me your legs. We are not interested in legs. Cover yourself. That is just glass."

Then she realized the truth of it and said, "I became a believer with Sulaymān."

This is the way of rulers. When they enter a city, they destroy everything and make those who were kings, slaves, and make those who were slaves, kings. Those who were raised up are cast down, and those who were lowly are exalted.

This is how the *awlīyā* enter the hearts of their followers. They are kings—rulers of those hearts—and so they enter as kings. The ego is controlling the city of your heart. It is debasing everything that is good, righteous, and related to Allāh ﷻ, and raising up everything that is evil and related to Shaytan. So what does the king do? He destroys and humiliates the power of that ego that was controlling your heart and he elevates all that is good

[110] Sūratu 'n-Naml [The Ant], 27:44.

and holy within you. Thus, *dunyā*—which was your master—becomes your slave.

That is *ma'rifah*, gnosis. That is what *ma'rifah* does. It gives control of your heart back to its heavenly power source, which is where it should reside. That is what *awlīyāullāh* do to the hearts of their followers. They entrust them with the power of these secrets and, through them, they are able to reach the presence of *Sayyidinā* Muḥammad ﷺ, and through the presence of *Sayyidinā* Muḥammad ﷺ they are able to reach the Divine Presence.

Saints Cast Down the Idols of the Heart

The ego places an idol in your heart. It builds it up year after year, and you worship this statue. We honor these idols and build thrones for them. How many statues are there in your heart? There are 800 idols there—one for each of the 800 actions prohibited by Allāh.

The saints of Allāh ﷻ enter the city of the heart and cast down these idols, just as *Sayyidinā* Ibrāhīm ؑ did with the statues that his people were worshipping instead of Allāh ﷻ. But just like *Sayyidinā* Ibrāhīm ؑ, they leave one standing to see if you are able to destroy it.

قَالُوا أَأَنتَ فَعَلْتَ هَذَا بِآلِهَتِنَا يَا إِبْرَاهِيمُ قَالَ بَلْ فَعَلَهُ كَبِيرُهُمْ هَذَا فَاسْأَلُوهُمْ إِن كَانُوا يَنطِقُونَ فَرَجَعُوا إِلَىٰ أَنفُسِهِمْ فَقَالُوا إِنَّكُمْ أَنتُمُ الظَّالِمُونَ ثُمَّ نُكِسُوا عَلَىٰ رُءُوسِهِمْ لَقَدْ عَلِمْتَ مَا هَٰؤُلَاءِ يَنطِقُونَ

Qālū a'ant fa'lta hādhā bi ālihatinā yā ibrāhīm, Qāla bal fa'alahu kabīruhum hādhā fa'salūhum in kānū yanṭiqūnā faraj'ū ila anfusihim faqālū innakum antum aẓ-ẓalimūn thumma nakisū 'alā ruūsihim laqad 'alimta mā hā-ulā'i yanṭiqūn.

They said, "Are you the one that did this with our gods, O Abraham?" He said: "Nay, this was done by this is their *biggest one! Ask them, if they can speak intelligently!" So they turned to themselves and said, "Surely you are the ones in the wrong!" Then were they confounded with shame: (they said), "You know full well that these (idols) do not speak!"*[111]

They said "Who did that with our gods?" He said, "Ask them. Their heads are gone and they have died. Ask the biggest of them, the only one whose head remains."

Then the people of *Sayyidinā* Ibrāhīm ؑ knew that they had lost their argument with him.

In the same way, the shaykh has the power to cut down the demigods that the ego has constructed in your heart, which you are worshipping in association with Allāh ﷻ. This is the hidden idolatry that the Prophet ﷺ warned about.

قُلْ إِنَّمَا أَنَا بَشَرٌ مِثْلُكُمْ يُوحَى إِلَيَّ أَنَّمَا إِلَهُكُمْ إِلَهٌ وَاحِدٌ فَمَن كَانَ يَرْجُوا لِقَاءَ رَبِّهِ فَلْيَعْمَلْ عَمَلًا صَالِحًا وَلَا يُشْرِكْ بِعِبَادَةِ رَبِّهِ أَحَدًا

Say: "I am but a man like yourselves, (but) the inspiration has come to me, that your Allāh is one Allāh . whoever expects to meet his Lord, let him work righteousness, and, in the worship of his Lord, admit no one as partner."[112]

أخوف ما أخاف على أمتي الشرك الخفي

The Prophet ﷺ "The thing I fear most for my community is the hidden idolatry,"[113]

قالوا وما الشرك الأصغر قال : الرياء

They asked, "What is the lesser idolatry?" and the Prophet ﷺ replied, "Lesser idolatry is to show off."

---

[111] Sūratu 'l-Anbīyā [The Prophets], 21:62.
[112] Sūratu 'l-Kahf [The Cave], 18:110.
[113] or in some narrations, "the lesser idolatry."

أما إني لست أقول إنكم تعبدون صنماً ولا حجراً ، ولكن شهوة خفية ، وأعمال لغير الله

And further, he said, "And truly I don't say that you will worship idols nor stone, but the hidden desires and actions done for other than Allāh ."

Thus the shaykh leaves the big one in its place, still standing, there for you to destroy yourself.

If anyone comes to the shaykh, he must treat him well. He must put him at his table and feed him, because he came to him. It means those who becamse old enough they reached the "age of maturity." Coming to him is the sign of seeking, and the sign of humility.

So there is, in addition to body care, heart care. In addition to feeding his body, the shaykh must care for that person's heart, because that is the true realization of the mercy of Divine Support.

So what happened in the heart? The shaykh destroys those statues which were before honored by the the seeker. He must topple those idols that were erected by the seeker's ego which were keeping that satanic image that is deeply rooted in the mud of the self; in that clay from which human beings are molded and created.

فيجعل اصنام قلوبهم اذلة، حيث كانت هذه الصور الشيطانية الكامنة في نفوس بني ادم المتداخلة في مجاري الدم، معززة من طرف انفسهم. فيدخل الله عز و جل في قلوبهم ملوك الاخرة الذين هم مؤيّدون بقوة جلاليه فهم اقوياء بالله، فيتبعون الشيطان في جسم المريد حتي يخرجوه صاغراً منكسراً ذليلاً. هم ادرى بخطط والعاب الابالسة. . انما الخلوة هي باب لترك الشواءب

المتعلقة بالدنيا ولترك علائق النفوس كحب الشهوات واتباع الشهوات الشيطانية. فطوبى لمن امر بالخلوة مرة في حياته. فبها يحصل له السلام و السكينة و الطمانينة.

Fa yajaʿlu aṣnāmu qulūbihim adhillatin ḥaythu kānat hādhihi ṣūr ash-shayṭānīyyah al-kāminatu fī nufūsi banī ādam al-mutadākhilati fī majāri 'd-dam muʿazzazatan min ṭarafi anfusihim. Fayudkhilullāh ʿazza wa jall mulūk al-ākhirah. Fa hum muayyadūna bi quwattin jalālīyyah. fahum aqwīyāu billāhi. ḥatta fayattabiʿūn ash-shayṭānu fī jismi murīdih. Ḥatta yukhrijuhu ṣāghiran munkassiran dhalīlan. Hum adrā bi khuṭuṭi wa alaʿābi abālisa. Inamā 'l-khalwati hīyā bābun li tark ish-shawā'ib al-mutaʿlaqati bi 'd-dunyā wa li-tark ʿalā'iqu 'n-nufūs fī ḥubbi 'sh-shahawāt wa atbaʿāu 'sh-shahawāti 'sh-shayṭānīyyah. Fa ṭūbā liman umira bi 'l-khalwati marratan fī ḥayātih. Fa bihā yaḥṣal as-salām wa 's-sakīnah wa 'ṭ-ṭumānīnah.

When the shaykh takes over the heart, he humiliates these satanic images that were honored by the ego, which are planted in the mud of the hearts of the Children of Adam and which mix in the blood of men. Shaytan and his reflections move through the millions of veins and capillaries of human beings. How are you going to destroy them by yourself? But the *awlīyā* can enter wherever the blood flows, and Allāh ﷻ has given permission to these kings of *ākhirah,* these inheritors of the secrets of the Prophet ﷺ , the saints, to enter these veins and save their followers from that hidden *shirk.*

That is why Allāh ﷻ said:

أَلا إِنَّ أَوْلِيَاءَ اللّٰهِ لاَ خَوْفٌ عَلَيْهِمْ وَلاَ هُمْ يَحْزَنُونَ

Alā inna awlīyā 'Llāhi lā khawfun 'alayhim wa lā hum yaḥzanūna

Behold! verily on the friends of Allāh there is no fear, nor shall they grieve;[114]

Allāh's saints have nothing to fear, at the end they will be victorious over the satanic idols built up in the hearts of their followers.They have good tidings in this life because Allāh gave them the power to fight Shaytan. Thus they will not grieve, and Shaytan cannot harm them.

Everyone who fights Shaytan is feaful, except the *awlīyā*, for Allāh ﷻ is saying to the *awlīyā*, "Never be sad and never be afraid. I am allowing you to enter a war against Shaytan supported with majestic power from My Power." In and of themselves they cannot be strong, but they are strong with Allāh ﷻ, and by Allāh ﷻ. Therefore they do not fear even to enter the veins and capillaries of their followers. Allāh ﷻ has given them permission and power to enter every drop of blood and follow every step of Shaytan in the bodies of their students. They track him, and he becomes their quarry. They follow him step-by-step. Allāh ﷻ gives them the power at the most sub-microscopic level, to detect and effect the minutest details of Shaytan's movements, and thus they are able to find him and drive him out—and along with him all these idols, humiliated, broken, belittled and defeated.

This is the strength of the *awlīyā*. They are experienced in the schemes of Shaytan and familiar with all his conspiracies. They know the tricks that he uses to gain mastery over the ego and how Shaytan uses it to build up these idolatrous effigies. Shaytan begins erecting such idols inside your heart when you are still a child. That is why guiding shaykhs tell their followers to recite 500 times "*Yā Ṣamad,*" to destroy these statues on whose worship you have been raised.

---

[114] Sūrah Yūnus [Jonah], 10:62.

The worst are those who are raised by the bottle. You do not know who is filling these bottles or what kind of power is put into them. Second worst are those that are breastfed, because the breastmilk of the mother creates veils in the heart of the child which come from the egoistic characteristics of both the mother and the father. For forty days after birth, the child is not veiled from the heavenly realm. If the mother and father never fight and never shout, then the child will grow up without any veils.

Grandshaykh said, "From the time that I was born until my passing, I was never veiled." That was because his mother was sister of his master, Shaykh Sharafuddin, so he was his uncle, and she knew how to raise him in such a way as to avoid veiling him from the heavenly presence.

One *murīd* came to Shaykh Sharafuddin, and the shaykh urged him to get married. He said, "Up to now you did not marry. Marriage is half of religion because it saves you from doing what is forbidden."

The disciple asked the shaykh, "Who am I going to marry?"

The shaykh pointed to a woman and said, "There is a lady. She is crazy, but you go and marry her."

This woman was feebleminded. She would stand in the street, take bread and distribute it to people. Sometimes, her legs would show. Sometimes, she had no veil on her head.

The student looked at her, and thought to himself, "How am I going to marry her?" But he loved his shaykh, and he knew that his shaykh would not tell him to marry her if that was not the right thing for him to do. He went and married her. She gave him two sons that grew up to be the two greatest scholars of their time. They were able to give legal rulings (*fatwa*) that no one could refute.

Shaykhs look to the future. They see what is written on the Preserved Tablet. So when you listen to them, they give you more.

Today, some say "our marriage did not work." Don't say that, rather it is your ego that did not work. She was not patient and he was not patient. In the case of this *murīd*, his wife was a mentally retarded woman, but that *murīd* was patient with her.

Today, neither the husband nor the wife are patient with each other. The wife must submit to her husband. She has to know his role in the family and respect it. The husband must respect his wife and treat her in the best way. If there is a problem, keep it to yourself. Talking about it with others, is simply the idols of the ego interfering to create difficulties in your life. That is why you see so many men and women complaining today.

The shaykh has the power to enter the hearts of his followers, cast out Shaytan, and topple the statues erected by the ego of the love of *dunyā* and its different branches. That is what happens in seclusion, but in order to benefit, you must be in a state that is prepared to enter seclusion and the seclusion you do must be with the ordered of the shaykh. If not, you are just wasting your time. The shaykh orders you into seclusion so that you can demolish the last and greatest idol, until you can tear aside that final thick veil. At that time you will find yourself in the Divine Presence.

You Must Earn Your Trust

The shaykh does not give you candy and say, "Here is your secret. Here is your trust." Many people today want everything to come this easily. Some say, I have been in *ṭarīqah* 15 years, 20 years, 30 years—I did not get it." Check if the statue in your heart is still there. The big one is still there. When you kill that big snake, then all other illusions will disappear. That is what *Sayyīdinā* Mūsā ﷺ did. His staff, *ʿasā*, stood forth and devoured all the statues of the heart. So, do not come to the shaykh and say, "I have been with you thirty years and still I am seeing nothing!"

Sayyīdinā 'Abdu 'l-Khāliq had a faithful student who always cut wood for the shaykh. One day, he sent this *murīd* to the cemetery, telling him, "Go there today and learn something."

When the disciple arrived at the cemetery the gate was closed, but there was an old man sitting on the fence nearby. He looked at him and said, "What are you coming here for?"

The student said, "I am coming for a visit, but the gate is closed. Do you have the key?"

Suddenly the gate opened on its own. Without hesitation, the *murīd* entered, recognizing the miracle of his master, and he was followed by the old man. The old man pointed to a grave and said, "This one died at the age of just one year."

The student, recognizing the name on the gravestone, a well-known scholar, said, "How can that be? He died at the age of eighty."

They proceeded on and stopped at another grave, again that of a well-known scholar, one of the disciples of his shaykh. The old man said, "This one died at the age of two years." Coming to another he said, "This one reached the age of four," and yet another, "that one died at ten years of age," and so on. According to him, not one of the dead whose graves they visited even reached fifteen years of age, the age of maturity, whereas to the knowledge of that *murīd*, most had reached old age.

The *murīd* looked at the man and said, "Who are you? Shaytan? I came to visit this cemetery by the order of my shaykh, and I knew all of these people. They were all disciples of my shaykh, and I know that all of them lived much longer than what you say!"

The student returned to his master, *Sayyīdinā* 'Abdu 'l-Khāliq, who asked him, "Did you see anything extraordinary today?"

The *murīd* said, "Yes, there was a person who came and said 'your *murīds* were very young when they died,' so I cursed him."

His shaykh said, "You animal, *yā ḥaywān*. You are an idiot. You do not know anything. I have to send you away, else you will contaminate all the other *murīds* with your illness!"

That old man was *Sayyīdinā* Khiḍr ﷺ, but he had veiled his identify from that follower. That is why the shaykh shouted at him. Today, you cannot shout at *murīds*. If Mawlana Shaykh shouts at a *murīd*, he will run away and not come back. Things were different back then. The shaykh shouted at that student, even though he had been cutting wood for him. But that *murīd's* heart remained connected with his shaykh. So, the Prophet ﷺ came and witnessed what he had achieved and bestowed on him his trust.

You do not receive your trust based on the number of years you have been with the shaykh, but based on the bond you have with him. Are you going to destroy that bond if he does not give you your trust? You must not be after rewards, *ʿiwaḍ*. You are going to the Prophet ﷺ. You are seeking the Divine Presence. You are coming to the shaykh for guidance on that journey. You are not coming to ask him to open this or that secret for you. When permission comes, they open your heart immediately. Butbefore that they will grind you first from Allāh's Love.

I have been with Mawlana Shaykh Nāẓim for fifty years, since 1957, and he never opened anything for me. I am still struggling. He may send something, but there is nothing coming from myself. If he throws something into my heart, it is there.

"Know, O ego, that there are 70,000 veils between you and the Prophet ﷺ. That is why you have to understand that it is impossible. When you realize that it is impossible, then that *ināyat* Divine Support comes, the Breeze of Youth, *rīḥ aṣ-ṣiba*. That breeze takes you to *ināyat Allāh*, Divine Support. There is where you will be able."

Shaytan asked Allāh ﷻ to leave him free until Judgment Day.

"I will mislead them all, every one," he vowed. "I will deceive them and cause them to deviate, and I will show you my power."

Allāh ﷻ said, "Do you want to challenge Me? No problem. If they follow you, I will throw you and them all into Hell."

These devils, *abālisa,* are in your heart trying to do that to you, and the *awlīyā* are given power to fight them. Seclusion is how Shaytan's power over you is broken, so good tidings to anyone who has been ordered into *khalwah* at least once in his life. If not, he is going to do *khalwah* in his grave, and that is not 100 times more difficult, nor 1,000 times more difficult, not even 100,000 more times difficult—Allāh ﷻ knows how much more difficult that is. So, good tidings to them because they will receive the greatest *baraka* and they will receive peace, tranquility and satisfaction of the heart.

Accept the Authority of the Shaykh

Sometimes people complain about those who are in authority over them. They criticize them, and this creates confusion and *fitna.*

The Prophet ﷺ said:

الفتنة نائمة لعن الله من أيقظها

al-fitnatu nā'imatan, la'an 'Llāh man ayqaẓahā.

Fitnah is dormant; Allāh curses the one who wakes it up.

To accept someone above you is difficult. That is why Allāh ﷻ ordered in the Holy Qur'an:

أَطِيعُواْ اللّهَ وَأَطِيعُواْ الرَّسُولَ وَأُوْلِي الأَمْرِ مِنكُمْ

Aṭī'ū 'llāha wa aṭī'ū 'r-rasūla wa ūli 'l-amri minkum

Obey God, obey His Prophet ﷺ and obey those who are in authority over you.[115]

If Allāh ﷻ has appointed someone to be the ruler of a nation, you must obey that one. You must obey the politicians and the police, because they are in authority. In addition, you must obey what Allāh ﷻ inspires in your heart, for He inspires the heart with the knowledge of what is good and what is bad. That is the authority of your heart. If you do not listen, then you are disobeying Allāh ﷻ, disobeying His Prophet ﷺ and disobeying those whom He has appointed as authorities over you.

But the ego never accepts this. It wants to be above everyone else.

Do not give yourself a title. Do not say, "I am a shaykh." If you do, you are imitating Iblīs. You are following the way of Shaytan, because he gave himself a title. *Dunyā* titles are different: you can be a doctor or an engineer, a plumber or a carpenter. That is okay. But *ākhirah* titles are different, and you must not apply them to yourself. Such titles can only come from heaven. They must be bestowed upon you by the Prophet ﷺ through your guide. Otherwise, you will be like Iblīs.

قَالَ أَنَاْ خَيْرٌ مِّنْهُ خَلَقْتَنِي مِن نَّارٍ وَخَلَقْتَهُ مِن طِينٍ

Qāla khalaqtanī min nārin wa khalaqtahu min ṭīn.

He said: "I am better than he: You did create me from fire, and him from clay."[116]

Iblīs gave himself a title. He said, "You created me from fire, and you created him from clay—from mud. I am better!" And Allāh ﷻ told him, "No. Now you are cursed."

Iblīs is cursed because Allāh ﷻ ordered him to make prostration (*sajdah*) and he refused.

---

[115] Sūratu 'n-Nisā [Women], 4:59.

[116] Sūratu 'l-'Arāf [The Heights], 7:12.

وَإِذْ قُلْنَا لِلْمَلَائِكَةِ اسْجُدُوا لِآدَمَ فَسَجَدُوا إِلَّا إِبْلِيسَ أَبَى فَقُلْنَا يَا آدَمُ إِنَّ هَذَا عَدُوٌّ لَّكَ وَلِزَوْجِكَ فَلَا يُخْرِجَنَّكُمَا مِنَ الْجَنَّةِ فَتَشْقَى إِنَّ لَكَ أَلَّا تَجُوعَ فِيهَا وَلَا تَعْرَى وَأَنَّكَ لَا تَظْمَأُ فِيهَا وَلَا تَضْحَى فَوَسْوَسَ إِلَيْهِ الشَّيْطَانُ قَالَ يَا آدَمُ هَلْ أَدُلُّكَ عَلَى شَجَرَةِ الْخُلْدِ وَمُلْكٍ لَّا يَبْلَى

Wa idh qulnā li 'l-malāikati 'sjudū li ādama fa-sajadū illa Iblīsa abā. Faqulna yā ādamu inna hādhā ʿadūwwun laka wa lizawjika falā yukhrijannakumā mina 'l-jannati fatashqā. Inna laka allā tajūʿa fīhā wa lā taʿrā. Wa annaka lā taẓmāū fīhā wa la tadḥā. Fa waswasa ilayhi ash-shayṭānu qāla yā ādamu hal adulluka ʿalā shajaratil 'l-khuldi wa mulkin la yablā.

And when We said unto the angels: Fall prostrate before Adam, they fell prostrate (all) save Iblīs; he refused. Therefore We said: O Adam! This is an enemy unto you and unto your wife, so let him not drive you both out of the Garden so that you come to toil. It is (vouchsafed) unto you that you hungerest not therein nor art naked, and you thirstest not therein nor art exposed to the sun's heat. But the Devil whispered to him, saying: O Adam! Shall I show you the tree of immortality and power that wasteth not away? Then they twain ate thereof, so that their shame became apparent unto them, and they began to hide by heaping on themselves some of the leaves of the Garden. And Adam disobeyed his Lord, so went astray.[117]

Allāh ﷻ told the angels to prostrate before Adam ﷺ. Iblīs looked at Adam ﷺ and refused because of his pride. We have that same pride in ourselves, that arrogance. All of us do—no one is free of that taint. It is the arrogance of seeing the self, giving a title to the self, taking pride in the self and wanting other people to respect yourself. You want people to look at you and say, "Oh!

---

[117] Sūrah Ṭā Ḥā 20:116-121.

We bow to you. You are our symbol." That characteristic comes into the self and dresses the self. It begins in childhood, and it grows with us until we die.

Awlīyāullāh, those who have authority from the Prophet ﷺ, ask their followers to cast off that bad trait that has been growing within them since childhood (*ṭifl an-nafs al-madhmūmah*) by reciting "*Yā Ṣamad*" 500 times. This eliminates that trait slowly. Then they order their student into seclusion to eliminate it completely. They want you to reach the level of humility, the opposite of arrogance and pride. If we cannot reach that, then we are carrying the character trait of Shaytan.

Iblīs was with the angels and his name then was ʿAzāzīl. He had always been faithful to his Lord. He was never absent from prostration to his Lord for even a single moment. He was the head of the angels and was known as "the peacock (*ṭāwūs*) of the angels."

The peacock is the most beautiful bird in this world, displaying the most beautiful and varied colors. Similarly, Iblīs was radiant with these myriad colors, always doing *sajdah*. Grand Shaykh Mawlana ʿAbdAllāh al-Fā'iz ad-Dāghestānī, may Allāh ﷻ bless his soul, said, "Iblīs did not leave one handspan in the heavens and earth empty of his *sajdah*. That shows his very exalted level."

What happened? He was the foremost amongst the angels, his chest decorated with brilliant medallions. He was like a king or a president, an official of high rank. What happens when you ask such a person to do something that requires them to show humbleness? They refuse. It is very hard for them to show respect to anyone they see as inferior to themselves. So it was with Iblīs. Allāh ﷻ, who is above all the angels, ordered them to make *sajdah* to Adam ﷺ. Iblīs refused, because for him it was an unacceptable act of humility. He said, "How can I bow to anyone other than Allāh? I cannot."

This is an important point: His first thought was not, "I will not bow to him because You created me from fire and him from clay." Rather, his first thought was, "How can I prostrate myself before anyone other than You, my Lord?" That was the first thing that entered his heart. That was why he hesitated.

If his train of thought had stopped there, that would not have been a problem, because *sajdah* is for Allāh ﷻ alone. But his animal, base and prideful character overthrew his better self and turned that good thought into something wrong. When he hesitated his pride overcame him. His first thought may have been, "How can I make *sajdah* to someone other than Allāh ?" But that arrogant character that was within him soon replaced that with, "How can I make *sajdah* to him? I am better than him!" That is when he was cursed and cast down.

However, we must reflect on this point: Was Shaytan really cast out of Paradise?

Adam عليه السلام was lonely in Paradise, and so Allāh ﷻ created Hawwa for him. For a time, they dwelt in Paradise together. Then Allāh ﷻ told them, "Do not eat from that tree." When they ate from it they saw their nakedness. Why did they eat? They ate because Shaytan whispered to them. That means Shaytan was still in Paradise.

Can Paradise accept the presence of a sinner? It cannot. If you allow a bad apple to remain in a basket of good apples, the rotten one will spread its rot to all the fresh ones. That is why it is only common sense to discard it.

Look at what happened with the avian flu. When one bird got sick, they threw millions into the fire. If they do this with birds today, they will do the same with humans tomorrow.

Yet, we see that Allāh ﷻ kept Iblīs despite having cursed him. He was left in Paradise to be a test for others, for Adam عليه السلام and Eve عليها السلام.

That is why the *awlīyā* keep rotten *murīds* around. They know that they are bad apples, but they give them power and *ijāzāt,* written authorizations, signed and stamped. They know that they are rotten and disobedient, that they are backstabbing the shaykh and other *murīds.* Yet, the *awlīyā* leave them to test their other followers, to see whether they too will become rotten or remain united. If one rotten apple can destroy the entire container, how much damage can one rotten *murīd* do—especially one who is given permission to lead *dhikr* and initiate people into *ṭarīqah*? That is why Mawlana said, "Two-thirds of my followers are going to leave me. One-third are going to stay, and out of that one-third, there are only fifty who are sincere."

That means that fifty of Mawlana's *murīds* will reach the level of sainthood. The rest of that third will be okay, those who carry humility instead if arrogance and pride. He will present them to them to the Prophet ﷺ and then to the Divine Presence. That is what we are hoping for from our guide.

Can Paradise accept sinners like you? No, it is impossible. Someone who sins must be cleansed before entering Paradise. Just as one must bathe and dress for work before going to the office, so we must be cleansed of our sins before entering through those holy gates. You cannot enter Paradise if the self is not clean. If you do not clean yourself in this world, you are going to do it when you die—and then it will be much harder. You have to go out of this world clean, otherwise you will be cleansed in the grave.

The proof of this is often found in the graves of saints. When they are opened, their bodies are still fresh—as if they had just been buried. That is because they were pure when they left this life, and they did not need to be cleansed. That is because they listened to the authorities that Allāh ﷻ ordered them to listen to and they obeyed.

ELEVEN

Shaytan's Traps

When you fall into the traps of Shaytān there is nothing to restore your respect in the Divine Presence. You lost your value, you lost your honor, and you lost your respect and your dignity in the Presence of *awlīyā*, in the Presence of the Prophet and in the Presence of Allāh, until you repent.

Adam listened one time to the whisper of Shaytān and Allāh took him out of Paradise for that and sent him to earth to live [*dār al-balā*].

And Adam requested forgiveness and Iblīs did not. So Allāh accepted the repentance of Adam but cursed Iblīs. Because of his character he was not accepted in Paradise. You lose all honor, all respect, all value when you fall into the trap of Shaytān.

يا بن ادم ان رءات ربك يتبعيو نعمه و انت تعصي فحضروا وا
علم ان افضل الزهد اخفي الزهد. لان ابشاعه يعلمك الغرور
بالنفس. واحذر الغرور بنفسك فيقتلك و يباعدك عن الحضرة
الالهية. لان كل منأ يتغطي عن اخطاءه و يعدها حفوات

Yā 'bn Ādam in rā'ita rabbuka yutabiʿiū niʿmahu wa anta taʿṣī fa-ḥadarū wʿalam anna afḍal az-zuhdi akhfā az-zuhdi. Li anna ibshāhu yuʿallimuka al-gharūr bi 'n-nafs. Waḥdhar al-gharūri bi nafsik fa yaqtuluk wa yubʿadiduka ʿan il-ḥaḍarat al-ilāhīyyah. Li anna kullu minnan yataghāṭa ʿan akhṭā'ihi wa yaʿudaha ḥafawāt.

As Sayyīdinā ʿAlī said, O son of Adam, if you see Allāh's Favor continuously coming to you and you are committing sins then beware what will happen to you. And know that the best asceticism is the hidden asceticism because ??ibshahu will teach you the prideof the self. Beware of self pride, for it will kill you and take you away from the Divine Presence. Each one of us conceals his defects and to consider them to be minor and insignificant and then he begins to think he has no defects.

It means you are rejecting your Lord's Favors; in fact it is as if you see them coming from Shaytān. That is for believers. It means you accept Allāh's Favors but commit sins at the same time, then beware the slip sending His ???

Al-Kahf [18:65 *ākhirah*, although you might have whole wealth of *dunyā* but to your heart you are not too attached to it, Allāh gave you from his favors and that can be of different kinds, giving wealth, giving knowledge, giving wealth and respect, giving honor and dignity and happiness, good life, good health, bless you with the mercy of Muḥammad that he gave to *Sayyīdinā* Khiḍr عليه السلام,

آتَيْنَاهُ رَحْمَةً مِنْ عِندِنَا

wa ataynāhu raḥmatan min ʿindinā.

We had bestowed Mercy from Ourselves.[118]

Sayyīdinā Khiḍr attained that mercy, because Allāh showed *Sayyīdinā* Khiḍr the reality of Muḥammad. That is why he could show *Sayyīdinā* Mūsā something he could not get, as *Sayyīdinā* Khiḍr was receiving from heart of *Sayyīdinā* Muḥammad from the realities that are coming in the Last Days.

The verse means, "Because We gave him mercy from heavens and we sent you not, O Muḥammad, but as a mercy to humanity." That mercy He showed to *Sayyīdinā* Khiḍr enabled him to reveal something from the secrets of the Last Prophet. This is related to what was mentioned in the *Ṭabaqāt* of as-Subkī, that

[118] Sūratu 'l-Kahf [The Cave], 18:65.

the Prophet was given three kinds of knowledge. One he was to for himself alone, and one he was granted and allowed to give as he likes to those he wishes and the third he gives to everyone, The last is the *ʿilm ash-Sharīʿah wa ʿilm al-Qur'an*, knowledge of Divine Law and the Qur'an. The *ʿilm* he gave to some was given according to the choice that Allāh gave the Prophet, and from that *Sayyīdinā* Khiḍr took out .

There is one knowledge that the Prophet will not open until the Last Day and that is mentioned in a hadith of Bukhārī.

> On Judgment Day the Prophet will make *sajdah* and Allāh inspire to his heart to make *duʿa* that were never opened before and he will make *duāʿ* and then Allāh will tell him "raise your head, ask and you will be given!" The Prophet asks, "*Yā Rabbī*, my Ummah, my Ummah!" and Allāh grants him to removeone third of the Ummah from punishment.
>
> The Prophet goes into *sajdah* once again and Allāh inspire to his heart to make *duāʿ* that were never opened before and he will make *duāʿ* and then Allāh will tell him "raise your head, ask and you will be given!" and he asks, "*Yā Rabbī*, my Ummah, my Ummah!" and Allāh grants him another third of the Ummah. A third time the Prophet goes into *sajdah* and Allāh inspires to his heart to make *duāʿ* that were never opened before and he will make *duāʿ* and then Allāh will tell him "raise your head, ask and you will be given!" and he asks, "*Yā Rabbī*, my Ummah, my Ummah!" and Allāh says, "Take your Ummah and go to Paradise."

TWELVE

Hide Your Asceticism

So Sayyīdinā ʿAlī described "the best of asceticism." Asceticism means to leave the pleasurely life completely, seeking one's journey through one's shaykh, to the Prophet and from the Prophet to Allāh . The seeker might be poor or he might be rich, that is Allāh's Favor. It might be he has no clothes except patched rags or it might be has everything. But if that person is rich it does not mean he is attached to *dunyā*. His goal is: *ilāhī anta maqṣūdī wa riḍāka maṭlūbī*—My God, my goal is to be in Your presence and Your happiness is what I seek." That person is thanking his Lord, poor or rich, and that is what is needed.

So if you are ascetic and you dropped love of *dunyā* and you dropped Shaytān from riding your ego, then at that time your soul is riding your ego. So at that time "the best of asceticism" is what Sayyīdinā ʿAlī described: "it is to hide your asceticism." The best of asceticism is to conceal your asceticism.

This means one must avoid showing off. True ascetics, *zuhhād*, hide their asceticism by possessing this thing or that, this wealth or that, cars, homes, horses, jewelry. And while they own all these material possessions they hold no attachment to these "toys". To them they have no meaning.

Your heart is always with Allāh ﷻ, you don't care for things. So the best of asceticism is to hide it for that makes it only to be between you and Allāh ﷻ. Then people look and say "look, he has all kinds of possessions; he is no ascetic." To hide it is best. How do you hide it? Be normal. Your heart is ascetic. But what is between you and Allāh is completely different from common people. Allāh knows your heart.

If you understand, you realize that is difficult; it is not easy. How do you hide something that is appearing on your face. People look, saying, "O he has rings on his hands, he has cars, he has this, he has that." That is what Sayyīdinā ʿAlī ؓ was like. Sayyīdinā ʿAlī ؓ was rich; *Sayyīdinā* ʿUthmān ؓ was rich, *Sayyīdinā* ʿUmar ؓ was rich; *Sayyīdinā* Abū Bakr ؓ was a business man and he was rich. *Sayyīdinā* ʿUthmān ؓ was able to offer seven caravans full of gold when the Prophet ﷺ asked for support.

Sayyīdinā Sulaymān ؑ asked:

قَالَ رَبِّ اغْفِرْ لِي وَهَبْ لِي مُلْكًا لَّا يَنبَغِي لِأَحَدٍ مِّنْ بَعْدِي إِنَّكَ أَنتَ الْوَهَّابُ

He said, "O my Lord! Forgive me, and grant me a kingdom which, (it may be), suits not another after me: for You art the Grantor of Bounties (without measure).[119]

Once the Prophet ﷺ began ask Allāh for wealth that no one had ever possessed, but he then remembered that this is reserved for Sulaymān ؑ, and so when Uḥud came offering to become gold for him, he refused and did not accept it, for that was for *Sayyīdinā* Sulaymān ؑ.

The Prophet ﷺ put forth all the wealth available to him to spread Islam. With the openings of Islam all the Sahāba became wealthy. Yet they never held onto their newfound wealth. So the best of asceticism is to hide your asceticism. If you display your asceticism, then that will teach you to be proud of your ego. "O I left *dunyā* and gave everything in Allāh's way. O look at me. Now I am a dervish, I have patches on my pants."

One time I was in California. It might have been in the early 90's when I first came to the States. And one person came to meet with me; it was the first time, in Palo Alto, near Stanford University. And one person entered with patches on his pants carrying a stick with two heads. Another followed, whose clothes had even more patches. Then a third came in who was also

---

[119] Sūrah Ṣād, 38:35.

wearing a patched shirt. I wondered, 'What is that? Perhaps they are poor."

However another time some months later, I saw one of them coming to me from his work, and he was dressed very well. So why are you wearing like clothes with patches? You cannot show your dervishhood, for that is showing off.

Use the Best of this Life for the Next

I remember Grandshaykh said, "Dress in the best clothes you are able; drive the best cars and don't buy cars that are not cheap, but get the best ones. We are a distinguished order and we have to show that we are not trying to be nothing for this is not the meaning of leaving everything. No, we have to show we spend in Allāh's way in order to attract more people. We must not make people become disgusted from our appearance." So we had the best and we were happy to come with the best car and take Grandshaykh around.

One time we went to Damascus but the car we brought was old and the tires were in bad shape. Mawlana Shaykh Nāẓim wanted to go to Latakia (in Syria), about 300 miles away. We left after breakfast and normally we reach there in four hours. It took to until after Isha to reach there, because the car had flat tire several times or broke down and Mawlana Shaykh Nāẓim was so upset, shouting and shouting. It took from morning until after Isha. Every 100 km. we got a flat tire. There were no gas stations there to go to fix a tire. So each time we had a flat, we had to wait for someone to take us; go and fix the flat; then return to the car and put it on.

So if Allāh gave you wealth it is acceptable to use it and to hide your asceticism. Don't say, "I gave everything in the way of Allāh ." If you gave, hide it. Why do you have to show it? "Hide" here is not meant in the sense of conspiracy but rather as a "conspiracy" (*makr*) against your Shaytān to break your ego down.

Sayyīdinā 'Alī said, "If you don't conceal and veil it and expose what your asceticism has done, then it will fill you with pride of the *nafs*, and make you arrogant." Beware of the pride and arrogance of *zuhd*; beware of exposing your asceticism. Only show it to your Lord, your Prophet and your shaykh. That is a secret you never want to reveal.

Beware of the pride and arrogance of exposing these secrets because doing so will "kill" your spiritual progress. Beware of the *zuhd* of the ego, thinking "O I am an ascetic. I perform my *awrād*, I do this and I do that." The ego will "kill" you and take you from Allāh's Presence. Because everyone of us veils our mistakes from ourselves and don't see them. Even if we were to see a fault we would consider it a *hafwah*, aminor slip, as if nothing. But to Allāh it is big and people see it as big. It is your ego which does not allow you to see it as big. In reality it is huge, until finally pride and arrogance overtake you and make you think you are without defect, completely spotless and perfect.

That is why everyone considers himself perfect. Every one of us thinks that he is above everyone else, and does not accept any advice from another. If you tell him hundreds of times "this is not correct" he will insist on doing it. Why?

Shaytān did not accept advice. Allāh ordered him to make *sajdah* and he refused. Advice is very difficult to accept. So when a seeker does not heed the good advice he is given, he begins to ignore and conceal from himself all of his own bad character traits. And though he is full of bad traits, he considers himself highly respected and begins to consider himself a professor, a PhD and a doctor.

Titles of Self-Aggrandizement

Something I saw in one country amazed me. Some professors there write in front of their name, "Professor", "Doctor" and so on. That is arrogance, for what purpose does that serve?

If such a person is also on the journey, seeking Allāh, and he is not hiding his asceticism, he wants to be known by one and all as professor, guide, master, shaykh, and to be designated with all kinds of titles, *luqāb*. He loves *dunyā* titles like *calipha*, senior *murīd*, senior this and that. It means, "You must listen to me else I don't want to hear from you."

If you are a shaykh, hide it. Rather let people run to you. Hide yourself. Then you become a spotlight. You don't want to cheat by going to other shaykh's *murīd*s and speaking to them and tricking them into following you. Go and find your own *murīds*.

Stealing Another Shaykh's Disciples is a Grave Sin

In the sight of *Awlīyāullāh* it is very grave mistake for a shaykh to take another shaykh's *murīds*. They don't like that. It is not acceptable to *awlīyā* for a shaykh to come to another who has *murīd*s and take the *murīds*. If they are both *walīs* they understand that secret and do not do that, but if one is not a *walī* he might come and take another shaykh's *murīd*s.

One time Grandshaykh gave this example of that problem, and it is striking. In normal life adultery is not allowed. If someone makes that sin of *zinā* it is from the *kabā'ir* and if someone commits that there are decisions to be taken there. And where the adultery between men and women is very hard and not acceptable, to *awlīyāullāh* it is similar if one shaykh comes and takes the *murīd* of another shaykh. That is not physical adultery, but in the spiritual dimension it is similar and for that reason it is tremendously hard on the hearts of *awlīyā* and forbidden to commit that kind of theft.

That is why the shaykh does not assign a *calipha*. He does that only when he is passing from this life. May Allāh give Mawlana Shaykh long life, he is our master. Everyone belongs to him. We are only bringing and presenting to him those whom we are looking after and bringing them to him. He is their master and their shaykh.

There are many who comes and call themselves masters and build kingdoms for themselves, and Allāh knows the heart.

When a seeker begins to see that he has no defects he begins to ignore and hide his bad actions until Shaytān will make him imagine that he has no more sins and that he is becoming completely free of faults. At that time he begins to exalt himself above everyone. You can see that sickness in a many of the guides who think they are *awlīyā* and in reality they have nothing to do with *wilāyah*. You see a lot of such guides today: people who think they have reached the highest level of *wilāyah* and imagine they are inheriting from the highest levels but in reality they are inheriting from Shaytān and he is making them to hallucinate and to imagine that they are perfect. The reality is such ones are far from perfect. They look only at the mistakes of others and never at their own mistakes. They never see what comes out of their mouths nor do they ever see what they are enjoying from the pleasures of life. They only sees the mistakes of others and correct them.

وَمَا أَظُنُّ السَّاعَةَ قَائِمَةً وَلَئِن رُّدِدتُّ إِلَىٰ رَبِّي لَأَجِدَنَّ خَيْرًا مِّنْهَا مُنقَلَبًا

Nor do I deem that the Hour (of Judgment) will (ever) come: Even if I am brought back to my Lord, I shall surely find (there) something better in exchange."[120]

This exchange shows the wealthy neighbor thought he would live forever.

The story of the garden can be interpreted the the garden's owner thinks his ego is a paradise now when in reality he is an oppressor to himself. Here Shayṭān is showing himself as perfect and pure, making him hallucinate that he is in the garden of Shaytān while thinking himself to be good.

That is what we see everyone has reached. Today no one is out of this delusion. He or she is full of that peackockness pride of

[120] Sūratu 'l-Kahf [The Cave], 18:36.

Satan, and everyone is proud, thinking, "I am doing this, I am doing that, that one spoke with me, that one spoke came to me." There is too much pride in every human being. How do you want to advise him about *ākhirah*? He doesn't want to listen. He thinks that he has no defects and that anything he does wrong he thinks is insignificant. That is the example of the neighbor in the story. One person said, "O it was a small issue like a grain and they blew it up to make it something big." Shaytān plays with him to consider a major defect as something insignificant. He wonders, "Why are they blowing it out of proportion." He does not realit that it is not insignificant; rather it is highly significant.

For example yesterday I was giving Jumʿah. That one was at the end and I was seeing that he was throwing his young son, who is three years old. To him it was insignificant but to the one observing it was significant.

Children teach you patience. It is good to teach them discipline. But sometimes you become angry and do something that is no longer accepted as good conduct and discipline but rather is harmful to the child. That is why every action teaches you patience and the last Beautiful Name of Allāh's Beautiful Names and Attributes is aṣ-Ṣabūr. From the beginning: Allāh u ar-Raḥmān ar-Raḥīm, al-Malik, al-Quddūs … all the way at the end that Allāh's last name is aṣ-Ṣabūr, the Most Patient One. To tell us "I am patient on My creation." Allāh is teaching us, that Allāh is patient with His servants badness. That tells us, "Don't you want to be patient with each other?" But because we have that character and we are molded with anger—we cannot accept anything. Even if something is Allāh's order, then we try to go around it to be sure it is not accepted by us, because we are proud and arrogant with ourselves; we don't want to follow what we are ordered by Allāh in Holy Qur'an and in holy hadith. *Mukhālifāt ash-sharīʿah,* leaving what Allāh ordered because we cannot accept. Obedience is always difficult on the self.

The Prophet was praying until his feet were swollen. They told him, "*Yā Rasūlullāh* you are praying until your feet are swollen, and Allāh forgave you your former and sins."

He said, "*alā akūna ʿabdan shakūra*—Should I not be a thankful servant?"

Today many people do not practice voluntary worship, the *sunan*, saying "it is not obligatory." That is obstinacy, not to accept any opinion except from yourself. That is why Iblīs challenged everyone saying, "O my Lord! Give me respite to live to the end and I will make sure to send all Your servants astray."

Look how patient Allāh is even with Iblīs. He gave him what he wants. Do you give anyone what he wants or she wants when he asks you? Instead we fight with each other.

In Arabic we have a saying, "*Ana bābā hasan*—I am Bābā Ḥasan!" and the other says "*antī bābā ḥasan*—No you are Bābā Ḥasan!" Bābā Ḥasan means the Aghā, the head of the town, the mayor a strongman, the chief, someone who is very tough. "You are chief?" "I am chief!" Even that boy will say, "I am chief!" No one will accept not to be chief.

Ask him and his wife, who is chief? That trap of Shaytān is teaching us his way which is to make us not see our own mistakes or to see them as insignificant.

Ten Excellent Character Traits

We have to know that the life of mankind is build on ten characteristics: knowledge, *al-ʿilm,* sincerity, *aṣ-ṣalāḥ,* piety, *at-taqwā,* humility, *at-tawadʿa,* patience, *aṣ-ṣabr,* thinking, *at-taffakur,* contemplation, *at-ta'amul,* meditation, *al-murāqabah,* and then on initiation, *murābiṭah* with the shaykh, which lead you, all together, *tadhalal li-rabbik,* to see yourself the lowest and to ask your Lord's forgiveness. If you don't have that attitude of self-deprecation you are going to fall into the trap of Shaytān.

So anyone who falls in the trap of Shaytān sees his mistakes as insignificant and he (*yataghādā*) overlooks his own bad behaviors. Although he has bad behaviors, he sidestep them and sees them as insignificant, thinking, "I don't have any kind of bad behavior." How is it that you don't have bad behavior? Everyone has bad behavior. A simple example: when they put the food, the one in middle can reach everything, but the one at the end wants to jump over everything to reach the dish that is farthest away. That is bad manners. "Give me, give me." Didn't you see that? What is in front of you is chicken and meat and vegetables. That dish at the other end is Baba Ghanoush full of garlic and onions. "O, Give me that." Though it is far you ask for it. That is a bad manner that makes us to fall into the trap.

Shaytān will begin to make his prey imagine that while he himself has no mistakes, but he looks at the mistakes of others and if theirs are insignificant he blows them up.

As we recited before:

"He entered his paradise and he was oppressor to himself, he said, as a tyrant, O I will think that this will be forever like that, green and fruitful and nothing can change it."

The interpreted meaning is that we imagine our physicality and spirituality are at their peak and nothing will change our conditions. Yes, it can be changed, when Shaytān traps you, then everything is taken. May Allāh forgive us and protect us.

THIRTEEN

The Worst Traits: Pride and Arrogance

Whoever allows pride and arrogance (*al-ghurūr wa 'l-ʿujb*) to enter his heart will be far away from spiritual realities and knowledge oceans. He will wear and display the peacock-like characteristic of Shaytan, because Shaytan entered his heart and occupied his personality. When pride and arrogance enter the self, the ego fashions a beautiful image of itself, like a resplendent rainbow-feathered peacock. Because of all the medallions and decorations that Iblīs has bestowed upon it, the ego attains a form of satisfaction and peace, thinking it has reached the highest level of achievement. These Satanic adornments make him forget the ocean of beauty of his Lord; he sees only these multi-colored peacock medallions instead of the radiant manifestations of Allāh's Beauty. By following Iblīs, the whispers of Shaytan penetrate his heart and take up residence there. That is how Shaytan catches people, and how he maintains his hold on them.

These characters are the peacockness characteristics of Iblīs that he has been molded with and that is why Allāh cursed him. Although as we said previously, Iblīs said, "I cannot do *sajdah* to anyone else, only to you yā Allāh ." Look how Iblīs was at the beginning, not accepting to make *sajdah,* except to Allāh . Then his bad characteristics overtook that good intention and flipped him. "You created him from clay and created me from fire." Clay. What is that fire? What is fire? Do you know what fire is?

Allāh created Iblīs from fire. That fire that can eat everything except water.

وَجَعَلْنَا مِنَ الْمَاءِ كُلَّ شَيْءٍ حَيٍّ

Wa jaʿlnā min al-māi kulli shayin ḥayy.

We made from water every living thing.[121]

Fire cannot conquer water, but water can conquer everything.

Ḥaqq al-hayāt, wa hayātan abadīyyah, the Real Life and the Eternal Life[122], the reality of the water is the reality of the Fount of Knowledge, that Allāh made everything that originates from water to be living. That is why our body is composed of 97 percent water. Nothing can destroy water but water can destroy fire.

If you can maintain a "watery" lifestyle, swimming in the waters of mercy then mercy will emerge. "Water" here is not the water that we drink and wash with. That is *dunyā* water. But there is another "water", the real "water". That means you have been submerged in Divine Oceans of Mercy, *buḥūr ar-raḥmah*; Oceans of the Water of Life, representing the Oceans of the Beautiful Names and Attributes of Allāh .

There is secret in H_2O. It is composed of two gases. Fire is gaseous so everything returns to its gaseous state.

Iblīs is created from fire. When he was ordered to prostrate before Ādam, immediately he came with his inane answer, demonstrating his bad characteristics by saying, "I am made from fire."

Fire Comes from Dumps

You don't go on the highway and see rubbish dumps where they are dumping the garbage? What happens then? Gas is generated and comes out and then the gas is burned off. So these rubbish dumps are being converted to fire. Iblīs' character is created from the dumps of the bad characteristics of the evil life of human beings. His character is a blend made from the bad characteristics of all human beings. That is his fire from which he

---

[121] Al-anbiya, 21:30.
[122] Abide, abode.

was created. Angels are not created from fire; rather they were created from light. The only one mentioned in the Quran as being created from fire is Iblīs. So that reality is that he is a rubbish dump being converted to a fiery gas that burns everything before it.

These garbage dumps are covered with pipes, above and below, and you see a stack sticking out from which a flame is blazing. That is the gas that is being burned.

So all these bad characters of Iblīs are being processed and produced under that dump emerging and becoming oil. That oil which comes forth is the urine of Iblīs. Because of oil, all kinds of problems have emerged on earth. If you look, you find most of the oil comes from those countries whose rulers and people are characterized by tyranny. This is one of the secrets that Mawlana is showing us through this explanation.

So that is what Shāh Naqshband showed Grandshaykh, revealing how Iblīs was created from fire and how he must carry all the bad character of all human beings. Everyone's bad character has to be dumped on him.

قَالَ أَنَاْ خَيْرٌ مِّنْهُ خَلَقْتَنِي مِن نَّارٍ وَخَلَقْتَهُ مِن طِينٍ

Qāla mā manaʿaka allā tasjuda idh amartuka qāla anā khayrun minhu khalaqtanī min nārin wa khalaqtahu min ṭīn

He said, "I am better than him; he created me from fire and created him from clay."

Fire of Intimacy

الَّذِي جَعَلَ لَكُم مِّنَ الشَّجَرِ الْأَخْضَرِ نَارًا فَإِذَا أَنتُم مِّنْهُ تُوقِدُونَ

Alladhī jaʿala lakum min ash-shajari 'l-akhḍari nāran fa idhā antum minhu tūqidūn

The same Who produces for you fire out of the green tree, when behold! ye kindle therewith (your own fires)![123]

He said from a green tree fire, and he described from the green tree, the live tree. I make from the life of eternity, fire that you can take warmth with it. That means the eternal life of knowledge. The green tree like pine tree. That is evergreen, when you submit to Allāh's knowledge always standing never dying. These guides are the green tree. They guide you to Allāh's love, which is the fire of infatuation. What *Sayyīdinā* Mūsā ﷺ saw was the fire of adoration.

إِذْ قَالَ مُوسَى لِأَهْلِهِ إِنِّي آنَسْتُ نَارًا سَآتِيكُم مِّنْهَا بِخَبَرٍ أَوْ آتِيكُم بِشِهَابٍ قَبَسٍ لَّعَلَّكُمْ تَصْطَلُونَ.

Idh qāla mūsā li-āhlihi innī ānastu nāran sa-ātīkum minhā bi-khabarin aw atīkum bi-shihābin qabasin laʿallakum tasṭalūn

Behold! Moses said to his family: "I perceive a fire; soon will I bring you from there some information, or I will bring you a burning brand to light our fuel, that ye may warn yourselves. [124]

He said, "I felt the flame of the fire of intimacy." What he felt was not a conventional fire but rather it is the fire of deep love, intimacy, *lahab*. He told his family, "Let me go and get something out of it or a piece of it that you may warm yourselves."

So that fire here comes from a green tree. That is not the fire blazing from the dump and it does not come from oil. Rather, Allāh says *The One Who produces for you fire out of the green tree.* This is a reference to living trees, for the Fire of Moses enveloped a living, green bush, without burning it It is not a fire from dumps, or dead trees. Oil underground is dead. But the fire here, comes from the green tree. Green represents guidance and

[123] Sūrah YāSīn, 36:80.
[124] Sūratu 'n-Naml, 27:7.

freshness.Moses was saying, "I bring you the real warmth and the real fire." To attain to real guidance can only come from humility. They teach you real humbleness, not arrogance. They want you to throw your evil characteristics on Iblīs.

He declared, "I am better than Ādam because I am fire. I am flame!" But what kind of fire is he? He is from the worst sort of fire. Thus we see all these countries that are governed by tyrants, mainly around the equator, are the headquarters of the devils, *abālisa*. That all comes from that area of the world, as do the majority of hurricanes and tornados. Look near the equator and you discover that is where the majority of oil is present, the urine of Iblīs and his group. And the people are now happy, saying "O that is nice. Now we produce everything from it. We makes clothes out of it, polyester. Everyone is "drinking" in the urine of Iblīs. That is where all evil characteristics are coming forth from these areas of oil. That is why no one is happy. Without our being aware, these bad characteristics are overtaking our bodies. This energy is all generated by burning fuel. All these huge TV stations are run by electricity and that comes from burning fuel. Some are even generated by atomic reaction, which is also contains a form of fuel. It was not like that in the past. Then they used to burn green wood or they would mine coal from the ground.

May Allāh guide us to learn humbleness. That is how they guide you in seclusion through such meditations, to understand the reality of all things. We can expand on it without end. This will reveal to us an understanding that we are helpless and we cannot do anything. Today the whole world is drunk with oil. Everything runs on it. Anywhere you want to go you must use oil. Angels consider oil the worst element, but humans find it the best because it is coming from Iblīs. And Allāh ﷻ knows best the wisdom behind what is happening.

To escape satanic whispers, and satanic drunkenness, one must humiliate oneself—and that is very difficult. For example someone says with which you strongly disagree. You immediately jump in his face with an answer. This comes from ego. If you were to think a little bit, you might remain silent.

The Heart's Boiling Pots

There are two pots in the heart. One pot is good, one pot is evil. The one that is good is peaceful and tranquil (*muṭma'innah*). It is always stable. The other one is bubbling with force, *ammāra*. It is forceful. When you hear something that you do not like, the forceful self jumps quickly to respond; it does not let the peaceful self to take it in, digest it, and then give an answer. So based on this understanding, do not answer quickly. It is a sign of our bad character when we jump quickly and fight back, when we answer from that boiling satanic pot. The other pot is simmering on a low flame. Meat that is cooked like that becomes tender. If you cook it rapidly over a hot fire, it becomes tough like plastic. One pot yields answers that are hard to chew and swallow; the other is accommodating and easy. In the beginning of his test Iblīs tried to be accommodating, but in the end, he blew his lid and said, "I am better than him!"

Humility Defeats Shaytan

All these powers by which Iblīs is trying to catch human beings will drop when you express humility. This means when you express the real taste of true humility, not simply expressing it by tongue. Claiming humility by mouth is easy, but true humbleness is not by word of mouth, rather it is by action. That does not come until the heart is boiling from the love of Allāh, *'ishq,* infatuation with Divine Love that makes the lid of the heart to shake, like the lid of a teapot on the fire, in order to bring that humbleness out, because as much as you are in the state of infatuation to the Divine Presence as much as you feel you are nothing. You are nothing. There is no presence and no existence to you; existence is for Allāh alone and of the entire creation that Allāh created, the only one that exists in that creation, the one who is responsible for all creation is *Muḥammadun Rasūlullāh.* So who are you to compare yourself to anyone else? Rather you must always see yourself lower than everyone.

That is how you train yourself—to know you are inferior to everyone else. It might be that Allāh makes you superior, but you have to show your ego, "You are nothing! You don't deserve that honor."This is what Allāh opened to Bayāzīd al-Bistāmī when he was seeking and begging Allāh, "Open for me Your door!" He heard a heavenly voice saying, "What did you do for Me?" He called out, "I am praying and fasting and worshipping for You, following the Sunnah of the Prophet ﷺ."

He did not say, "I know." People today say, "I know," in response to anything they aretold. If that arrogance emerges in daily life, what would happen if you say that in presence of Allāh? So in seclusions they teach you not to do that.

Be a Dump

Awlīyāullāh carry the burdens of people. They take these bad characters which is described as what is dumped from people. Every one of us is carrying these characters without realizing it. We are unaware that we are accepting and allowing our body to carry these bad characters. Thus our body becomes a dump to carry these bad characters and we don't let these ugly aspects go. Instead we are holding on to them.

Awlīyāullāh understand this dumping process in a different way. For them it means to take on from people their bad characteristics and and dissolve them. Normal people keep them. They take on these bad traits and then and keep them and hold them, like possessions. They see such traits as the decorations of this worldly life, *dunyā;* what we perceive as a beautiful way of life.

There were *awlīyā* who are completely ascetic, such as Bahlul. His food was only milk and bread. He said, "If Allāh asks me on Judgment Day what I did, I will reply,"I was keeping a goat, eating barley bread and drinking milk."

For the majority of people their whole occupation are the desires of the mouth and the desire of the lower half. The desire of the mouth is to be always hungry. There are even people who eat and vomit then eat and vomit again. They are bulimic. For them eating is their pleasure.

Then there is the normal sexual pleasure.

قال رسول الله : من يضمن لي ما بين لحييه وما بين رجليه أضمن له الجنة.

> That is why the Prophet ﷺ said, "who can guarantee what I between his jaws and between his legs I guarantee him Paradise."

So when all these characteristics of Iblīs are being dumped on us, we are happy. That is our problem. But *awlīyā* will put you in seclusion in order to make these harmful traits to disintegrate.

Keep Your Love to Your Shaykh Alone

Grandshaykh, may Allāh bless him, was usually in seclusion. He used to do seclusion in the upper floor, of his house, and his wife, who would serve him during the seclusion, stayed downstairs. She used to serve him tea and food. When time for a meal comes she cannot bring it until he knocks on the floor to inform her, "now is the time, you may bring it."

In one such secluion many months passed. One day she did not hearing Grandshaykh's stick tapping on the floor for her to bring up his meal. And she did not hear it for all that day. She kept quiet. Since it is seclusion she must not open the door or to go in and check. So a second day passed, without the signal. A third day passed and she became concerned. She went to Shaykh Sharafuddin, saying, "O Shaykh Sharafuddin! For many days

Shaykh Abdullah is not tapping for me to bring food or water or tea." He said, "Leave him and don't worry. He will call you back."

Grandshaykh related to us this story. This story contains very important lessons for us. He said this went on for seven days. In these seven days he went through a vast experience in his seclusion. Shaykh Sharafuddin often used to speak about Shāh Naqshband and about his *manāqib*, the stories from his life and its many events and his specialties as the founding saint of the Naqshbandī order.

During the course of hearing these stories, some of Shaykh Abdullah's love shifted towards Shāh Naqshband, because of the attraction to the high stations that Shaykh Sharafuddin was describing. Because of this shift, the love for his shaykh decreased slightly. That is a state like a scale. In a barometer, for example, the pressure has to increase until it hits the roof. Similarly roller coasters go up and up and up, even as high as 100 feet and then they come down with tremendous speed. Now if you don't reach up to the top level you cannot come down with full power. So Grandshaykh's love began to shift.

So in order to learn the importance of his Shaykh, Shāh Naqshband appeared in his spiritual form. *Awlīyāullāh* can move freely, even beyond time. Past, present and future are the same for them. Shāh Naqshband came to Mawlana Shaykh ʿAbdAllāh al-Fā'iz ad-Dāghestānī in the place he was doing and from the window said, "*Yā* ʿAbdAllāh come with me."

One time Grandshaykh showed me *Sayyīdinā* Shāh Naqshband, how he looked.

Sayyīdinā Shāh Naqshband ق has a huge beard which reaches all the way to ground for it has never been cut. From the back you can see his beard coming very wide from the back, like two handspans in width. I saw him one time with this huge beard just as Grandshaykh ق described.

So *Sayyīdinā* Shāh Naqshband ق took Grandshaykh on a journey which took seven days and seven nights. That is why he was not calling his wife for food and tea. He was not there, gone. It meansThe spirit was gone from the body and the body remains there. *Awlīyāullāh* have that power.

Today many people in west say they have out-of-body encounters. What they experience is only imitational, but it indicates there is something real behind it. Theirs is the plastic fruit but it indicates the real fruit exists. This is one way in which Allāh gives signs.

So Shāh Naqshband took Grandshaykh on a journey spanning seven days and seven nights But there travel was not according to ordinary means—wherever horizon his glance would reach they would reach there in the blink of an eye. They reached a place after seven days and nights of travelling with that incredible speed. What that means is they were traveling at the speed of light, which is 300,000 km per second. Count in seven days: 24 hours multiplied by 60 minutes, multiplied by 60 seconds, now multiply by 300,000, multiplied by seven: that is 180 billion miles. Where is that in the universe? The moon is 300,000 km. So where did he take him? The sun is 100 million miles from earth. So where did they go?

They finally arrived at their destination and Shāh Naqshband said, "Look on the horizon, as far as you can see." Grandshaykh was looking and seeing some kind of form in the distance, but because it was far away, he could not distinguish what it was clearly. Shāh Naqshband said, "O my son! Do you know who that is?" Shaykh ʿAbdAllāh replied, "You know better."

That reply was the correct *adab*, good manners, in front of the shaykh. In front of the shaykh don't say "I know." Say, "You know better." In everyday issues, yes, you may say, "I know," because in worldly terms, the shaykh doesn't reveal that he knows how to do plumbing, electricity or carpentry. In such cases, when he asks you something, give the appropriate answer. But when it comes to issues of spirituality say, "you know better."

Shāh Naqshband said, "Now you can see. Do you know who that is?" Shaykh ʿAbdAllāh replied, "You know better." He did not jump to give the "correct" answer. Today we jump to give an answer, but that is only a display of egoism.

Shāh Naqshband said, "That is Shaykh Sharafuddin, your shaykh." Of course Shaykh ʿAbdAllāh knows that distant form is his shaykh but keeping discipline, he showed ignorance. Shāh Naqshband asked, "And what is that big animal with him?" Shaykh ʿAbdAllāh replied, "You know better." He said, "This is Iblīs. Allāh gave your shaykh the authority to hold Iblīs with a bridle, and all the evil deeds of servants done in every 24 hours he is dumping on Iblīs."

That is one of the specialties that Allāh is giving to one *walī*. That is one of the hundreds of thousands of characteristics that each *walī* carries. He continued, "That level, no *walī* reached it. He is able to dump all the sins of human beings on Iblīs and bringing the followers to the Prophet ﷺ clean every single day."

FOURTEEN

Three Levels of Spiritual Attainment

You have to know the best of deeds, *ʿamāl,* is to leave the hidden sins—those things that are forbidden, but which are known only to the self. If you leave these hidden sins, then you will already have turned your back on those that are open and overt.

انَ افضل العمال المعاضي الباطن لانَ الباطن اذا تركت كان

صاحبها لالمعصي اترك

Inna afḍal al-ʿamāl tark al-maʿsīy al-bāṭina li anna al-bāṭina idhā turikat kāna ṣāḥibuhā li ʾl-maʿsīy atrak.

Truly the best of deeds is to give up hidden sins because when the inner sins have been discarded, it means their owner has discarded the outer sins.

In seclusion, you come to realize there are many hidden sins that you are committing. They attack you like wild beasts, because they are afraid you will leave them behind. The self can accept leaving overt sins, because they put you in a shameful position before others. Hidden sins are another matter; the self cannot release them. That is why they attack you in seclusion, when you are trying to cast them out of yourself.

These hidden sins are the source of the frightening visions, strange dreams and scary voices that haunt you in seclusion. We speak here, again, of the real seclusion—the one that is ordered by the shaykh. You might perform a hundred seclusions and not see anything, but that is because those are seclusions done to make the self happy.

Anytime you are doing *dhikrullāh* and you feel happy, you must immediately stop and do something else. That is because you must not become self-satisfied. When the self becomes satisfied, the ego becomes happy. If that happens during *dhikr*, you must stop and change to some other form of worship. The ego will find that unacceptable, and that is what you want the ego to feel—you are fighting against it. That is why Mawlana said, "when you feel pleasure in doing *dhikrullāh*, stop and do something else." For example read the Qur'an. Do not let yourself feel pleasure, even in *awrād*, or in any form of worship. Thus you will always be fighting and struggling against the ego.

There are three levels in fighting the ego.

First Level

فمن كانت سريرته خير من علانيته فذلك الفضل من الله

> *Faman kānat sarīratahu khayrun min ʿalānīyyatihi fa dhālika al-faḍlu min allāh.*
>
> When the inner self, becomes clean and perfect—more polished even than the visible, outer self—that is a grant and a favor from Allāh ﷻ.

You lift up your inner self—which is invisible to everyone accept you—by putting down your ego, by stepping on it, by coming against it and by saying "no" to its desires. That is a struggle between you and yourself. No one can see that. Yet, the more you perfect your inner character, the better your outer character will become. That is because polishing your heart is more important than how you live your exterior life, for Allāh ﷻ likes you to be clean on the inside.

Today, we see people spending more time worrying about how their external appearance. We see people wearing a big turban and *jubbah*, growing a long beard and carrying a walking stick. People say, "That is a big shaykh. Let us go to him and take *baraka*." They do not know what is hidden inside that shaykh. It is better to drop that outer form and dress your heart instead with a turban, *jubbah* and stick.

Consider a clock. It may have an elegant face, an ornamented dial and decorated hands. However, if its battery is dead, what good is it? Its external appearance is impressive, but it does not tell you the correct time. Today, people are dressing very well, but they are not charging their batteries. The Prophet ﷺ said that Allāh ﷻ does not look to your form (*ṣūwarikum*), but to your heart.

How do you charge your battery? Think about a cellular telephone. It comes with a charger and connector—a stick—that plugs into the phone. To give a heavenly staff to the heart is to connect it with the heavenly charger, to connect it with the Divine Presence. That "stick" is the Staff of Divine Oneness (*tawḥīd*).

Either you point with your finger which is like a staff, or you point with a cane or today they point with something like a small antenna, which stretches and becomes a long pointer. Professors carry them. The point opens and extends. There is a pointer in the heart, when you open it grows wider. The heart has something even better than that. Today they have pointers that open and shoot out a laser beam. That is what you need: alaser pointer. That will be the staff of the heart.

Similarly, you wrap the heart with a "heart" turban, adorn it with a"heart" *jubbah* and decorate it with a "heart" beard? Adorning the heart with all these forms of Sunnah spiritual dress is from Allāh's ﷻ grants to you.

Second Level

فذلك عدل من تساوي سريرته علي علانيته

man tasawā sarīratahu ʿalā sarīratahu fa dhālik ʿadlun

Whoever makes his inside and his outside the same that is justice.

The first level was to guide you to sainthood. Then next level is is to balance what is outside and inside and that is justice. You are giving for *dunyā* and for *ākhirah*. As Sayyīdinā ʿAlī said:

اعمل لدنياك كانك تغيش ابدا وعمل لاخرتك كانك تموت غدا

āʿamal li-dunyāka ka-annaka taʿayshu abadan wa āʿamal li ākhiratik ka-annaka tamūt ghadan.

"Work for your *dunyā*, worldly life, as if you are living forever and do for your afterlife, *ākhirah*, as if you are dying tomorrow."

If you seek this life, you will achieve the level of a student but you will not become a professor. Even after receiving your PhD you need another ten years to become a professor, doing research and publishing papers and books. With a PhD you can become a teacher but you need ten years residency to become tenured professor.

So if you cannot achieve the balance suggested in this saying of Sayyīdinā ʿAlī, it means you desire only the basic Paradise level. You are not seeking the highest station:

فِي مَقْعَدِ صِدْقٍ عِندَ مَلِيكٍ مُّقْتَدِرٍ

fī maqaʿdi ṣidq ʿinda malīkin muqtadir.

In an Assembly of Truth, in the Presence of a Sovereign Omnipotent.[125]

Living in such a manner is as if saying, "I don't want to be with those four groups: the prophet s, the veracious ones, the martyrs and the righteous," of whom that assembly consists. I want to be in the level of normal people."

In that case you are at the third level, which is what most people, if we don't say all, achieve. It in only a rare few who are able to surpass that.

125 Sūratu 'l-Qamar, 54:55.

Third Level

فمن كانت علانيته افضل من سريرته فذلك ظلم و جور

Faman kānat ʿalānīyyatihi afḍalu min sarīratahi fa dhālika ẓulmun wa jawr.

When the outer self becomes better than the inner self—that is a oppression and injustice.

When someone's external character is better than his internal character—the one who looks after his body, his daily life, his pleasure more than he looks after his inner self and those things which are required to raise it and purify it—that is oppression and injustice (*ẓulman wa jūra*).

Today, people are concerned about oppression, that one group of people is oppressing another group. However, they do not see how much they are oppressing themselves on the inside by not improving their inner character in the Way of Allāh ﷻ. They are following the Jālūt of the *nafs*, the enemy of Ṭālūt. Ṭālūt represents the inner and Jālūt the outer.

أَلَمْ تَرَ إِلَى الْمَلإِ مِن بَنِي إِسْرَائِيلَ مِن بَعْدِ مُوسَى إِذْ قَالُواْ لِنَبِيٍّ لَّهُمُ ابْعَثْ لَنَا مَلِكًا نُّقَاتِلْ فِي سَبِيلِ اللّهِ قَالَ هَلْ عَسَيْتُمْ إِن كُتِبَ عَلَيْكُمُ الْقِتَالُ أَلاَّ تُقَاتِلُواْ قَالُواْ وَمَا لَنَا أَلاَّ نُقَاتِلَ فِي سَبِيلِ اللّهِ وَقَدْ أُخْرِجْنَا مِن دِيَارِنَا وَأَبْنَآئِنَا فَلَمَّا كُتِبَ عَلَيْهِمُ الْقِتَالُ تَوَلَّوْاْ إِلاَّ قَلِيلاً مِّنْهُمْ وَاللّهُ عَلِيمٌ بِالظَّالِمِينَ

Alam tara ila al-malāi min banī isrāīla min baʿdi mūsā idh qālū li-nabīyyin lahum 'ubʿath lanā malikan nuqātil fī sabīlillāhi qāla hal ʿasaytum in kutiba ʿalaykumu 'lqitālu allā tuqātilū qālū wa mā lanā allā nuqātila fī sabīlillāhi wa qad ukhrijnā min dīyārinā wa abnā'inā fa-lamma kutiba ʿalayhimu 'l-qitālu tawallaw illa qalīlan minhum w'Allāhu ʿalīmun bi 'ẓ-ẓālimīn

Have you not turned your vision to the Chiefs of the Children of Israel after (the time of) Moses? They said to a Prophet ﷺ

(that was) among them: "Appoint for us a king, that we may fight in the cause of Allāh ." He said: "Is it not possible, if you were commanded to fight, that that you will not fight?" They said: "How could we refuse to fight in the cause of Allāh, seeing that we were turned out of our homes and our families?" but when they were commanded to fight, they turned back, except a small band among them. But Allāh Has full knowledge of those who do wrong.[126]

The Children of Israel asked their Prophet ﷺ to request Allāh ﷻ to send them a leader to guide them so that they might fight in the Way of Allāh ﷻ. He sent Ṭālūt.

As we have said, we must always ask Allāh ﷻ to send us a king. That means asking Allāh ﷻ to guide us. But what kind of king? A king that can lead us in our fight against the enemy: "*Yā Rabbī,* send us guidance and the power to fight our ego and the devils that are overtaking us, the tyrants of our selves!"

[126] Sūratu 'l-Baqara [The Heifer],2:246.

FIFTEEN

Exercise and Its Results

When we sit for any spiritual undertaking we recite the following intention:

نويت الأربعين نويت الاعتِكاف نويت الخلوة نويت العزَلة

نويت الرِياضَة نويت السلوك، لله تعالى في هذَا المسجد

Nawaytu 'l-arbā'īn, nawaytu 'l-'itikāf, nawaytu 'l-khalwa, nawaytu 'l-'uzla, nawaytu 'r-riyāḍa, nawaytu 's-sulūk, lillāhi ta'ala fī hādhā 'l-masjid.

I intend the forty (days of seclusion); I intend seclusion in the mosque; I intend seclusion; I intend isolation; I intend discipline (of the ego); I intend to travel in God's Path for the sake of God in this mosque.

This is our intention (*nīyyah*). Mawlana Shaykh taught us to make this intention in every association, because every association is a seclusion. We are secluding ourselves from the outside world. In this way, you get the same benefits of seclusion when you sit with the shaykh for an association.

This intention is composed of six different levels:

- The intention of forty days
- The intention of secluding oneself in the sanctity of the mosque
- The intention of the seclusion itself
- The intention of isolating oneself from the rest of the world
- The intention of training the ego
- The intention of traveling on Allāh's Path for His sake

There are also six spiritual poles (*qutb*) responsible for maintaining balance in this creation:

- ❖ The pole responsible for keeping the Earth balanced on its axis
- ❖ The pole of nations, without whom countries would collapse
- ❖ The pole of guidance
- ❖ The pole of universal governance and administration
- ❖ The pole of poles
- ❖ The *Ghawth*, who is over them all, monitoring them all and taking directly from the Prophet ﷺ

The discipline or training (*riyāḍah*) refered to in the intention means exercise, but not physical exercise such as jogging, running, dancing or martial arts. These are exercises for the body, not for the soul. Many of these martial arts from the East claim to be for the soul, and they may give the practitioner the ability to perform amazing physical feats. But they have their limits. Exercise for the soul guides you through different kinds of *dhikrullāh,* teaching you different Holy Divine Names and recitations that put your soul through an intensive course of spiritual training.

Thus, *riyāḍah* in the terminology of Sufism is *riyāḍatu 'n-nafs,* training and exercising the self to the point that you can ride it, instead of it riding you.

That is the point of all of our training and associations: to tame our egos so that we may ride them like horses. These are spiritual martial arts. They involve training the heart, not the body. By mastering these, you can accomplish much more than is possible through physical martial arts. Some saints can move mountains by merely pointing with their fingers. Moving a mountain is easy compared to moving the heart. To move the heart of one *murīd* toward its reality is harder than moving a mountain from one place to another.

Consider the Earth, spinning on its axis. In physics, the earth rotates around a hypothetical axle. That axle is one finger of a *walī* who is responsible for this planet, the first *quṭb*. His finger is the axis around which this world turns. Moving the heart of a person is more difficult than that. The heart of the believer is always rotating. Speaking metaphorically, we can say that Allāh ﷻ is spinning it between His Two Fingers.

When you make the intention of training (*nawaytu ar-riyāḍah*), you are intending to be one of the disciplined ones (*ar-riyāḍiyūn*), those who can carry everything and can survive without anything. They have the power to stay forty days without food and water. Even if they stay one year without food and water it does not matter, because they do not need it. Allāh ﷻ gave them exceptionally strong spiritual powers. That is the power of spiritual martial arts. It can only be achieved through seclusion.

Mastering these spiritual martial arts means mastering the conduct and control of the soul. That is why it precedes the next level of intention, the intention to travel Allāh's Path (*nawaytu 's-sulūk*), for you cannot make that journey until you control your soul. This is the sixth level of intention, and its parallel among the Poles is the *Ghawth*.

When these six levels come together, they bring you to the presence the Prophet ﷺ (*al-ḥaḍarat an-nabawīyyah*). It is an easy thing to say, but it is a difficult thing to do. To go through all these steps is not simple. This is not to discourage you, but you must recognize that we are moving like ants, not like rockets. Even that is enough though, for as long as you do not stop, when Allāh's Care (*rīḥ aṣ-ṣibā ināyatullāh*) reaches you, it will carry you like a rocket to the Divine Presence.

Some people have been moving in this way for ten or fifteen years without seeing anything. That is okay; but you must keep progressing. You still have to eat in this *dunyā*. You have not yet reached the level of *ar-riyāḍīyūn*. You still need food and whatever you are in need of is your master. If you need food, then at that moment food becomes your master. *Ar-riyāḍīyūn* know that.

Allāh said:

كَانَا يَأْكُلاَنِ الطَّعَامَ

kāna yākūlūn aṭ-ṭʿam.

(Christ the son of Mary and his mother)both used to eat their (daily) food.[127]

Thus, they train themselves and are not slaves to anyone except their Lord.

Success in this spiritual exercise is predicated on humbleness. It is humbleness that enables *ar-riyāḍīyūn* to reach this level. Humbleness allows you to do what is very difficult for others to do. You must also stay away from people, both when you meet them and when you leave them (*al-ʿirād ʿan-il khalqi fil-iqbāl wa 'l-idbār*). You cannot depend on anyone in anything, in your going and facing others or in your turning away and giving them your back. That means complete disconnection. You cannot connect to anything in this *dunyā* because you cannot associate anything with Allāh ﷻ.

Of course, you still need a guide because you cannot do any of this without one. The guide is the teacher who leads you to an understanding of Allāh's Oneness by taking you to the City of Knowledge. There, you begin to observe that reality that the Prophet ﷺ observed when he went on Isrā and Miʿrāj. You begin to see with the Eye of Truth (*ʿaynu 'l-yaqīn*). It is the power of the six levels of intention that allow you to see what they put into your heart.

The highest level of the intention is walking the Path of Allāh ﷻ. That path is like a railway, and Mawlana Shaykh is the engine of the train that plies it. He will take you on that journey, but it is not without obstacles. Know that you are going to face

---

[127] Sūratu 'l-Mā'idah [The Spread Table], 5:75.

many challenges on this Way. He wants you to taste bitterness. When you do, he is watching you to see if your heart remains true.

The shaykhs have been trained to turn their faces away from you. When they do that, you will feel like you do not want to live on this earth anymore. They cast you down, and then they look to see if you are taking it or running away. If you think you have tasted bitterness already, what do you think you will taste if the shaykh says, "I am taking my *baya*ʿ from you. I am throwing you away!" That is real bitterness. They crush you into pieces and make you dust under their feet. Then they scatter you.

Through it all, you must keep your heart connected to the shaykh, and from the shaykh to the Prophet ﷺ and from the Prophet ﷺ to Allāh ﷻ. You must remain constantly pleased with whatever Allāh ﷻ gives you, whether it is a little or a lot.

Do not come to the shaykh complaining that you have lost half your pension, that your wife or husband cheated on you, that they took everything you own. If it was written for you, no one could take it away. But it was not written for you. Allāh ﷻ is the best of planners. He wrote what He wrote for you. It is not your concern. You still have to say, "Thank You, Allāh ! You are still giving me breath." Money goes and comes, but you cannot live without breath. Perhaps Allāh ﷻ took that money from you to cleanse you so that you can enter Paradise.

All of this is easy to speak about, but it is hard to do. It is easy to count the lashes, but it is hard to take the whip. Yet, we must be happy with whatever Allāh ﷻ gives us, whether it is a little or a lot, and we must turn to Allāh ﷻ in both hardship and ease. If it is hard, it is because He wants it to be hard; if it is easy, it is because He wants it to be easy. To do that requires training. This training is what is important in Sufism, not speeches or lectures. What does it benefit you if listen for half an hour but do nothing?

You have to learn where to place your feet so that your steps are always on solid ground. Look at these tightrope walkers in the circus. Not everyone can do what they do. If any movement is unbalanced, they will fall. If they loose that balance for even a moment, they will fall. That sort of balance requires training, and that is just to walk on a rope over a net. What do you think about the Straight Path (*ṣirāṭ al-mustaqīm*), the bridge over hellfire on Judgment Day? It is said that, for believers, it will be wider than this world. For unbelievers, it will be as thin as a hair—and there is no net underneath it.

We need spiritual training to balance our actions (*ʿamal*). The physical training taught by the martial arts might give you an idea about spirituality, but that is not sufficient. Real spiritual training requires you to take the hand of perfect shaykh and let him lead you through all kinds of forms of remembrance (*adhkār*), reciting the Holy Qur'an and remembering Allāh's Beautiful Names and Attributes. You must know that the best of deeds is leaving disobedience, that the best of actions is leaving hidden or unseen sins (*al-maʿasīy al-bāṭinah*).

Physical training is just an imitation of this spiritual exercise. When you free your spirit from its imprisonment in the body and build it up through seclusions and *awrād*, then you are able to defeat Jālūt. Then you are able with one stone to kill the devil within yourself. You can kill it with one shot, but you have to know where to shoot.

Today, they have games for children that require them to shoot at a target. If they hit it, they win a prize. A child will spend money and keep spending it in order to keep shooting until they hit that target and win a prize, even if it is just a small piece of candy. Even a small candy from your Lord is enough to open the Seven Heavens for you. The experiences He sends you in seclusion are enough to keep you happy for the rest of your life. So, keep shooting until you hit. Even if your prize is just a small piece of candy, it will be enough.

SIXTEEN

Adam and the Tree of Life

وَعَلَّمَ آدَمَ الأَسْمَاء كُلَّهَا ثُمَّ عَرَضَهُمْ عَلَى الْمَلاَئِكَةِ فَقَالَ أَنبِئُونِي بِأَسْمَاء
هَـؤُلاء إِن كُنتُمْ صَادِقِينَ قَالُواْ سُبْحَانَكَ لاَ عِلْمَ لَنَا إِلاَّ مَا عَلَّمْتَنَا إِنَّكَ
أَنتَ الْعَلِيمُ الْحَكِيمُ

Wa ʿallama ādama al-asmā kullāha thumma ʿaraḍahum ʿala al-malā'ikati faqāla anbiūnī bi-asmā'i hāulā'i in kuntum ṣādiqīna. Qālū subḥānaka lā ʿilma lanā illa mā ʿallamtanā innaka anta al-alīmu 'l-ḥakīm.

And He taught Adam all the names, then showed them to the angels, saying: Inform me of the names of these, if ye are truthful.They said: Be glorified! We have no knowledge saving that which You hast taught us. Lo! You, only You, art the Knower, the Wise.[128]

It says that He taught Adam all the names. Which names? The names of all creation.

Every creation has a name. Look at the Periodic Table. Every element has a name, which means that every atom has a name. The Sun also has a name, and so does every atom that comprises it. If one of those atoms goes, part of the Sun disappears. So, too, the Moon and the Earth. That is because every atom has a name, and with that name, it is functioning. Moreover, all of those atoms complete each other. And Allāh gave the knowledge of all their names to Adam.

Then Allāh called the angels and asked them to tell Him the names of these things. They said, "We have no knowledge except what You have taught us."

---

[128] Sūratu 'l-Baqara [The Heifer],2:31-32.

Who is higher, Adam ﷺ or *Sayyīdinā* Muḥammad ﷺ? It means that Allāh ﷻ gave Adam ﷺ the ability to receive this knowledge from the reality of the Prophetic Heart—Prophet Muḥammad's heart. From that wellspring, he was receiving the knowledge of these names. Adam ﷺ could not receive this knowledge directly. This is an important point, for it was by this knowledge that He taught him. That demonstrates that you cannot get anything without knowledge. That is why the *awlīyā* are always asking for that knowledge.

There is no end to this knowledge. It is *al-akbar*, which means that there is no end to its greatness:

لَخَلْقُ السَّمَاوَاتِ وَالْأَرْضِ أَكْبَرُ مِنْ خَلْقِ النَّاسِ وَلَكِنَّ أَكْثَرَ النَّاسِ لَا يَعْلَمُونَ

La-khalq as-samāwāti wa'l-arḍ akbar min khalqin-nāsi wa lākinna akthar an-nās lā yʿalamūn.

Assuredly the creation of the heavens and the earth is a greater (matter) than the creation of men: Yet most men understand not. [129]

The mind cannot comprehend this greatness, yet Allāh ﷻ taught *Sayyīdinā* Adam ﷺ all the greatness of creation through the heart of *Sayyīdinā* Muḥammad ﷺ. And Allāh ﷻ said to him, "If Muḥammad comes in your time, follow him. Do not think that you are the boss. Do not think that you are on top. My Musṭafā, My Chosen One, he is the one who I chose to be the center of this circle, and all of creation is on its circumference."

What is between the center of that circle and its circumference? It is void. Thus, everything exists within a void, and the void does not exist. What exists then? Muḥammad ﷺ. He is the center: *lā ilāha illa-Llāh Muḥammadun Rasūlullāh. Faḍā* is a void, he is not inside the circle and not on its circumference.

---

[129] Sūrah Ghāfir [The Forgiver of Sin], 40:57.

Allāh ﷻ taught Adam ﷺ about the Light of Muḥammad ﷺ, so he knew that reality. Yet, with that wisdom, he committed the sin. For that wisdom, Allāh ﷻ sent mankind to *dunyā*.

Allāh ﷻ does not sit and plan it; when He says, "Be" (*kun*), it is. When His Will (*irāda*), His Attribute of "The Knower" (*al-ʿAlam*) drafts the blueprint and the Attribute of His Name "The Creator" (*al-Khāliq*) executes that design and the Ocean of the Attribute of "The Capable" (*al-Qādir*) makes it appear. That is how His Will is manifested, only through His Attributes. He is able to do everything.

So that Allāh ﷻ might accept his repentance (*tawbah*), Adam ﷺ asked for forgiveness for sake of the Prophet ﷺ Muḥammad ﷺ. That is an important piece of knowledge that Allāh ﷻ gave us to use. Everyone should know the *hadith*:

اللهم اني اسلك و اتوجه اليك بنبيك محمد نبي الرحمة. يا محمد اني

اتوجه بك الئ ربي في حاجتي هذه لتقضئ لي اللهم فشفعه في.

> *Allāhuma innī asaluka wa atawajahu ilayk bi-nabīyyika Muḥammad. Yā Muḥammad innī atawajjahu bika ila rabbī fī ḥājatī hādhihi li-tuqḍā lī allāhuma fashafiʿhu fīyya.*
>
> O Allāh! I am asking You and turning to You through Your Prophet ﷺ Muḥammad, the Prophet ﷺ of Mercy. O Muḥammad! [*Yā Muḥammad!*] I am turning to My Lord, taking you as a means for my request to be granted. O Allāh, grant me his intercession.

The Prophet ﷺ himself was using this means, as were his Companions. All of the *awlīyā* are using it, too. All of the Prophet ﷺs are coming to Prophet ﷺ Muḥammad ﷺ through his intercession for that *duāʿ*. But who is memorizing this today?

People memorize songs, but they do not memorize this hadith. The six verses of Surah Yāsīn, who is memorizing them?

The first ten verses of Surat al-Kahf and the ten from the end will save you from the Dajjāl, the Anti-Christ, and take you to Paradise. Who is learning them?

Whenever you need something, use the intercession of the Prophet ﷺ.

In the words of the Prophet ﷺ himself:

وَقَالَ لَهُمْ نِبِيُّهُمْ إِنَّ آيَةَ مُلْكِهِ أَن يَأْتِيَكُمُ التَّابُوتُ فِيهِ سَكِينَةٌ مِّن رَّبِّكُمْ وَبَقِيَّةٌ مِّمَّا تَرَكَ آلُ مُوسَى وَآلُ هَارُونَ تَحْمِلُهُ الْمَلآئِكَةُ إِنَّ فِي ذَلِكَ لآيَةً لَّكُمْ إِن كُنتُم مُّؤْمِنِينَ

Wa qāla lahum nabīyyuhum innā ayāta mulkihi an yatīyakumu 't-tabūtu fīhi sakīnatun min rabbikum wa baqīyyatun mimmā taraka ālu mūsā wa ālu hārūna taḥmiluhu 'l-malāikatu inna fī dhālika la-āyatan lakum in kuntum muminīn.

And (further) their Prophet ﷺ said to them: "A Sign of his authority is that there shall come to you the Ark of the covenant, with (an assurance) therein of security from your Lord, and the relics left by the family of Moses and the family of Aaron, carried by angels. In this is a symbol for you if ye indeed have faith."[130]

What is *mulk*? It means "kingdom"—the kingdom of Allāh ﷻ in the heart. The sign of His kingdom is to carry the ark that contains tranquility, to follow the *awlīyā* and to be guided to door of the Prophet ﷺ. Rebuilding the heart is how the new kingdom is constructed. The Shaykh who inherits from the Prophet (*Shaykh al-wārith*) has to to win and possess the ark of the heart (*yazfar bi 't-tābūt*). He has to take it out of the possession of Shaytan. Then the tranquility of the Lord will fill it. That is the peacefulness of *maqām al-iḥsān*.

---

[130] Sūratu 'l-Baqara [The Heifer],2:248.

Choose Your Goal

If your external life—that which is visible, that which you do with your physical body—is geared more to the pleasures of *dunyā* than for the benefit of your soul, then your hidden, inner self is not going to be doing anything for *ākhirah*. If your goal is *dunyā*, your *ākhirah* will be diminished. That is the source of oppression (*ʿayn aẓ-ẓulm*).

If you balance *dunyā* and *ākhirah*, that is justice. However, if you do more for the pleasures of your worldly life, commit all kinds of sins and forget Allāh ﷻ and what He has ordered you to do, that is injustice and self-oppression. You may still appear to be a good person in the eyes of people, but inside you are not. If you are immersed in the filthy ocean of *dunyā*, do you think Shaytan is going to let you escape from the ocean of filthy hidden sin?

Hidden sins come with the whisper of Shaytan:

فَوَسْوَسَ لَهُمَا الشَّيْطَانُ لِيُبْدِيَ لَهُمَا مَا وُورِيَ عَنْهُمَا مِن سَوْءَاتِهِمَا وَقَالَ مَا نَهَاكُمَا رَبُّكُمَا عَنْ هَـٰذِهِ الشَّجَرَةِ إِلاَّ أَن تَكُونَا مَلَكَيْنِ أَوْ تَكُونَا مِنَ الْخَالِدِينَ

Fawaswasa lahumā 'sh-shayṭānu li-yubdīya lahumā mā wūriyā ʿanhumā min sawātihimā wa qāla mā nahākumā rabbukumā ʿan hādhihi 'sh-shajarati illa an takūna malakayni aw takūna min al-khālidīn.

Then began Satan to whisper suggestions to them, bringing openly before their minds all their shame that was hidden from them (before): he said: "Your Lord only forbade you this tree, lest ye should become angels or such beings as live for ever."[131]

Paradise is only for clean people. If you are dirty, you cannot enter its gates. That is why Allāh ﷻ, out of His Mercy, will

---

[131] Sūratu 'l-ʿArāf [The Heights], 7:20.

cleanse people on the Day of Judgment. Those who did too much wrong, Allāh ﷻ will send them to Hell (*jahanam*) to clean them. After that, they are admitted to Paradise, though Allāh ﷻ will leave some there.

That is why you must leave hidden sins. You must not say, "No one is seeing me, so who cares?" You must not approach that which Allāh ﷻ has commanded us not to approach. Yet, Shaytan whispers to us, just as he whispered to Adam ﷺ. That was enough to sway him; he did not need to do more.

Shaytan said, "I will guide to eternal life, the Tree of Eternity. After you eat from it, you will never die and you will be given a kingdom that will never disintegrate."

Adam ﷺ and his wife were already in kingdom that will never disintegrate. They were in Paradise. Is it any different with human beings today? If Allāh ﷻ gives a man paradise in this world, still he wants to commit sins. Even though Allāh ﷻ is giving us plenty to eat and drink, still we want to abase ourselves in filth. That is oppression. The body can carry oppression, but the soul cannot. That is why people become depressed. They become depressed because they oppressed themselves.

Grandshaykh said that, in general, Allāh ﷻ gave human beings a life span of 137 years. In earlier times it might have been longer, but this is what he gave to the nation of the Prophet ﷺ (*ummat an-nabī*). So, why do people die younger? Because every sin you commit reduces the span of your life. That is why people die at 50, 60, 70 or 80. That is why they never reach 137 years of age.

Now, people's whose hearts are not accepting may ask why the Prophet ﷺ died at age 63. That is because the Prophet ﷺ shared his life with other people.

Jibrīl ﷺ came to him and said, "Do you want to stay or go? Allāh ﷻ is missing you (*mushtāqun lak*). Do you want to come now, or live out the rest of your life?"

The Prophet ﷺ said, "I will come."

Jibrīl ﷺ asked, "What will you do with the rest of your life?"

The Prophet ﷺ said, "I will share it with my *ummah*."

That is the life of the Perfect Man. What was left of it, he divided among the entire nation of believers. Some got one second, some got one hour, some got one day. All of those who received a portion of his holy life will appear on Judgment Day with those deeds of the Prophet ﷺ and they will be shining with the light of that worship. Grandshaykh said all of them would be sent to the Paradise of the *Muḥammadiyūn*. All of them there will be blessed with Prophetic features that they carry from *Sayyīdinā* Muḥammad ﷺ. That is why the *duāʿ* of the *awlīyā* is, "O Lord, let us share with the Prophet ﷺ in his servanthood (*ʿibādah*), his prayer, his fasting, his pilgrimage (*hajj*), his recitation of the Holy Qur'an. Let us share with the Prophet ﷺ in everything he did." They ask that in their *duāʿ*, and so they will be dressed with that for which they have asked.

Human Beings are Built on Mistakes

The nature of human beings is built on mistakes. If not, *Sayyīdinā* Adam ﷺ would never have succumbed to the whispering of Iblīs and would never have eaten the fruit of the tree that was forbidden. He was a Prophet ﷺ, so he repented and Allāh ﷻ forgave him. Yet, Allāh ﷻ created us perfect and revealed to us what is good and what is bad:

فَأَلْهَمَهَا فُجُورَهَا وَتَقْوَاهَا

Fa-alhamahā fujūrahā wa taqwāhā

And He inspired us to do the good and to avoid the bad.[132].

Allāh ﷻ inspired us with the knowledge of right and wrong, but we like to make mistakes. We run after what is bad.

---

[132] Sūratu 'sh-Shams [The Sun], 91:8.

We never run toward what is good. Thus, we are those who err (*khaṭā'ūn*).

To eliminate these mistakes and free yourself from these errors, you need to follow a guide. Without a guide, it is impossible to learn and understand. You can learn the theory, but you will not be able to put it into practice. A guide can give you the taste, the reality, by teaching you how to stop sinning and eliminate bad characteristics from the self. The wise ones do this by putting their followers through difficult training in order that they might taste the reality of the journey they are longing to make and show them the Way.

The Tree of Life

What is the tree that Adam ﷺ ate from? It is the Tree of Life (*shajarat al-khuld*). It is the everlasting tree that will never perish.

In the Holy Qur'an, trees are things that give life to mankind. In Surat Yāsīn, Allāh ﷻ said:

الَّذِي جَعَلَ لَكُم مِّنَ الشَّجَرِ الْأَخْضَرِ نَارًا فَإِذَا أَنتُم مِّنْهُ تُوقِدُونَ

alladhī jaʿala lakum mina 'sh-shajari 'l-akhdari nāran fa-idhā antum minhu tūqidūn.

Who hath appointed for you fire from the green tree, and behold! ye kindle from it.[133]

Allāh ﷻ put the Tree of Life off limits for Adam ﷺ and his wife. He told them, "Do not touch that tree. You are free to enjoy all of Paradise, except for this one tree." Yet, they left everything else that was in Paradise and went to that tree.

It is the same with us. The Prophet ﷺ said there are 800 forbidden things, both great and small (*al-kabā'ir wa 'ṣ-ṣaghā'ir*). He told us not to approach them. What do we do? We approach them. Everyone runs to these sins. That is oppression. We may speak of one people oppressing another, but the true oppression is

133 YāSīn, 36:80.

the oppression of the self by the self. That is what Allāh ﷻ does not like. That is what diminishes the life of people.

Sometimes, children die. When they do, they carry the sins of their parents and grant them entry into Paradise. Sometimes, they die in the womb of the mother in order to take these difficulties upon themselves. Allāh ﷻ planned everything in order to send His servants to Paradise. Allāh's Mercy is greater than His anger.

Be careful of oppression, of both others and of the self, for it will take you far from humbleness.

SEVENTEEN

Prophet Muhammad is Allah's Caliph

The Prophet ﷺ has been given the knowledge of every smallest detail because he is *Muḥammadun Rasūlullāh.* Allāh ﷻ is the Creator and Muḥammad ﷺ is the *calipha,* His representative, for all creation. He is the sulṭān that Allāh ﷻ appoints to represent Him here on this earth—or indeed upon all the earths in all the universes—and thus he has to know every detail for, if something is missing from his vision or knowledge, then he would not yet have reached the highest level of kingship. Without a doubt, Allāh ﷻ perfected *Sayyīdinā* Muḥammad ﷺ and raised him to the highest level of kingship, and He took him on Isrā and Miʿrāj, the invitation to the Divine Presence. No other prophets were taken to that highest level, but Allāh ﷻ was showing his predecessors His signs on earth.

وَكَذَٰلِكَ نُرِي إِبْرَاهِيمَ مَلَكُوتَ السَّمَاوَاتِ وَالأَرْضِ وَلِيَكُونَ مِنَ الْمُوقِنِينَ

Wa kadhālika nurīyya Ibrāhīm malakūt as-samāwāti wa 'l-arḍ

So also did We show Abraham the kingdom of the heavens and the earth that he might have certitude."[134]

Allāh ﷻ showed *Sayyīdinā* Ibrāhīm ﷺ the heavenly kingdom and the earthly kingdom from this planet. But He raised *Sayyīdinā* Muḥammad ﷺ.

سُبْحَانَ الَّذِي أَسْرَى بِعَبْدِهِ لَيْلاً مِّنَ الْمَسْجِدِ الْحَرَامِ إِلَى الْمَسْجِدِ الأَقْصَى

الَّذِي بَارَكْنَا حَوْلَهُ لِنُرِيَهُ مِنْ آيَاتِنَا إِنَّهُ هُوَ السَّمِيعُ الْبَصِيرُ

Glory to He Who did take His servant for a Journey by night from the Sacred Mosque to the farthest Mosque, whose

---

[134] Suratu 'l-Anʿam, (Cattle), 6: 75-79.

precincts We did bless,- in order that We might show him some of Our Signs: for surely He is the Hearing, the Seeing.[135]

وَالنَّجْمِ إِذَا هَوَى مَا ضَلَّ صَاحِبُكُمْ وَمَا غَوَى وَمَا يَنطِقُ عَنِ الْهَوَى إِنْ هُوَ إِلَّا وَحْيٌ يُوحَى عَلَّمَهُ شَدِيدُ الْقُوَى ذُو مِرَّةٍ فَاسْتَوَى وَهُوَ بِالْأُفُقِ الْأَعْلَى ثُمَّ دَنَا فَتَدَلَّى فَكَانَ قَابَ قَوْسَيْنِ أَوْ أَدْنَى فَأَوْحَى إِلَى عَبْدِهِ مَا أَوْحَى مَا كَذَبَ الْفُؤَادُ مَا رَأَى أَفَتُمَارُونَهُ عَلَى مَا يَرَى وَلَقَدْ رَآهُ نَزْلَةً أُخْرَى عِندَ سِدْرَةِ الْمُنْتَهَى عِندَهَا جَنَّةُ الْمَأْوَى إِذْ يَغْشَى السِّدْرَةَ مَا يَغْشَى مَا زَاغَ الْبَصَرُ وَمَا طَغَى لَقَدْ رَأَى مِنْ آيَاتِ رَبِّهِ الْكُبْرَى

By the Star when it setteth, your comrade errs not, nor is he deceived; Nor does he speak of (his own) desire. It is naught save an inspiration that is inspired, which one of mighty powers has taught him One vigorous; and he grew clear to view. When he was on the uppermost horizon. Then be drew nigh and came down till he was (distant) two bows' length or even nearer.

God revealed to His servant what He revealed. The Prophet's heart in no way falsified what it saw. Will you then dispute with him about what he saw? And he saw Him again another time at the Lote-tree of the utmost boundary, at the Garden of Abode. Behold the Lote-tree was shrouded with what shrouds. His sight did not swerve or waiver. Indeed he saw of the Signs of his Lord, the Greatest.[136]

Allāh ﷻ took the Prophet ﷺ all the way to show him every detail. *Sayyīdinā* Ibrāhīm ﷺ was not given every detail. Thus, *Sayyīdinā* Muḥammad ﷺ became Allāh's representative on Earth.

---

[135] Suratu 'l-Isra, (The Night Journey), 17:1.
[136] Suratu 'n-Najm (The Star), 53: 10-19.

السلطان ظل الله في الارض فمن اكرمه اكرمه الله ومن اهانه اهانه الله

> *as-sulṭān dhilullāh fil-arḍ, man akramahu, akramahullāh, wa man ahānahu ahānahullāh.*
>
> The Sultan is the Shadow of God on earth. Whoever honors him, Allāh ﷻ will honor; whoever dishonors him, Allāh ﷻ will dishonor.[137].

To honor the Prophet ﷺ is to remember him, and to remember him is to recite *dhikru 'n-Nabī* with the tongue. Those who keep up this rememberance are honored, which is why the *awlīyā* are honored.

As for those who dishonor the Prophet ﷺ, we do not refer here to the unbelievers, but to those believers who neglect the rememberance of him, or worse, call that *bida*ʿ. They are dishonored.

That is why it is important to be connected to a perfect shaykh, as he is aware of all the details of these secrets of secrets of creation. He understands not only the creation, but also the wisdom of why it was created. He recieves all the hidden heavenly details that have been secured in the Ocean of the Essence, and he is the one who is receiving from the hidden reality of that Essence that is veiled from everyone in the name of *Hūwa*.

The Meaning of *Huwa*

Hūwa is a pronoun. So, when when Allāh ﷻ says, "*Qul Hūwa Allāh,*" He is referring to a level preceding "Allāh". Allah is the Name encompassing all the Holy Names and Attributes. The level preceding it is "*Hūwa,*" and it is entirely unknown. It is beyond description. It can only be described by the Beautiful Name that encompasses all the other Names and Attributes, but the Prophet ﷺ is able to take from its realities through the secrets of the *wa* he was addressing his Lord.

---

[137] Aṭ-Ṭabarānī in his *Kabīr* and al-Bayhaqī in *Shu'b al-Īmān*.

Sayyīdinā Muḥammad ﷺ was in the Divine Presence and Allāh ﷻ said, "Who are you?" there was no "there" existing except Allāh ﷻ. The Prophet ﷺ was completely annihilated in that Presence. He was not seeing himself. "*Man Anta,* who are You?" He said, "*Anta,* I am You!" There was no more *Sayyīdinā* Muḥammad ﷺ. When Allāh ﷻ sent him back, he went in the station of *baqā,* in Allāh's Presence there is no *sharīk*. Everything and everyone else becomes zero. That is the secret of *Hūwa Anta, wa Anta Hūwa,* and that is why the *awlīyāullāh* recite it.[138]

Consider a piece of metal: iron, gold or platinum. If you take one atom away from it, it remains iron, gold or platinum. That atom is still the same substance as the original piece—iron, gold or platinum. If you return it to the original piece, its composition is also unchanged. The part is the same as the whole.

Thus, the source of all things lies in this unknowable level, for all creations can be rendered back to the Holy Names *al-Qādir* (The All-Powerful) and *al-Muqtadir* (The Determiner). That is why it is said that everything is Allāh ﷻ, for Allāh ﷻ created everything. The source of all things lies in those Beautiful Names and Attributes that describe the Essence. That is why we say, "O Allāh ﷻ, take us from our partial will to Your complete Will." The saints have been dressed in the raiment of these realities, for this is Islam: to submit and surrender.

Today, they say that Islam is peace. Piece of what? Piece of the heart; Peace of the heart. That is what comes from surrendering to Allāh ﷻ.

That is why the saints say, "That *Hūwa* that created everything is You, and *Anta* is You the Unknown." If you are clever, you will understand. If you are from the people of witnessing (*ru'yā*) and those who can remove the veils (*kashf*), you

---

[138] Sayyīdinā Abdul Qadir Jilani ق was always reciting the majestic prayer: "*Hūwa Anta, wa Anta Hūwa*—You are He and He is You; You are the Complete Unknown and the Complete Unknown is You).

can comprehend what these saints mean. But we cannot, for we are veiled. Allāh ﷻ removed their veils.

When the *awlīyā* come to the presence of the Prophet ﷺ, he removes veil after veil. Then he takes them to the Presence of Allāh ﷻ. Thus, the realities are uncovered for them. It is as though they were covered with a blanket and someone pulled it away. The lid of the pot is removed, so they can see inside. That is why they are people of *ru'yā,* because they can see. Next comes the knowledge of what is seen *(dirāyā).*

The people of these three levels have doven into the Ocean of Divine Knowledge. They have become hidden, just as one disappears from sight when they dive beneath the waves. Yet, they are still there and they may emerge at any time. The *awlīyā* dive into these Oceans, take what they want and return with it. You may see them, but they are not here—they are there, exploring the depths of that Sacred Knowledge like divers on a coral reef.

Just as divers need oxygen, the saints need these three levels in order to dive into the Oceans of Divine Knowledge. For this reason, the followers of the *awlīyā* cannot accompany them on these dives unless the saints assist them. They must teach them to dive slowly. First, they must teach them to swim. Then they teach them how to make quick dives without oxygen. They may go under for a few seconds. Only when they have become strong do they give them these three levels: *kashf, ru'yā, dirāyā.*

However, not every diver in this world can go deep into the depths of the ocean. Most cannot. To do so requires special equipment and training. Moreover, such deep dives require a slow ascent and a long decompression. For the same reason, if someone is in *ḥālat al-jaẓbah,* the State of Attraction, and comes out quickly, his tongue will be completely frozen or he may begin to say things that people cannot accept. That is what happened in the case of Muḥyīddīn Ibn 'Arabī. Spiritual decompression means keeping these secrets in the heart and releasing them slowly.

The Divine Essence is Utterly Unknowable

It is important to understand that these Heavenly Secrets are not revealed directly to the saints from the Divine Essence. Rather, these *awlīyā* are in the Oceans of the Treasures of *Bismillahi 'r-Raḥmani 'r-Rahīm*. Everything comes with the Name of Allāh ﷻ, thus everything comes from the Name "Allāh ." Only *Sayyīdinā* Muḥammad ﷺ gets this Divine Knowledge directly, and even he cannot take from that Essence that is Utterly Hidden, (*al-ghaybu 'l-muṭlaq*). That is because Allāh ﷻ has no partner.[139] Allāh ﷻ sends from the *alif* to the *lām, lām, hā*.

The *walīullāh* have been hidden and locked in the treasure houses of *bismillāhi*, and the key to the locks of these vast storehouses that are likes oceans unto themselves are the trusts that Allāh ﷻ is keeping:

إِنَّا عَرَضْنَا الْأَمَانَةَ عَلَى السَّمَاوَاتِ وَالْأَرْضِ وَالْجِبَالِ فَأَبَيْنَ أَن يَحْمِلْنَهَا
وَأَشْفَقْنَ مِنْهَا وَحَمَلَهَا الْإِنسَانُ إِنَّهُ كَانَ ظَلُومًا جَهُولًا

Innāā ʿaradnā al-amānata ʿalā 's-samāti wa 'l-arḍi w'al-jibāli fa abayna an yaḥmilnāhā wa ashfaqna minhā wa ḥamalaḥā'l-insāna innahu kāna ẓalūman jahūla.

*We did indeed offer the Trust to the Heavens and the Earth and the Mountains; but they refused to undertake it, being afraid thereof: but man undertook it;- He was indeed unjust and foolish*When Allāh ﷻ asked the the earth and the mountains to carry that trust, they refused. Human beings said, "Yes, we will take it." They knew no what was behind those locks. They accepted it and defiled it with their sins. But the saints protected their trust. They kept it clean, and they were able to see by means of spiritual unveiling (*kashf*) and knew what they were

---

[139] Muḥammad al-Busayrī said, "Praise Muḥammad as much as you like, but do not say as they did of Sayyidīnā ʿĪsā, (i.e. that he is God or the son of God).
[140] Sūratu 'l-Aḥzāb [The Confederates], 33:

seeing. Allāh ﷻ gave them the key to these locks, and that key is "There is no strength except through Allāh " (*lā quwatta illa billāh*).

That is why the *awlīyāullāh* say, "We are weak, we are helpless." They have confirmed that to their egoes. Everything is in Allāh's Hands.

The Prophet Muḥammad ﷺ said:

انا عبد عاجز

anā 'abdun 'ajiz.

I am an helpless slave.

If Muḥammad ﷺ is saying this, what about the rest of us?

These saints receive such Heavenly Knowledge in their seclusions and from their training. They become teachers and give initiation (*baya'*) to their students. This is how it has worked from the time of the Prophet ﷺ up to the time of our own master, Mawlana Shaykh Nāẓim, who is the perfect guide and the guide of this age. All of these teachers know that there is no power except with Allāh ﷻ, which is power that comes from Divine Energy (*qudrah*).

When one can tap into that Heavenly Power and focus it with intention, then that energy can become manifest in a zeal that can move mountains. For it is said:

همة الرجال تقلع الجبال

Himmat ar-rijāl taqla'u al-jibāl

The zeal of men takes mountains from their roots.

And also:

علو الهمة من الإيمان

'Ulūw al-himmat min al-īmān

The highest of zeal is from faith.

The *awlīyāullāh* have the *'ulūw al-himmah,* intense zeal. They are not lazy like us. Their enthusiasm is like a laser that can cut through mountains. They are like these giant cranes that are used to erect skyscrapers. They are the heavy lifters of the *Ummah,* its power. Yet, they know that there is no power except that which comes from Allāh ﷻ.

With the power that Allāh ﷻ gives them, these saints are able to rise through the different levels of Divine Knowledge, penetrating deeper and deeper into its secrets. However, each one can only advance to a certain limit, beyond which they do not have the necessary clearance to enter. They clean themselves, and through this purification of the heart, they are able to raise the level of their clearance until they are able to enter into areas that were never opened to those teachers that came before them. Thus, the *awlīyā* of today are getting the accumulated knowledge of those who came before them in addition to what they are receiving from the intercession of the Prophet ﷺ.

Without that intercession, they would get nothing. But with it, they are given what no eyes have seen and what no ears have heard. This means they are given what has never even been imagined, what has never even entered into the heart of another human being. With these understandings, they are able to dive deep into the oceans of the Beautiful Names and Attributes of Allāh ﷻ.

As we have said, these Oceans of Divine Knowledge are hidden, and they are only revealed through Allāh's Ancient Generosity, which is related to His Greatness. There are levels upon levels of Allāh's Greatness, and the *awlīyā* are able to advance through them according to their own level of purification. Through them, Allāh ﷻ reveals the Hidden of Hiddens. Then they become knowers of Allāh's Knowledge, true gnostics. They are able to perceive Allāh's Light engraved upon all species of creation and read what He has written on each one. They are able to see these designs (*nuqūsh*) that are the mark of Allāh's Power which designed all things. You are a design, trees are a design—everything is a design of Allāh ﷻ.

These designs are engraved with Allāh's Light (*nūr*):

اللهُ نُورُ السَّمَاوَاتِ وَالْأَرْضِ

Allāh u nūru's-samawatī wa'l-arḍ.

Allāh is the light of the heavens and the earth.[141]

[141] Sūratu 'n-Nūr [The Light], 24:35.

EIGHTEEN

Divine Blueprints

The *walī,* who, under Allāh's mercy was unveiled to him all the realities that by means of all the angelic powers bestowed on him he is able to grasp and understand the heavenly structures that are created from heavenly plans. These heavenly structures are unlike any earthly structures where you see forms, walls, roof and ceiling.

Heavenly forms cannot be understood, just as human begins cannot begin to understand this universe, for every day they say they are discovering something new and extraordinary. We are like an ant before an elephant. And they are unable to go to the nearest portion of outer space without space shuttles. They go up yet how far do they reach? It might be 100 km, 80 miles, and they say "O we are in that highest place where we are rotating around the earth."

Beyond the earth they cannot go. They send shuttles, as we go with what they say that it went to Mars or to the Moon. Let us say "yes, you did, but what they did you come up with" They came up with a little information. What do you think about when Allāh said He created seven heavens and seven earths? And these heavens are not in this universe. That universe is *samā ad-dunyā,* the earthly sky, not the lowest heaven. It is the sky of this earth. This whole universe has a sky that wraps it together. What is beyond that? Where are these seven heavens that Allāh structured with heavenly structure? No one knows. They are not like planets and galaxies in this universe.

How many galaxies, are there, as they theorize? They say there are 6 billion of them and each galaxy contains around 80 billion stars. And they understood nothing from any star or planet except a tiny bit of knowledge gleamed about Mars. Look at all these constellations how symmetrically they are arranged, and each is moving in its their orbits, gracefully and without interference or disharmony.

كُلٌّ فِي فَلَكٍ يَسْبَحُونَ

Kullun fī falakin yasbaḥūn

Each (just) swims along in (its own) orbit (according to Law).[142]

What is that swimming? It means dancing and singing, the Beautiful Names and Attributes of Allāh . So when that *walī* is approaching, and they are giving him, and when he begins to penetrate into these heavenly structures, he is stunned, finished. There are no words to explain what he is seeing. Only the heart can understand what that *walī* is tasting and seeing. For the body the tongue tastes, for the spirit, the heart tastes.

So the heart is tasting. When you have a problem or someone dies, what do you do? You cry. The tongue does not taste the sadness, nor does the tongue taste the happiness of a person when happy. There are different senses for the spirit, which are reached through the heart. The body perceives through the five senses, but the heart has different kinds of senses that no one can describe.

Power of the Kidney

Take for example, the kidney of a human being. It contains millions and millions of pores. These pores are able to differentiate between different kinds of minerals; what is good for body is kept and what is not good it eliminates. When they put someone on a dialysis machine, it does not determine what is good and what is bad. It eliminates everything and then they must give back to the patient potassium, calcium and all other elements that are needed to maintain the blood chemistry.

---

[142] Sūrah YāSīn, 36:40.

Who gave that power of differentiation to the kidney? Who gave that incredible scientific ability to the kidney? It is like a doctor all by itself. That is in the body. If the kidney can distinguish through millions of pores, what is good and keep it and what is bad and eliminate it, what do you think about the heart?

الاان فى الجسد مضغة اذا صلحت صلح الجسد كله و اذا

فسدت فسد الجسد كله الا و هي القلب

Alā inna fi 'l-jasadi muḍghatan. Idhā fasadat idhā ṣaluḥat, ṣaluḥat al-jasad kulluh wa idhā fasudatfasad al-jasada kullahu. alā wa hīyā al-qalb.

That is why the Prophet ﷺ said, "There is piece of flesh in the body, if it is good the entire body is good and if it is corrupt the entire body is corrupt—verily it is the heart."

There are no words to express what the heart feels. There are no words of tongue, but there are words of the heart. There is a special language between them that cannot be decoded and they speak with it. Through *rābiṭah* and telepathy a *walī* can reach and talk. That is why normal scholars, who have not the reached level of *wilāyah,* cannot understand. They don't have language of heart. That language of the heart is related to heavens. That is how *awlīyāullāḥ* can taste and understand what Allāh wants them to understand and taste.

Heavenly Coma

The movements of the constellations by the angelic powers reaches the heart of the *walī* through this language which cannot be described. Then that *walī* becomes stunned; then something new is opened. As he is progressing, further and further levels are unveiled and thus his presence in that heavenly structures, that has a certain taste that he tastes through his heart, he will no longer to be able to take himself out and he will then be yearning and moaning for more. At that time his spirituality will be molded with godly infatuation. At that time, the *walī* who is standing at the threshold will be thunderstruck, awestruck from these manifestations of the realities that come to him and that will strike him and put him in a "heavenly coma". If you speak with him about *dunyā* he doesn't care. If you give him $1,000,000 he spends it and if you give him clothes they are gone. He has no more love to this world, *dunyā*. He is in complete love of *ākhirah,* the next life. He goes into a complete "coma" where only his heart is working.

In physical life, when a person enters a coma, only his heart is pumping. His mind is gone. Some come back while other go on to the next life. If you don't have a perfect guide that guides you constantly, you might fall into that sort of coma that keeps you out of *dunyā*. That is why many *awlīyāullāh* leave *dunyā* for *ākhirah* and become ascetic in their lives. They no longer care for *dunyā* and they leave and those we call *zuhhād*, ascetics.

Those who are under a perfect guide are lucky, for when they emerge from their coma, the effects of that coma will disappear and they will become as Grandshaykh was described—*khalwatī, jalwatī.* That means "with people and with Allāh at the same time." "With Him" does not mean partner with Him, *ḥāshā,* rather it means being in His presence and at the same time being present with people.

At that time if you give him 100,000 dollars it doesn't disappear. If you give him any *matā ad-dunyā,* as Allāh described *matāu 'd-dunyā qalīl,* it is worthless, he has it but it does not overwhelm his heart. He does not care if he has it or not, he might give it or keep it, at that time his system is balanced.

This is that state that when Shaykh puts you in seclusion the shaykh will make you first to smell. As when you are cooking, the first thing you notice is the smell, whether it is good or not? That is why you put in different ingredients and you take a whiff.

Does it have a pleasant smell? Then once it is cooked somewhat you will taste.

So the first thing a *walī* experiences is smell, and if they are able to continue in their journey, neither looking right nor left at the desires of the *dunyā* then they will begin to taste. If they continue from there they begin to taste more and more.

Heavenly Pictures

These thoughts which were noted by this pen, on Tuesday, the 26th of Rajab, were enlightenments and lights of realities that governed and took complete hold of my thoughts, my brain and my mind, then took me over completely so that I was no longer able to control myself. They entered into my heart with Mawlana Shaykh's company and support, to emerge from that pen. At that time the pen was able to write and draw, but it is not really writing, in the normal sense, because you are not thinking about what you want to write. The pen was drawing designs and the pen was drawing letters. These letters. From that pen was emerging designs, what we call *rasamāt*, pictures, in Arabic. So the pen began to draw these letters and these letters composed these words and these words composed what we wrote of sentences and paragraphs. In truth these words were poured on me on the night of Isrā and Miʿrāj out of the lights of the realities which took hold of my thoughts and mind and then entered my heart to emerge to the pen drawing what I felt and what I saw with the eye of my heart. Because whatever is unveiled from enlightened realities you cannot draw with the mind. You can write. Lecturers write words and letters, but with the heart it is what drawings emerge. So what comes out is letters and these letters are actually designs.

Grandshaykh said that every letter of the Holy Qur'an has at least 12,000 oceans of knowledge and every ocean has no beginning and no end. How many verses 6326, or 6666, and how many words? 323670 or so.

So if there are 12,000 oceans of knowledge on every letter then think, O servant, what kind of knowledge is there to pick up if we are on the right track?

So what I felt in the eye of the heart is by Allāh's grace and thanks be to Him for that. And, O my master; O Messenger of Allāh, to you is the grant and the greatness.

When someone gives you a grant you feel you owe him gratitude. Those emanations I received that nihgt were granted from the Prophet ﷺ and we have to express the immense gratitude we feel for receiving them. That is a *minā*, a grant.

Sayyīdinā 'Alī said, "Whoever taught me one letter I become a slave to him." Even if you paid someone money to teach you, you must keep gratitude. That is why *awlīyāullāh* teach discipline and respect to their followers.

For you O Prophet, is the gratitude and greatness. You are the Beloved of Allāh, Ḥabīballāh, and the owner of the secrets that Allāh gave to you that cannot be revealed without you! O Prophet of Allāh, and O my Shaykh! It is a grant from you and you have done me an immense favor and Allāh bless you that you accompanied this poor servant who is sitting between four walls and connecting his heart through *rābiṭah* to you, and stayed with him in that journey. May Allāh grant and connect us with the Owner of the Time, whose time is near at hand, *Sayyīdinā* Mahdī, and we are seeking and asking from the essence of this seclusion, as Mawlana requested, the essence of this seclusions is to ask Allāh for a king that comes supported with Divine Support.

وَقَالَ لَهُمْ نَبِيُّهُمْ إِنَّ اللهَ قَدْ بَعَثَ لَكُمْ طَالُوتَ مَلِكاً قَالُوٓاْ أَنَّى يَكُونُ لَهُ
الْمُلْكُ عَلَيْنَا وَنَحْنُ أَحَقُّ بِالْمُلْكِ مِنْهُ وَلَمْ يُؤْتَ سَعَةً مِّنَ الْمَالِ قَالَ إِنَّ اللهَ
اصْطَفَاهُ عَلَيْكُمْ وَزَادَهُ بَسْطَةً فِي الْعِلْمِ وَالْجِسْمِ وَاللهُ يُؤْتِي مُلْكَهُ مَن يَشَاءُ
وَاللهُ وَاسِعٌ عَلِيمٌ

Their Prophet said to them: "(Allāh) hath appointed Ṭālūt as king over you." They said: "How can he exercise authority over us when we are better fitted than he to exercise authority, and he is not even gifted, with wealth in abundance?" He said: "(Allāh) hath Chosen him above you, and hath gifted him abundantly with knowledge and bodily prowess: Allāh Granteth His authority to whom He pleaseth. Allāh careth for all, and He knoweth all things."[143]

It means fight with that king that Allāh will send away the evils of the ego and the devils of this *dunyā*. That is first. What is meant here is not to fight one another. The first battle is with the devils of your ego and the veils of the ego. Fight and eliminate them. It means we need a king, each and every one of us. Even though we gave initiation to our Shaykh, Shaykh Muḥammad Nāẓim ʻAdil al-Ḥaqqānī, we are not asking through the heart and with the language of the heart for him to appear to us as a king. If we ask that through the tongue of the heart using the language of the heart, then that king will be granted to us to fight the evil of this *dunyā* and its devils.

Allāh sent *Sayyīdinā* Muḥammad as mercy for all humanity. That mercy is for everyone. That is why he wants to save people in the Last Days, which is a time of second ignorance. To someone who is not a prophet, as Prophet Muḥammad ﷺ is the last prophet, but who is a *walīullāh* carrying secrets of safety and security for all human beings more and more understanding will come to his heart in seclusion. Inspirations will come and open up all these realities to the heart.

In one of these dreams I was present and I saw Mawlana Shaykh was coming and he saying to me, "These *munajāt*, intimate discourses, that you are making daily as I ordered you to do, are more powerful than the *munājāt* of fifty *walī*s. With that power I

---

143 Sūratu 'l-Baqara [The Heifer],2:247.

am putting you in that situation." And from these *tajallis* he said, he was worried that I would pass away. For that reason he was always monitoring and controlling my state.

In Bukhārī's *Tārīkh,* Abū Hurayrah relates that they said to the Prophet ﷺ, *"Yā Rasūlullāh, idu'Allāh ta'ala 'alā al-mushrikīn*—ask Allāh to remove the unbelievers and to destroy them. "

What was the answer of the Prophet ﷺ? This shows the greatness of *Sayyīdinā* Muḥammad ﷺ. This is one of the biggest arguments made by *awlīyā* today. He said, "I was sent as a mercy and I was not sent as a punishment or as a destroyer."

Fal-yata-amal al-muta-amil. Let the meditating one reflect and observe, how was the prophet *raūfun bil-'ibād,* caring and kind with human beings in their totalities. This was his way not only with the Muslims, but with all. He is *Raūfun Raḥīm,* Kind and Merciful. Allāh dressed him with these two Names: Kind and Merciful.

So that *raḥmat* that Allāh put in the heart of the Prophet ﷺ, the Prophet ﷺ gave it , depending on the level of these *awlīyā,* he inherited it to them. That is why high level *awlīyā* never come against any unbeliever. They try to get them into their association or in their area, try to bring everyone in that mercy. They don't want anyone to be left behind. To bring everyone under their protection. That is why these seclusions teach you and give you the reality of these kinds of mercy.

The Prophet ﷺ guided these *awlīyāullāh* to the *ṭarīq al-hudā,* the Path of Guidance, *ṭarīq ar-raḥmah,* the Path of Mercy, and to *ṭarīq as-sirāṭ al-mustaqīm* to the Path of the Straight Way. That is the straightforward path, which Allāh ﷻ described in Sūratu'l-Fātiḥa, for Allāh wants us to be on the Right Path. He does not want us to be deviated. Therefore the Prophet ﷺ shows us the way of mercy, the way of guidance and the right path.

So Allāh is addressing us, His servants, with His love. When you speak to your children, you speak with love to them

You feel how much you love them when you tell them, "Don't do this, do that."

How Do We Repay Our Lord?

So Allāh is speaking to us, "O sons of Adam I created you and you are worshipping someone else, either yourself or Iblīs. What did I do wrong to you? I gave you life and happiness and I gave you everything you have in your life. I gave you the very breath that comes in and out each second. Is this is how you repay My generosity?"

This is how we are repaying our Lord. We repay Him by running away from Him.

"I remember you always and you forget Me. You are My servants."

وَعَدَّهُمْ عَدًّا

Aḥsāhum wa 'addahum' adda.

He does take an account of them (all), and hath numbered them (all) exactly.[144]

Allāh knows their total number and He counted them one by one.

Allāh saying in Holy Qur'an that He knows their totality, He knows what He created without looking into it. That is something beyond mind. If you have a company or a bank and you want to count how much money. You have a machine to count for you. They don't know how much is in that box. That is only to give an example.

So these universes all seven heavens and what is in them, He knows without counting and yet He then said, "counting them". Why? He knows them all. Does He need to count them? Why does he mention that: *'Addahum 'adda,* means, to count 1, 2, 3, 4, 5, these secrets in these numbers. That means he gave that

[144] Sūrah Maryam, 19:94.

authority to the prophet that assigned for the prophet angels that will count every detail of creation in this universe.

That is why the Prophet's name is beside Allāh's name. *lā ilāha ill-Allāh* is "There is no god except Allāh, without any partner." And then *Muḥammadun Rasūlullāh*. With every creation that Allāh created Muḥammad is *rasūl*—messenger.

It means, "I remember you" and He mentioned them and He counted them through angels assigned to count and gave that to the Prophet ﷺ. "So when an angel comes and touches you in order to count you that is also a blessing, yet you forget Me, forgetting the peaceful touch with which I touched you."

Each human being is born on innocence. His parents make him what he is. But Allāh touched him, He gave to them whatever is there.

> "You forget Me. When I call you to My presence I will answer you. No you run away and you deny Me, *tanfaw*. Why are you running away? For what? I am giving you heavenly paradises.
>
> I only created Shaytan to run after you and test you: are you going to follow him or Me? He is only doing his job. What is his job? It is to take away everyone."
>
> "This is great oppression. You hate Me while I love you. You stab Me when I love you. Not physically, but you stab My orders to you and My words to you."
>
> "I come to you and you run from Me. So what greater oppression is there than that? I created you only to worship Me. So don't think about your *rizq*, provision. When your thinking is only to worship, I will guarantee your provision. Don't be tired running for this world, *dunyā*. Whatever is written it comes to you."

That is why when *awlīyā* reach a certain level, they leave *dunyā*, *dunyā* comes to them. They are working to fight their egoes and to being back people to the mercy of *Sayyīdinā* Muḥammad ﷺ.

"Seek Me you will fine Me." It means, "Seek Allāh you will find Him."

"If you find Me you find everything. You don't need anything else, it is finished. But if you did not find Me or you lose Me because you did not seek me, you are finished. There is a border between Me and you. I am more beneficial to you than anything else."

Our Lord is our refuge and his door is our Prophet, and the way to Him is our guide. So let us keep good manners with *awlīyāullāh* and take from their lessons examples, and not be stubborn with our opinions and our wills. Submit, surrender. Don't use your mind in the presence of your shaykh. If you want to use your mind be away from your shaykh, come back later and say, I repent.

They will try to crush you. Not crash course. That means quick course. They give a crush course. Crush their opinions. The Shaykh makes himself ignorant. "Don't do this don't do that." Throwing away what you think is correct. It may be correct, but they reject it because they try to correct it. They want to make sure you suffer. When you suffer you are raised up and they take away your will; then you have to surrender. May Allāh forgive us and may He give our Shaykh long life.

Bi hurmatil Fāṭiḥah.

NINETEEN

Three Levels of Fruitfulness

Allāh ﷻ is *mal'adhunā,* he is our refuge and the door of our refuge is our Prophet *Sayyīdinā* Muḥammad ﷺ, and the way to reach that door and traverse that long tunnel is by means of a guide. We need a guide who has a flashlight that he can turn on so that we see where we are going. And we have to be respectful to our guides and learn from their knowledge and take them as our example and not be stubborn holding onto our thoughts and opinions. Rather we must leave our wills behind. If you are going to stand on your opinion and your will you are going to be in a gave situation. That will not result in a happy situation.

Consult Others

Do not be stubborn in your opinion. You can give your opinion to your guide, which is the meaning of:

وَأَمْرُهُمْ شُورَى بَيْنَهُمْ

wa amruhum shūrā baynahum.

Those who (conduct) their affairs by mutual Consultation. [145]

You may give your opinion, but don't be stubborn on holding to it as if to say "my way only. I don't accept anyone else's opinion."

Keep to the way of the Prophet ﷺ, for although he is higher than *Sayyīdinā* Jibrīl ﷺ in station and in every goodness, Allāh caused him to follow the guidance of *Sayyīdinā* Jibrīl ﷺ. This is to show humbleness. The Prophet was demonstrating this level of utter humility by accepting someone to guide him. It means, "No one can be a guide to himself."

---

[145] Sūratu 'sh-Shūra [Mutual Consultation] 42:38.

Today if you want to write your resume, you need someone to correct it for you. Even if you know all that you accomplished throughout your life, you still need to send it to someone to go through and check it.

Don't say, "I am not in need for another." Don't be stubborn. We are all in need of one another.

The wife is in need of her husband and the husband is in need of his wife. Parents are in need of their children, and children need their parents. When children are young, they need you for everything and when you become "young" then you need them.

وَمِنكُم مَّن يُرَدُّ إِلَى أَرْذَلِ الْعُمُرِ لِكَيْلَا يَعْلَمَ مِن بَعْدِ عِلْمٍ شَيْئًا وَتَرَى الْأَرْضَ هَامِدَةً فَإِذَا أَنزَلْنَا عَلَيْهَا الْمَاء اهْتَزَّتْ وَرَبَتْ وَأَنبَتَتْ مِن كُلِّ زَوْجٍ بَهِيجٍ

wa minkum man yuṭawāffā wa minkum man yuraddu ilā arthali al-ʿumuri likay lā yaʿlama min baʿdi ʿilmin shayan Wa tarā al-arḍa ḥāmidatan fa-idhā anzalnā ʿalayhā 'l-mā ihtazzat wa rabat wa anbatat min kulli zawjin baheej.

and some are sent back to the feeblest old age, so that they know nothing after having known (much), and (further), you see the earth barren and lifeless, but when We pour down rain on it, it is stirred (to life), it swells, and it puts forth every kind of beautiful growth (in pairs). [146]

Some of us, and this means most of us, go back to the worst situation in old age; you become like a child, either falling severely ill or losing mental faculties, or becoming physically clumsy. When you reach old age you need your children.

Wa tarā al-arḍa ḥāmidatan—you see the earth barren and lifeless.

---

[146] Sūratu 'l-Ḥajj [The Pilgrimage], 22:5.

You see the earth flat on Judgment Day. That means the body can no longer carry life as you did when you were young. Then Allāh sends water to rejuvenate yourself. That means your children, those whom you can trust. Not to throw you in senior home. How many you see there in this gathering? Hundreds and hundreds. Islam and spiritual discipline teaches us to take care of our parents in old age.

In the same way, the spiritual guide takes care of his students and in return they must "take care" of him by listening to his decisions. You give your opinion and then listen to what he says. That is *tawada'*, humbleness. To reach spiritual realities, you need humbleness. If you are humble, you sleep on the floor or you sleep on the bed and you thank Allāh . Then you advise people and then they thank Him also.

So it means if you have wealth you use it, buy a bed. But if you don't, you sleep on the floor. When there is nice food you eat it, but if there is something you don't like, don't say "what is that?" The Prophet ﷺ never said "what is that?" He still takes a portion of it.

Honor the Prophet

The most happy time was when the Prophet ﷺ was invited to a meal by one of his companions. That companion was a wealthy one, and he was so happy that the Prophet ﷺ was honoring him by coming to his house. He was preparing for many many days. He doesn't know what to slaughter from cows, sheep, goats and oxen. He was doing everything to make the Prophet ﷺ happy and bringing all kinds of fruits. Then he invited the Sahaba.

As the Prophet ﷺ was entering inside with Abū Bakr aṣ-Ṣiddīq ؓ and all this food was everywhere, ready for the Prophet ﷺ. It was difficult in those times to prepare so much food. But due to his wealth he was able to do so.

When the Prophet ﷺ entered, the host said, "what I have done does not befit you. What I have done is very little to befit you."

When the Prophet ﷺ heard this, he backed out, he said, "let the Sahāba eat" and he backed out.

That Sahabi did not know what he did and *Sayyīdinā* Abū Bakr ؓ said, "O Rasūlullāh what happened?" The Prophet said, "When I saw that *niʿam,* blessing, I saw all those angels prepared, then I saw all that blessing and then when he said 'that it is not befitting me' it was so tough on me, as if when he is saying it is not befitting you, for your honor, yet I saw all the honor that Allāh was bestowing on that food, it did not work with me. It was like crossfire."

So they were hungry, the Prophet ﷺ and *Sayyīdinā* Abū Bakr ؓ, so they were going for some dates or some stones to tie to their stomach to relieve the hunger.

As they were walking, an old lady came and said, "*Yā Rasulullāh,* my husband was sick and he believes in you, though he never saw you. And I was praying that Allāh will send you to pass by me so that I can invite you and my husband will see you."

So the Prophet ﷺ accepted and went in. She brought cups and a jug of water and some bread, made from barley. It was not fine bread like we have today. It was coarse and had stones in it. For that reason the Prophet ﷺ used to advise to keep water nearby, in case you choke.

So this is humbleness, this is *tawāḍaʿ*. So the Prophet ﷺ was putting the bread in water and then dipping it in the salt. Then he told Abū Bakr ؓ, "Eat as much as you can." And he said, "I never ate in my life as I ate today."

It means when you thank Allāh for His favors where that woman was trying to do her best even though she had nothing, so Allāh sent angels to that food, more than He sent on the other place. That is for humility, for humbleness. If we keep that humbleness that will take us to the realities we described before. Let us leave all pleasures of this *dunyā*.

Those who claim they know and proclaim, who speak as if they know everything, but they never tasted, that comes from *ʿilm al-awrāq*, knowledge of writing. Those who proclaim they know everything, they are running after *dunyā*. They want the chair to be ready for where they sit, according to protocol, one higher, one behind, one a little higher, and so forth.

اجلس كما يجلس العبد وآكل كما ياكل العبيد

> *Ajilus kamā yajlisu 'l-ʿabd wa ākulu kamā yākulu 'l-ʿabd.*
>
> I eat as a slave eats and I site as a slave sits.

The Prophet ﷺ used to sit on the floor and he used to eat bread with his hands. Those scholars claim they know and understand Islam, yet they are chasing *dunyā*. Allāh will rob them of the fountains of wisdom and extinguish the lights of guidance in their hearts because of their greed for *dunyā*. Greed for *dunyā* removes wisdom from the hearts of people. If wisdom goes away humbleness goes away.

Levels of Fertility

You have to accept the guidance of your shaykh and seek his advice because the levels for the seekers in the journey of a seeker are of three different kinds.

The first level is like that of seeds. When these seeds are planted at the right time they will flourish but if you plant seeds at the wrong time they will not grow.

When you plant seeds in the correct season their fruits can be harvested but one time. Crops like this are wheat, which is harvested only once or barley. These are crops from which one produces flour. These are harvested only once a season, not two or three times.

When you are a beginner in this journey the guide will plant in your heart seeds and these seeds will grow up with *dhikrullāh,* Allāh's remembrance. When these seeds develop up by Allāh's remembrance and by Allāh ﷻ's grace, you need to harvest their fruits and they are only harvested one time.

So the shaykh knows who are going to be in the first level, who in the second and who in third. Therefore if you like to be harvested one time, there are many farmers. They say we harvest only one crop, corn. This state we live in is famous for corn. After the crop is harvested nothing else comes; you get it one time per year.

There are students who say, one harvest is enough. They do *dhikrullāh,* 1500 Allāh and 300 *ṣalawāt* per day. And that is sufficient, like the light of a candle let us say.

But if you want to go to the second level, you have to keep that reality in your heart that you are going to try to make further progress. In this way the shaykh will observe and know what level of aspiration you have. Today you find there are many people who consider themselves as representatives and shaykhs, yet despite this they say "one harvest is enough."

But there are those who want to reach higher and higher. So the shaykh plants in them a seed that is not for a single harvest; rather it is a special seed. It grows like a tree, and then you take the saplings and they grows and they do not die after they are harvested. For corn or wheat, watermelons and tomatoes, the plant is harvested only once. But there are fruit trees which are not like that.

The masters will plant in your heart a small plant that if you water it, it keeps growing. This small plant is growing in your heart from these seeds and it becomes a small tree that he then roots firmly in your heart. Because you are ready and when he checks you, and is satisfied with you achieving the first level of a single harvest he then says, "Yes, you are ok." At that time you have reached the level of *muḥibbūn (lovers of the shaykh).* You like to be near the shaykh. But if you want more he plants in your heart a tree that will grow and does not die after one season. It grows up from year to year.

The water for that plant is *dhikrullāh* as well as your good behavior and good manners. They observe your progress in struggling with your behavior and to develop good manners. It means in addition to your five prayers and other mandatory worship you are seeking a higher level, the level of perfection.

In that level your tree will be producing fruits and you will be able to harvest those fruits and as it keeps growing it also keeps giving.

Today there are four seasons' trees, and in the same tree, for example an orange or lemon, it gives you in summer, in fall, in winter and in spring. Different parts, each give at different times. That keeps continuously giving throughout the year. That tree is like the tree the shaykh plants in the heart that it is constantly giving and you are tasting.

Level of *Murid*

If you continue on that level, you reach the level of *murīdīyyah fī ṭarīqati 'l-'alīyyah.* To be a student or apprentice in the Most Distinguished Sufi Way. You went through the first phase, that yields a single harvest, and he then plants a tree that gives multiple harvests. Then, finally, he will plant the tree of knowledge, of gnosticism. That tree will be able to feed an entire nation; a complete country of citizens. You will teach a huge number of people—it mean you become a spotlight, a guide by the permission of your master, to guide people to their lives and how they must function through their lives in such a way to improve their *ākhirah,* afterlife. You become like a stormy ocean, like a roaring lion of an ocean. You wish to go and show its power to everyone. Like an ocean that has a unending series of waves crashing on the beach, continuous without stopping. Then you become a tsunami that goes into the heart of everyone bringing them into the circles of lovers, then inside the circle of beginners and then bringing them into the circle of followers. You will tie them to the way of your shaykh and to door of your Shaykh and he takes them to the door of the Prophet ﷺ and the Prophet ﷺ takes them to the Door of Allāh . Your harvest at that time will be unlimited, continuous and never-stopping.

So all this comes from what? From being humble. That humbleness causes you to reach these levels. Without humbleness no one arrives there. Without humbleness no Sahāba would go to the Prophet ﷺ. The Prophet ﷺ was humble, coming to *Sayyīdinā* Jibrīl ؏.

Humbleness flows with the blood. Blood is written by Allāh ﷻ to be humble and the blood is pushed by the heart. Allāh gives the order to blood to move by the power of the heart. As an example, when you are not humble you get a blood clot. At that time you need heart surgery. So the shaykh knows where you have clots in your spiritual soul, and that is where he makes a spiritual surgery. He tells you, "Do this *awrād* today, do this tomorrowm" guiding you to open the heart-blockages that you have developed in your life.

So in every drop of blood Allāh gave angels to make sure that drop is circulating and moving through the body. Without blood you would immediately die. That blood carries oxygen to every part of the body, without which everyone dies. Through the flowing of the blood in the veins of the body, the doors of the heavens and earth will open from the gnosis of the secrets of creation. Through the flowing of that blood, containing the light of Allāh's remembrance, you begin to receive all these different secrets and wisdoms that Allāh places in His creation.

من تواضَعَ لله رفعَه

The Prophet ﷺ said in a hadith "Whoever humbles himself to Allāh, Allāh will raise his station."

So that is what our goal is. When you are humble Allāh will raise you. That is when all manner of secrets will open to you. These secrets will cause you to think, meditate and contemplate on the creation of heavens and earth.

الَّذِينَ يَذْكُرُونَ اللهَ قِيَامًا وَقُعُودًا وَعَلَىٰ جُنُوبِهِمْ وَيَتَفَكَّرُونَ فِي خَلْقِ السَّمَاوَاتِ وَالْأَرْضِ رَبَّنَا مَا خَلَقْتَ هَذا بَاطِلاً سُبْحَانَكَ فَقِنَا عَذَابَ النَّارِ

Alladhīna yadhkurūn 'Llāha qiyāman waquʿūdan wa ʿalā junūbihim wa yatafakkarūna fī khalqi 's-samāwāti wa'l-arḍi rabbanā mā khalaqta hādhā bāṭilan subḥānaka faqinā ʿadhāb an-nār.

Those who celebrate the praises of Allāh, standing, sitting, and lying down on their sides, and contemplate the (wonders of) creation in the heavens and the earth, (With the thought): "Our Lord! not for naught Hast Thou created (all) this! Glory to Thee! Give us salvation from the penalty of the Fire.[147]

Those who are remembering Allāh, that humility, *tawādaʿ*, comes to their heart and they remember they are nothing. O Allāh ! You did not create it for nothing, so protects us from punishment. Don't punish us in the Fire of Regret by taking us far from You; rather make us near to You.

When that happens you come to [the realization/reality that] no one can be worshipped except Him. He is the one who created everything and everyone else is His servant. And since *lā maʿbud siwā,* there is none else to make a prostration. He is the Unique One Who has the right to pray to Him the five prayers and you make *sajdah* to Him alone.

So for that reason when you enter the prayer you must be in the Divine Presence, else how are you going to perfect your

[147] Sūrat Āli ʿImrān [The Family of ʿImrān], 3:191.

standing, sitting and laying down. All these will follow in sequence.

And now we remind ourselves of what Muʿadh told his son, "O my son when you pray, pray as if it is your farewell prayer; as if it is the final prayer you are praying. And know, O my son, the believer is between two goodnesses or two rewards: (*ḥasanāt*) he will die between these two good things: one that he reaches quickly and one that comes later."

For example: if a person is praying as if it is his farewell prayer, and if he dies he will leave this life at that high level and he is waiting to pray the next prayer in the same level as the last. That means he has no love of *dunyā* in his life. May Allāh drop the love of *dunyā* from our hearts and from Allāh comes all success.

TWENTY

Exemplars of Humility

The pious ones were exemplars of humility. 'Urwah ibn az-Zubayr related that he once saw *Sayyīdinā* 'Umar ❀ walking on the street in Madina, carrying a clay jar filled with water on his shoulder. 'Urwah ibn az-Zubayr called to him, "O Amīr al-Muminīn, it is not acceptable for you to carry that. I will carry it."

"No," said 'Umar ❀. "I will."

'Urwah ibn az-Zubayr insisted, "No. You are the Amīr. I will carry it."

Sayyīdinā 'Umar ❀ would not relent. He said, "No. I will carry it."

"O Amīr al-Muminīn, Prince of the Believers," the other begged, "It is strange, it is not appropriate to your status."

Thus, they debated, each one asking the other to let him carry the jar. That is humility.

Today, we are not humble. We are not leaders, and yet we fight with each other. We spread false rumors in order to create confusion about other people, and this is what the Prophet ﷺ prohibited. This is lying and backbiting (*namīmah* and *ghībah*). The Prophet ﷺ prohibited it, and we still do it.

Namīmah is something that is not real. It is a lie that you create in your subconscious, and it spreads to your conscious mind. You imagine something happened that never, in fact, occurred. Then you spread that lie. Or perhaps, in order to give an excuse for something that you are doing, you accuse someone else of doing it. Someone may ask you, "Why are you doing that?" and you may say, "Because that one did it, so I have the right to do it, too." That is *namīmah*. That is how Shaytan plays with people.

That is why it is said:

arfaʿu 'n-nās qadran man lā yarā qadra nafisih.

> The highest in dignity are those who do not give themselves importance.
>
> *Wa akthar an-nāsi faḍlan man lā yarā faḍla nafsihi.*
>
> The one's with most favored of people are those who do not see themselves favored.
>
> *Wa lā tasma' li man namaka lianna Allāh yākhudhu ḥaqqak.*

Don't listen to the one who backbites you nor come against him, nor cut him off and stop speaking with him, and do not separate and created distance between you and him, because Allāh will take your right from him. What you take of your rights is limited but if Allāh takes your rights he leaves that one with nothing, either in this life or the next. Therefore say, "*lā ḥawla wa lā quwatta illa billāh*—there is no might and no power except with Allāh. O my Lord I want my innocence from You." At that time Allāḥ ﷻ will take everything from those liars who oppressed you. If He doesn't take it in this life, in the next life He will take all their deeds and give them to you.

We have to leave these bad characteristics. They are what prevent us from approaching the Presence of the Prophet ﷺ. That is what keeps you from achieving sainthood.

Though *Sayyīdinā* 'Umar ؓ was the Amīr al-Muminīn, the highest level of authority in Islam, yet he was still afraid. He did not want to let his ego grow. This was during the time of Islam's great expansion. Countries were opening up and accepting Islam, and each nation was sending a delegation to pledge their allegiance to *Sayyīdinā* 'Umar ؓ. He told 'Urwah ibn az-Zubayr, "When the delegations of tribes came to, listening and obedient, I felt pride and arrogance in myself (*dakhala nafsī nafwah*)."

When pride entered his heart, *Sayyīdinā* 'Umar ؓ moved quickly to cast it out. He realized that these delegations were not coming because of anything he had done but they were coming because Allāh ﷻ inspired them to enter Islam. He knew that Allāh

ﷺ sees what is in his heart, and he was afraid that pride had entered his. To break that, he took up that clay jar in front of all those delegations and was taking the water to the front of the masjid for people to wash and drink.

Sayyīdinā 'Umar ؓ was not wrong; he was calling to the way of the Prophet ﷺ. He was teaching us how to be humble and break the ego down. Can you find anyone like that today?

Today, there is a disease spreading among young and old, a disease of pride. When people defeat someone they shout, "Yah!" They growl and pump their fists in the air. You see this all the time in sports. However sports should teach you to be humble. You also see it in politics. Look at what happens in elections. The politician gives a speech when he is elected, and his supporters raise their hands and shout, "We won!" You even see people exulting like this when they take over a company or win a seat on the board of directors. They say, "We are in control now!" When someone wins today, they put him on a chair and give him a gold trophy. They kiss the trophy and keep on kissing it, as if it was their ticket to Paradise. When they are finished, they take it from them and put it in a museum.

Sayyīdinā 'Umar ؓ was afraid to attribute anything to himself, but today people are so eager to attribute all kinds of good actions to themselves that they lie to impress others. When pride enters your heart, it will take you away from divine realities and knowledge. This is what came to me when I was in seclusion.

فيصبح العبد بعيدا عن الحقاءق والمعارف و يطرد من حضرة الحق

Fa yuṣbiḥu al-'abdu ba'īdan 'ani 'l-ḥaqāiqi wa 'l-ma'ārif wa yuṭradu min ḥaḍrat al-ḥaqq.

The servant becomes far from reality and gnosis and he will be expelled from the Presence of The Reality, Allāh .

Such a one will be kicked out of the Divine Presence (*La yalīk bika hādha 'l-maqām*). Why? Because that station does not befit one who has pride in his heart.

There are people in government that begin with piety, but as they rise higher and higher in rank they lose their *īmān*, faith. When they realize what has happened, they leave those high positions. *Awlīyā* test their followers in this way. They raise them up higher and higher until they realize that they are going in the wrong direction. Some turn back, but they are very few.

Attacks by the Delegations of Pride

You must even be careful that pride and arrogance do not enter into your worship or they will destroy what you have gained. The servant of Allāh ﷻ can draw nearer to the Divine Presence by excessive worship in the middle of the night, *qiyām al-layl*, but there are many people who stay up all night doing this and yet sleep in the morning. They say, "We are doing our *waẓīfah* at night." If you are asking to be closer to your Lord, be careful of pride and arrogance. Come closer to your Lord by performing the night vigil, prayers and meditation (*at-ta'amul wa 'l-murāqabah*) in the early hours between midnight and *fajr*—the time of supplication, *duāʿ*, and heartfelt invocation, *munājāt*, but be careful there that the delegations of pride do not come to your heart. All delegations supported by devils and his army will be sent to your heart and at that moment they will try to trick you. At that moment, their tricks are very dangerous, because you are alone. No one is with you. Your family is sleeping. You are doing what must be done, but that is a critical moment when Shaytan will try to attack you and destroy you.

We have to be careful of the whispering of Shaytan, especially in the stations of contemplation, reflection and meditation (*ta'amul wa 't-tafakkur wa 'l-murāqabah*). When you contemplate on the Oneness of Allāh ﷻ, contemplate on His creation as the Prophet ﷺ instructed. When you make that the subject of your reflection it will take you to a deeper level of meditation. However, you must be careful, for that is also the time at which Shaytan may attack you.

That is what happened to *Sayyīdinā* Āḥmad al-Badawī. He was deep in such a state of contemplation and reflection when his guide came to give him the key to his spiritual trust. At that time Shaytan tricked him, telling him, "Don't take it from that guide—that is a form of *shirk,* idolatry. Take your key directly from your Lord!" Then he heard a Heavenly Voice calling him, "O Āḥmad! Go and take that key from My servant. You need to keep to the way of causes, *asbāb,* so go to him and take it."

Endless Oceans of the Divine Essence

When you run from Shaytan, then your teacher will open for you the oceans that have no bottom (*lā qaʿr lahā*). You can dive into these oceans and keep diving. They never end. You will always be in these oceans of knowledge, oceans of infatuation, oceans of beauty, oceans of majesty. These are the oceans of Allāh's Names and Attributes, the oceans with which Allāh ﷻ dressed His Prophet ﷺ.

النور الذاتي و السر الساطع

An-nūr idh-dhāti wa 's-sirr as sāṭiʿ

The Light of the Divine Essence and the Shining Secret

These oceans accumulate the light of this Essence. You cannot gather the Essence itself. That is known only to Allāh ﷻ. Yet, from these oceans of the Beautiful Names and Attributes, the essence of the Prophet ﷺ has gathered the Light of Allāh's Essence and manifested it. From this emerges the Lights of the different Divine Names and Attributes. The Divine Names and Attributes are not limited to 99 in number, rather they are uncountable. In these Lights which He bestowed on Sayyīdinā Muḥammad, Allāh has gathered the secrets of each Beautiful Name and Attribute, for there is something hidden in each of these. Every Name from each of the infinite Names and Attributes contain infinite Divine Secrets. That is why Grandshaykh said that every letter of the Holy Qur'an contains 12,000 oceans of meaning. One *walī* has the knowledge of one of these oceans, another has the understanding of another. You cannot limit Allāh's Knowledge.

The heavenly dew that we referred to earlier is from these Divine Oceans of Knowledge. The guide sends this heavenly dew to you in your seclusion. The drops are infinite in number, and all are gathered from the ocean of *Sayyīdinā* Muḥammad ﷺ. These secrets have no beginning and no end. They are derived from the Secrets of the DivineEssence.

هذه الاسرار حملتك ثم اغمستك ثم اغرقتك

> *ḥamalatka, thumma aghmasatka, thumma aghraqatka.*
>
> These Secrets will take you and carry you, immerse you and drown you.

Tasting Will Make You Progress

What they reveal to you in seclusion is a taste of these Oceans of Manifestations of Divine Secrets. When you teach a child to swim, you must also carry him. You dip him into the water and this gives him a taste of it. In the same way, they will carry you and show you a glimpse of these heavenly knowledges. As you progress, they will show you more. When you go to the beach, you are anxious to touch the water. Some people roll up their pants and dip their feet in, splashing in the waves. That is enough for them; they are happy. If you take a child to the sea and hold his hand as he plays and splashes in the water, he is so happy. He thinks the whole ocean is his. In reality, he is just playing on the edge. In the same way, the saints carry the one in seclusion to the edge of these Divine Oceans of gnosis and allow him to taste them.

They carry you and thus give you a taste to encourage you to continue. You need to progress more and more in order to reach that ocean. They let you touch that water with your feet, but not taste it with your tongue. If you taste it with your tongue, you will drown. You will fall faint into a coma, for you cannot endure the intensity of these manifestations of Divine Secrets while still in this life, *dunyā*. Yet, if you keep progressing, they will give you more. First they will teach you how to swim. Once you learn to swim, they will let you swim on your own. They will let you enter those oceans that were gathered by the Prophet ﷺ and let you swim near the shore. They will carefully monitor you, as a lifeguard does, so that when danger comes they can dive in and save you. This is a dangerous time, because Shaytan is angry that he is losing you to Allāh ﷻ. They watch you constantly, ever ready to save your life from the tricks of Shaytan.

After you have become a proficient swimmer in these oceans of heavenly knowledge, you will yearn to go deeper. Then they will give you a snorkel and fins—not yet an air tank, but just enough for you to see under the surface. They will allow you to see the treasures hidden beneath the waves of those oceans, but you will still not be able to dive down to reach them. Only after you have mastered snorkeling will they teach you how to dive like a whale and reach those sunken treasures. You need special training to go deeper.

When you do, you will be drowned in this ocean. But there are deeper oceans than this. There are the Oceans of Divine Oneness, *biḥār al-wāḥidīyyah*, and, beyond those, Oceans of Divine Uniqueness, *biḥār al-āḥadīyyah,* and then they shape you from the Manifestations of Divine Unity (*ashkalatka min awḥāl at-tawḥīd*). *Awlīyā* want to go deeper and deeper. They want to reach these far oceans of Uniqueness. That is a high station (*maqām*), and you must be very careful not to commit hidden idolatry, *shirk al-khafī,* there. In that station everything is directed and directing to Allāh ﷻ, but the tricks of Shaytan are also strong in that region.

Sayyīdinā Bilāl ؓ was saying, "One, One (*Āḥad, Āḥad*)!" while they were torturing him. He had attained the Ocean of Vision (*mushāhadah*), and the Station of Witnessing. He had reached the Station of the True Gnostics (*maqām al-'arifīn*).

The Light of the Absolute Essence and the Station of the Gnostics

The light of the Prophet ﷺ is gathering all of the lights of the Divine Essence (*an-nūr adh-dhāt*), the secret that is running through all of the Names and Attributes. This light is beyond description, but we can compare it to a volcano. When a volcano erupts, all of this lava and fire that was hidden inside the Earth comes out, flowing this way and that. Whatever it touches melts—even rocks. That is an analogy to help you understand.

The Light of the Absolute Essence is beyond even the knowledge of the Prophet ﷺ. When it erupts in his heart it fills it with all of these oceans of enlightenment. These are oceans of light. They flow like mighty rivers, cutting through rock and polishing it. They create their own shape and flow through it. This light flows to the *awlīyāullāh*. It runs in their spirits—runs through their souls—and it carries them, dipping and drowning them, to the Divine Oceans of Unique Oneness (*buḥūr al-Āḥadīyyah*). In this way, the saints are raised from the taste of oneness to the taste of witnessing, as happened to *Sayyīdinā* Bilāl al-Habashī ؓ.

This is the station of the gnostics. When you reach that station, these oceans will open their treasures and stores to you. The floodgates of these oceans will burst forth, and just as the tsnunami took away everything in its path, they will carry you to the center of the ocean of unity (*'ayn al-waḥdat*). There, everything you see will indicate the Creator, and you will see that everything is coming from Allāh ﷻ. There, you will experience complete submission. You will not be able to hear, see or sense anything other than your Lord.

The approach to your Lord is through your shaykh and through the Prophet ﷺ. The Shaykh will take you to a station where you do not see, hear or sense anything other than that which comes through *Sayyīdinā* Muḥammad ﷺ. Then he will take you to the station where you do not see, hear or sense anything other than Allāh ﷻ. That is the final anhiliation in the Beloved (*fanāun fillāh fanāun fil-ḥabīb*).

The Shaykh who takes you there is the light of your soul. When it was created, your soul was blended with the soul of your shaykh, and he is the life of your soul (*ḥayāt rūḥik*) and his soul is the secret of your reality. That is because your reality is coming from his soul, for you were assigned to him on the Day of Promises. Through him you understand your reality and through his reality comes all knowledge and understanding of the universe. Nothing can come outside his reality, for just as his soul is the secret of your reality and his reality is the knowledge of what is around you, so too his soul is from the reality of the Prophet ﷺ. Thus, it is like a chain reaction. As he is to you, the Prophet ﷺ is to him. As he is the life of your soul, the Prophet ﷺ is the life of his and the life of the Prophet ﷺ is coming from Allāh ﷻ.

Such knowledge cannot be understood except through a state of humbleness. To grasp such ideas, you must humble and humiliate yourself, just as Sayidina 'Umar ؓ did. Only then will you be able to learn and understand. Otherwise, you will be far away from the understanding of such knowledge.

This humbleness and humility does not come from outward displays. It does not come from eating on the floor, or dressing in rags, or sleeping on the ground or doing this and that to show that you are humble. These are simple things that anyone can do. True humility is within you. When you forgive those who harms you, that is true humility. Anyone can sit on the floor, but to forgive someone and be kind to someone who is irritating you, aggravating you or doing something that you dislike, that is true humility.

Once, a wrestler spit in the face of Sayyīdinā ʿAlī ﷺ. He was about to kill him, but Ali ﷺ said, "If I kill you now, then humility will be gone."

The Prophet ﷺ had a neighbor who, for seven years, was dumping garbage on his door. Yet, when that man was dying, the Prophet ﷺ visited him.

Like the ones who asked *Sayyīdinā* Mūsā, how many years does our neighbor have of life, who was a tyrant? Then he said, "*Wa lā ḥawla wa lā quwatta illa billāh il-ʿAlīyyi 'l-ʿĀẓīm.*"So the man said, it, the wife said, and the son said. Then that neighbor died. Then *Sayyīdinā* Mūsā said, "How *yā rabbī,* you said 300 years. Allāh ﷻ replied, "When they rendered to me, then I must respond."

These are examples of true humbleness and humility.

You have to eliminate arrogance and pride, and you have to replace these with humbleness and humility. That will elevate you and give you patience. Then these oceans of knowledge can flow into the heart. You must also be humble with your shaykh.

How do you show humbleness to the shaykh? It is not by giving him his shoes. That is love. Humbleness is to leave everthing to the shaykh and to accept whatever he says. When you do that, your heart will be polished and cleansed, and he will be able to fill it with knowledge.

TWENTY-ONE

Bitterness Training

What will the shaykh do if you are patient and humble with him? He will feed you bitterness in order to teach you. When he sees that you have reached the level of not objecting, he will try you with bitterness by preventing you from enjoying the things you desire of this world. He will make everything difficult for you and see how much you can bear.

Everyone likes to have a video camera. Everyone likes to have a cell phone. Those are from the pleasures of *dunyā*. We are like children in eyes of the shaykh. We like candies like cell phones, but the best cell phone is the spiritual one that connects your heart to the heart of the shaykh. Everyone wants a reward for following the shaykh. No one says, "I am following the shaykh to polish my heart." That is why there are many students who follow the shaykh for thirty or forty years and then, at the end, begin to go astray. They are filled with doubts and begin to question the shaykh because, from the beginning, they were seeking something and they did not get it. That is becoming a dangerous issue.

Today, people come to the shaykh for many reasons, but most of them are related to *dunyā*. No one is coming to learn from the shaykh. When the shaykh sees that, he gives them one sip of bitterness to check them. He does not give them a big cup, for that would kill them. They would run away. He gives them just a taste to test them and then checks to see if they are struggling. That struggling is a sign of faith.

The Shaykh denies you worldly pleasure because he wants you to enjoy the pleasures of *ākhirah*. We say, "Why is he doing this to us when he does not do this to others we know? They are around him getting all the crumbs from him and we are getting only bitterness. Why is he not giving that to them? Why is he only giving it to us? Why does he keep petting them, giving them what they like, letting them stay with him, sitting with them in his room." He is giving these things to them because he wants to reward them in *dunyā*. For you, he gives bitterness in *dunyā* in order to reward you in *ākhirah*.

What do you want from the shaykh? Do you want money for business? How much? Take it and go. If that is what you want, that is what he gives. But for you, he gives you that which will upset and frustrate you. He is training you. He is not training them. He does not care for them. That is very difficult on the self, and that is why in Sufi training the master may give some *murīds* more than others. When he does this, some students will ask, "Why is he preferring them over us? They are wasting what he gives to them. They are not praying as much as we are. They are not doing *dhikr* as much as we do. Yet, he gives them more attention than us, and when he speaks to us, he shouts." That is the Way. If you like it, accept it; if not, struggle like a salmon trying to make its way upstream. Everyone must struggle according his capacity and according to his level.

The Shaykh's Disdain Raises You

The Shaykh wants you to enjoy the pleasures of *ākhirah* and the pleasures of *jannah*. He wants for you what was promised to the Prophet ﷺ: the highest level of Paradise, the station of truthfulness in the Divine Presence (*maqām aṣ-ṣidq ʿinda malīkin muqtadir*). So, be patient when the shaykh turns away from you. Be patient when he does not give you attention (*jafā*). Be patient when he mistreats you, when he ignores you completely, when he appears to be disgusted with you. Be patient when he does not talk to you, when he will have nothing to do with you, when he treats you as though you were the worst of his followers. That is where the secret is. The epicenter of knowledge is between his grimness and his disdain, between his huffing and puffing. Allāh

ﷻ hid it there. He gave it to the Prophet ﷺ and the Prophet ﷺ gave it to the *awlīyā* and told them to hide it.

That is why Allāh ﷻ said in the Holy Qur'an:

عَبَسَ وَتَوَلَّى أَن جَاءهُ الْأَعْمَى

ʿabasa wa tawalla in jā'ahu al-āʿamā

He frowned and turned away because the blind man came unto him.[148]

Allāh ﷻ said, "It might be that blind man will come and get knowledge." The Prophet ﷺ grimaced and turned away from the blind man in secret in order to quickly polish that man's heart and raise him that he might receive those secrets for *ākhirah*.

When the shaykh grimaces, he is trying to take your pride and dump it in the ocean of disdain. He is trying to strip you of that peacock character of Iblīs and cast it into that sea. When the shaykh grimaces at you, especially if you know him very well and have spent many years with him, you can think of nothing but, "Oh! The Shaykh is angry with me." At that moment, you can take knowledge.

If you do not taste bitterness in childhood, you will never reach anywhere in adulthood. Childhood means your first years in *ṭarīqah*. If you do not learn the bitterness then, when the shaykh is trying to polish you, then you cannot become an adult in *ṭarīqah*, because it is nearly impossible to change anything when you are older. When you are older, it is difficult to learn and grow. Then you will have reached your capacity and cannot expand beyond it. That is why those who come to *ṭarīqah* when they are young are better than those who come when they are old.

If you do not taste bitterness in your *dunyā* life, you are going to drink from the fountains of ignorance forever. Imam Shāfiʿī said:

---

148 Sūrat ʿAbasa [He Frowned], 80:1-2.

Fa man fāttahu 't-ta'līm fī waqt shabābih fa kabbir 'alayhi arba' takbīrāt.

Whoever misses learning in his youth, make four *takbirs* over him.

That means that he is dead. It means, perform the funeral prayer over him.

It is very difficult to change someone when he becomes old if he was not trying to change his life when he was young. That is why you see many people who are moving on the right path turn away in the end. That is a great danger. That will destroy us.

You are not yet perfect. The Prophet ﷺ is the only perfect one. After him, the next in rank are the Companions and the saints. You must remember that summation of the life of a human being, *khulāsaṭa ḥayāt al-insān* is connected with knowledge, and that knowledge reveals the best of ways. We advance as humans through knowledge, *'ilm*, righteousness, *ṣalāḥ*, piety, *taqwā*, humility, *tawaḍa'*, patience, *ṣabr*, reflection, *ta'amul*, meditation, *taffakur*, contemplation, *murāqabah*, and finally through connection (*rābiṭah*), which is the initation you take from the shaykh. All of these—*'ilm, ṣalāḥ, taqwā, tawaḍa', ṣabr, ta'amal, taffakur, murāqabah, murābiṭah*—are wrapped by self-effacement before your Lord (*tadhallul li-rabbika*). That takes you to the place where you see your lowness and your Lord's Generosity with you. You then realize that you are the lowest of the low. Even then, you must be on guard against the sin of pride. You must believe that peacock character of Iblīs is still contaminating you and that you are not yet truly good. Then there is no recognition of your self by your Lord, by the Prophet ﷺ and by your shaykh.

TWENTY-TWO

Exemplars of Guidance

Bayazid al-Bistami

The mother of *Sayyīdinā* Bayāzīd al-Bistāmī sent him to study when he was young. She sent him to a school to study and the teacher, on the first day, was reciting a verse from Surah Luqmān:

وَوَصَّيْنَا الْإِنسَانَ بِوَالِدَيْهِ حَمَلَتْهُ أُمُّهُ وَهْنًا عَلَى وَهْنٍ وَفِصَالُهُ فِي عَامَيْنِ أَنِ اشْكُرْ لِي وَلِوَالِدَيْكَ إِلَيَّ الْمَصِيرُ

wa waṣayna al-insān bi wālīdayhi iḥsānan ḥamalathu ummuhu wahnan 'alā wahnin wa fiṣālihi fī 'amayn an ishkur lī wa li-walīdayka ilayyā al-maṣīr

And We have enjoined on man (to be good) to his parents: In travail upon travail did his mother bear him, and in years twain was his weaning. (Hear the command), "Show gratitude to Me and to your parents: to Me is (your final) Goal."[149]

Luqmān ﷺ was teaching his son that Allāh ﷻ advised human beings to look after their parents and to take care of them. When Bayāzīd heard this verse, he immediately left the school and went to his mother.

She said, "Why are you coming back early?"

He said, "I cannot continue now."

"Did the teacher scold you?" she asked. "Did he beat you or do something else to you?"

"No," said Bayāzīd. "He recited a verse of Surah Luqmān, and Allāh ﷻ is saying to take care of you."

She was confused and asked her son to explain.

---

[149] Sūrah Luqmān, 31:14.

He recited the verse to her and said, "Allāh ﷻ is asking me to fufill my responsibility to my parents and He is asking me to fufill my responsibility to Him. But I cannot be the protector of two homes. I have only one heart. So, I am coming to you, my mother. If you release me from my responsibility to you, I will be able to fufill my responsibility to my Lord. If you want me to do that, then you have to ask the Lord on my behalf to release me from my responsibility to you. Only then can I focus on my responsibility to Him."

Though he was still just a child, Bayāzīd was in a spiritual trance. When his mother saw this and heard his words, she began to cry.

"O my son, I am releasing you from your responsibility to me," she said. "Go in your way and protect the House of Allāh — the house that He referred to when He said:

وسعني أرضي ولا سمائي ولكن وسعني قلب عبدي المؤمن

> *mā wasi'anī samā'ī wa lā arīi wa lākin wasi'anī qalbī 'abdī al-mu'min.*
>
> Neither My sky nor My earth can contain Me, but the heart of My believing servant contains Me.' You are right. You cannot divide your attention; your focus must be one."

That is an example of the perfect guide. Bayāzīd did not want to be away from his Lord for one second. O you who believe and are pious, accompany such trustworthy people. You cannot be like that, but you can be with those who are.

When Bayāzīd al-Bistāmī's mother freed him from his responsibility to her, he was able to direct his heart completely toward Allāh ﷻ. Before that, he could not because he wanted to make his mother happy. If his mother did not release him from that obligation, he would never have left her.

The Prophet ﷺ said, "Paradise is under the feet of mothers." Bayāzīd knew that if he sincerely devoted himself to his mother that would take him there.

Who among us is making his mother happy? Today, when children are still teenagers, they run from their mothers and go to live in dormitories. Bayāzīd's mother freed him not so he could run off and spend his time in discos and nightclubs, but so that he could advance spiritually and become her guide to Allāh ﷻ. She also knew her responsibility to her Lord, and so she did as as ibnat 'Imran, the mother of the Virgin Mary, who said:

إِذْ قَالَتِ امْرَأَةُ عِمْرَانَ رَبِّ إِنِّي نَذَرْتُ لَكَ مَا فِي بَطْنِي مُحَرَّرًا فَتَقَبَّلْ مِنِّي إِنَّكَ أَنتَ السَّمِيعُ الْعَلِيمُ

Idh qālati imrātu 'imrāna rabbī innī nadhartu laka mā fi baṭnī muḥarraran fa taqabbal minnī innaka anta as-samī'u 'l-'alīm

Behold! a woman of 'Imrān said: "O my Lord! I do dedicate unto You what is in my womb for Your special service. So accept this of me: For You hearest and knowest all things."[150]

She made an oath, offering the child that was in her belly to Allāh ﷻ that he might follow His Way. When she delivered a girl, she remained true to her promise and released her to Allāh ﷻ, even though she was a girl. Allāh ﷻ provided for that girl in her niche and made her the mother of *Sayyīdinā* 'Isa ﷺ.

When *Sayyīdinā* Bayāzīd al-Bistāmī received that permission from his mother, he dedicated himself to pleasing his Lord. He said, "*Yā Rabbī*, I am coming to your door!"

Later, he related the story of his spiritual journey:

At the beginning of my life, Allāh ﷻ made me stand at the door of the scholars. I accompanied the '*ulamā* for a long time and learned from them all the knowledge of Islamic law (*Sharī'ah*) until my ego began to whisper, 'Now you have reached the

[150] Sūrat Āli 'Imrān [The Family of 'Imrān], 3::35.

highest level of knowledge. You do not need more than that. You have become a gnostic of the highest order.' I reached a place where I saw too many others like me standing at that door and waiting for it to open. Too many of these scholars were crowded into the same place and I could not find a way to reach the door. All of them were struggling to be the first to enter. I did not find a place to put my feet because of their great number (*Wa lām arā li nafsī mawḍiʿ*). I decided it was impossible to get in.

I realized that knowledge (*ʿilm*) and divine understanding (*maʿrifah*) is worthless if it is not real and acquired through the actual tasting of it. I was thinking that knowledge and scholarly reasoning (*ijtihād*) were real, but I learned that by themselves they are not. I saw that I was like everyone else waiting outside that door, and I saw that door was not opening. Thus, I realized I had not yet reached the truth, the reality (*ḥaqīqah*), the knowledge of certainty (*ʿilm al-yaqīn*), the eye of certainty (*ʿayn al-yaqīn*), the reality of reality (*ḥaqq al-yaqīn*). I knew there had to be another way, so I began to follow the backroads.

I found myself following those who are worshippers, those who are constantly praying (*al-muṣalīn fi 'l-jamaʿāt*). I came to every prayer and I never missed even the first *takbīr* of my five in congregation (*jamaʿat*) for a long time. As soon as the imam said, 'Allāh u Akbar,' I was there, five times a day. Then another vision came to me, and I saw that I was in the midst of a huge crowd at a door similar to that of the scholars. Before this door, everyone was prostrating. Once again, I could not find a place to put my head, and once again, this door did not open. I knew that I would never reach that door, so I left them and went away.

I decided to go with those who are always fasting (*ṣā'imūn*). I fasted the whole year with them. I ate and drank with them at the fast-breaking meal (*ifṭār*) every evening and at the pre-dawn meal (*sahūr*) each morning until I once again found myself facing a similar door, this one surrounded by so many fasting people that I could find no place to put my feet. Once again, I crept away.

Then I went to Mecca and I began to circle (*ṭawāf*) the Kaʿbah. I continued this rite for many years with every pilgrim that came. I persisted in my circumambulation for many years until I again had vision, this time of pilgrims lined up before a similar door. Each was asking that it be opened and I could not find a place to put my feet. In that vision, Allāh ﷻ showed me all of these pilgrims standing before that door crying, "*Labayk Allāhuma labayk, labayk la sharīk lah.*" They were coming from every far place, putting on the seemless cloth (*iḥrām*), coming to the House of Allāh and asking for entrance before that door. Yet again, that door never opened.

Then Allāh ﷻ led me to those who are struggling against their egos (*jihād an–nafs*). I was fighting along with the others who were fighting sitting in association and trying to reach as far as they could. Yet, in the end, I found myself at a similar door with all of them standing there, carrying their spiritual swords against their egos, but there were too many of them that I could not reach my Lord's Divine Presence. Once again, I realized that this was not going to be the way, that Allāh ﷻ had something else destined for me.

So, I went into my room, into my prayer niche, and I said, "O my Lord, send your mercy on me. I am confused. I do not know what to do. Put me in a situation there is no competition, as I cannot compete[151]. Guide me to a place where there is not so much competition, where it is not so crowded. Do not send me to another place filled with people who have already surpassed me, who are already stronger than me, who I can never hope to pass."

I was asking with a burning heart, until I heard a voice, saying, "*Yā* Bayāzīd. No one can approach Me with something that does not belong to Me. You have to approach Me with

[151] Competition is difficult. When you compete with other people it, it makes you arrogant.

something that belongs to Me." He said, "you cannot come with something that is not for Me. You have to come with something that does not belong to My description."

That means Allāh wants His servant to approach Him by means of something that belongs solely to creation, the Lord is above that. It is a characteristic that does not belong to Lordship. The servant must use such a characteristic as a means of approach. It means, "Prayer is for Me, fasting is for Me, and supererogatory worship is for Me. But you have to come to Me through those attributes that belong to human beings throught the taste of an experience you approach Me."

Bayāzīd said, "O Allāh ! What is that thing that is not Yours by which I can come with it to You and You will not let anyone reach You without coming through it? Teach me." Then I heard a voice saying, "*Yā* Bayāzīd, *laysa lī fāqatun wa lā faqrun*. I have no needs and I am not poor.'"

Allāh is al-Ghanī, He is the Rich. *Faqr*, poverty, cannot be used to describe Allāh . You cannot describe Him with *fāqah*, neediness.

> "You have to come through that. There is nothing I am in need of from creation and I have nothing to do with poverty. If anyone wants to come to Me, then this is the way to come."

I said, "*Yā Rabbī,* show me these people who are impoverished and in need and You are not in need of them."

I looked and I saw that there are very few people who are poor that are are coming to their Lord asking to approach Him through their need[152]. So I followed the way of spiritual poverty

[152] People do not want to be poor. They want to be rich. That is why poor people do not approach Allah ﷻ through their need. Their mind is playing with them. Shaytan is telling them, "You have to be rich." What Bayazid is referring to then is not material poverty, but spiritual poverty. He was coming to his Lord saying, "*Yā Rabbī,* I am coming with complete helplessness to Your door. I am not coming to you like a scholar proud of what I know, nor like a fasting person proud of what I have given up for you, nor like a pilgrim proud of the journey I

until I came to a door like the others, but this one had very few waiting before it. There was plenty of room for me to stand.

Then the voice said to me, "Now you must experience poverty. You have only grasped the theory. So, go and make yourself a trash bin for My servants. Carry their difficulties and accept all of their garbage.[153] Be a rubbish dump and show your complete humbleness and poverty to Me. Then I will open to you My door."

From that moment on, I made myself a trash bin for all humanity and I promised my Lord, "O Allāh, I will come to you with poverty and weakness." From that moment, every second of my life became a miracle (*karāmah*). These miracles are beyond the reach of everyone except those who accept to show weakness and helplessness, who are willing to demonstrate their poverty to their Lord and are patient with it.

From *Sayyīdinā* Bayāzīd al-Bistāmī's righteous example, we can see the difficult experiences a perfect guide must endure in order to reach Allāh's door.

The Holy Qur'an says:

وَاللَّهُ الْغَنِيُّ وَأَنتُمُ الْفُقَرَاء وَإِن تَتَوَلَّوْا يَسْتَبْدِلْ قَوْمًا غَيْرَكُمْ ثُمَّ لَا يَكُونُوا أَمْثَالَكُم

---

have made to Your House." He had become one of those rare people who cast away everything and come to their Lord with nothing, those pure souls who have turned their backs on *dunyā*. He did not find many like him waiting before that door.

[153] Poverty teaches humility. Homeless people eat from garbage cans in the street, just like cats. They are happy with whatever they find. Allah ﷻ took pride and arrogance from them. They go and eat from the garbage and Allah ﷻ gives them immunity from all of the diseases that are in that discarded food. We cannot eat that. We are very delicate. If anyone ate from a spoon, we cannot eat form it. Yet, they eat what other people have already tasted and thrown away. They are experiencing poverty, and Allah ﷻ gave them immunity from sickness and immunity from Shaytan. You do not see that, but that is the reality.

w'Allāhu 'l-ghanīyyu wa antumu 'l-fuqarāu wa in tatawallaw yastabdil qawman ghayrakum thumma lā yakūnū amthālakum

But Allāh is free of all wants, and it is ye that are needy. If ye turn back (from the Path), He will substitute in your stead another people; then they would not be like you![154]

Allāh ﷻ is the Endlessly Rich and you are poor. If you do not accept this reality, Allāh will take you and bring another people in your stead. Bayāzīd al-Bistāmī accepted that reality of spiritual poverty, and that is how he became a perfect guide.

Spiritual Poverty

Spiritual poverty means approaching your Lord through humility. You must not strut with your head up, but walk with your head always down. This is necessary if you hope to find a perfect guide and be guided by him to what you need and what is needed from you in order to reach the Door of the Divine Presence. Of course, you must practice the Five Pillars of Islam—you must testify to your faith, perform the five prayers, fast during Ramadan, pay the poor-tax and perform the Pilgrimage to Mecca if you are able—but these alone will not open that door. You can only reach that door through humility.

Spiritual poverty, *faqr,* is to be completely hopeless of having anything. Then you can approach Allāh ﷻ with your extreme need. You must demonstrate to your Lord that you know that He is Rich and everything other than He is poor and in need of Him. You must accept that all of your actions (*'amal*) amount to nothing. That is why the Prophet ﷺ was worshiping day and night until his feet were swollen.

Fa 'l-faqru hunā laysa al-faqr māḍḍīyan

"the meaning of poverty here is not physical poverty."

[154] Sūrah Muḥammad, 47:38.

This spiritual poverty means accepting that you are spiritually bankrupt, that you have absolutely nothing and are utterly dependent on your Lord for everything. You must not congratulate yourself for your acts of piety and worship. Rather, you must ensure that these actions—all of your prayers, your fasting and other acts of worship—do not become a source of pride by reminding yourself that, even in these actions you remain entirely dependent on Allāh ﷻ for everything. In your feelings, in your dealing with other people, in every movement of your life you have to maintain a connection with your Lord. You must keep this connection in your heart, even when you are dealing with other people. *Antum al-fuqarā—"ye are the poor."*

The best knowledge is not that which makes you proud of yourself, but the knowledge that makes you realize you are utterly needy of Allāh's support. How does that happen? By freeing the soul and the spirit from the ego. As Bayāzīd himself said, that comes from forgetting the ego and remembering the Fashioner of the ego (*maḥw an-nafs ʿinda dhikr bārī an-nafs*). You must forget your self and remember the One who created your self. He fashioned it in the best of ways. If you return to Him with humility, He will give you the strength to let go of your ego so that you can ride it instead of it riding you. This comes from remembering your Lord, Who has the power to weave your self in different ways and purify it.

Bayāzīd was no longer worshipping Allāh ﷻ in the hope of receiving a reward; he was worshipping his Lord as a humble servant. He was worshipping because he had no choice, because he was happy to be nothing but a servant to Allāh ﷻ. Today, people are worshipping Allāh ﷻ to save themselves from hellfire, but Bayāzīd was not like that. He said, "It is not my choice, whether He puts me in Hell or in Paradise, regardless I have to be a true and grateful servant."

The Prophet ﷺ said that he was never happier than when Allāh ﷻ called him "servant" in Surat al-Isrā:

سُبْحَانَ الَّذِي أَسْرَى بِعَبْدِهِ لَيْلاً مِّنَ الْمَسْجِدِ الْحَرَامِ إِلَى الْمَسْجِدِ الأَقْصَى
الَّذِي بَارَكْنَا حَوْلَهُ لِنُرِيَهُ مِنْ آيَاتِنَا إِنَّهُ هُوَ السَّمِيعُ البَصِيرُ

subḥān-alladhī asrā bi ʿabdihi laylan mina 'l-masjidi 'l-ḥarāmi ila 'l-masjidi al-aqṣā 'Lladhī bāraknā ḥawlahu li-nurīyahu min ayātinā innahu hūwa as-samīʿu 'l-baṣīr.

Glory to (Allāh) Who did take His servant for a Journey by night from the Sacred Mosque to the farthest Mosque, whose precincts We did bless, in order that We might show him some of Our Signs: for He is the One Who heareth and seeth (all things).[155]

This level of servanthood is the station of slavery, *maqām al-ʿubudīyyah*. You must be a complete slave to your Lord. A slave has nothing. He is in the hand of his Master. His Master tells him what to do, and he does it.

Station of Slavery

Once, they came looking for Bayāzīd. He told them that Bayāzīd was not there. They asked Bayāzīd, "Who are you then?"

He said, "I do not know. I forgot my name. I am not Bayāzīd anymore."

"Then who are you?" they asked.

"I am a slave to my Lord," he said. "That is what I know. I do not know who Bayāzīd is. If you find him, ask him. He is gone."

"Where has he gone?" they asked.

"Why are you asking me?" he said.

"Why do you not travel?" they continued.

"My Friend is not traveling, so why should I travel?" he replied. "I am already there."

---

155 Sūratu 'l-Isrā [The Night Journey], 17:1.

Bayāzīd said that because he had already made the journey to his Lord. When he reached that destination he said:

Yā *Rabbī*! You created creation. It is Your creation, not anyone else's. They are all Your shadow. So, why have You put a Balance on Judgment Day to see what they have done? You created them. What You have done is perfect, so when You weigh what You have done, it will be perfect and they are safe."

You put that Path (*ṣirāṭ*) over hellfire, and they must cross it on Resurrection Day to reach Paradise. We are Your shadow[156] and Your image. You walk there and pass before us; You will find us there with You.

That is how Allāh ﷻ brought him nearer and nearer.

Bayāzīd said:

I divorced *dunyā* three times and went to my Lord by myself, with only the guidance of my shaykh and the guidance of my Prophet. I told *dunyā*, "In no way I will return to return to you; I am only going to Allāh ﷻ." I never looked back to what I had of positions (*jāh*) nor to what Allāh ﷻ had granted me of knowledge (*ʿilm*).

Bayāzīd had been a great scholar (*ʿalim*) in his life and held high positions. He said, "I am not looking back. I am going to my Lord. And I am praying that there is no one left to me except You. There is no way to go right or left, only to You."

He continued:

At that moment, Allāh's words came to my heart: "O My servant, I accepted your *duāʿ*."

When that inspiration came to my heart, He made me to forget completely myself. I no longer knew who I was, I knew only that I was a servant to my Lord. And the entire creation was displayed between my hands. He brought the whole *dunyā* before me. I left it, but as soon as He accepted me and it came to my heart that He accepted my prayer, I saw all creation coming to me. But I never looked at it.

---

[156] Allah ﷻ created human beings in His Image.

Allāh ﷻ made *dunyā* a slave to Bayāzīd because he had turned his back on it. He said, "You left *dunyā* and became My slave, so I have made *dunyā* a slave to you."

Bayāzīd said to Allāh ﷻ, "What do I want with *dunyā*? I want You." So Allāh ﷻ said, "Now I give *dunyā* back to you. Separate from yourself and come to Me. You will find Me."

When someone dies, the soul separates from the body (*fāriq ar-rūḥ min al-jasad*). Thus, Allāh ﷻ was saying, "Divorce yourself and come to Me."

Bayāzīd al-Bistāmī demonstrated how to be a perfect shaykh. We know that we have to find and follow such a perfect guide. *Alḥamdulillāh* that Allāh ﷻ guided us to Shaykh Nāẓim.

Salman al-Farsi ؓ : Examplar of Servanthood

Look at *Sayyīdinā* Salmān al-Fārsī. He was the servant of a Zoroastrian, searching for reality. He was with his Lord, but still he was a slave in *dunyā*. Later, he became a slave in a monastery. He said, "I never did anything against the wishes of the monk [his master]. I served him more than I served myself." The Prophet ﷺ was training him even before he met him. He was training Salmān ؓ through his heart.

Training and knowledge of the Prophet that comes through the heart is more powerful than that which comes through a physical meeting. That is why, when he finally came to the Prophet ﷺ, *Sayyīdinā* Muḥammad ﷺ said, "He is from me, Āhl al-Bayt."

When you approach Allāh ﷻ and His Prophet ﷺ through your heart, not looking at anything else, the whole of *dunyā* will come after you, but you will drop it from your heart. Even if you possess all the wealth of this world, you will be bankrupt before your Lord:

يَا أَيُّهَا النَّاسُ أَنتُمُ الْفُقَرَاءُ إِلَى اللَّهِ وَاللَّهُ هُوَ الْغَنِيُّ الْحَمِيدُ

Yā ayyuha an-nāsu antumu'l-fuqarā ila Allāhi w'Allāhu Hūwa al-ghanīyyu 'l-ḥamīd.

O ye men! It is ye that have need of Allāh . But Allāh is the One free of all wants, worthy of all praise.[157]

When you reach that station, you will feel less than the weight of a mosquito.

You may be richer than anyone, but if Allāh ﷻ afflicts you with cancer, what use will all your wealth be to you? There are many rich people who have no health, so we must thank Allāh ﷻ for giving us health. You must show that you are in extreme need to your Lord, even if you have everything.

After long service to several masters, *Sayyīdinā* Salmān ؓ sold himself to some Arabs going to Madina, for he had been informed by his last master that it would be in Madina he would find the last Prophet. He sold himself, gave up everything and sought to go to his Lord. They cheated him and they sold him as a slave to someone else. So he went from being the slave of a Zoroastrian to the servant of a Christian monk to the slave of a Jew. That Jew sold him to another Jew, and he served him faithfully. He did not say, "This is a Zoroastrian. This is a Christian. This is a Jew." He was listening and obeying. He was listening and keeping awareness, *asmaʿū wa āwū,* in the station of "listening and obeying". In the end, the Prophet ﷺ said, "Come, you are part of my family."

What is better than that? When Allāh told Bayāzīd, "Come to Me, I am opening My door to you."

When you come to your Lord through truthfulness (*ṣidq*), you will reach Him as those before you reached Him. The point of all of this is to leave the self and what it desires. You must turn your back on what it likes and forget about yourself completely.

---

[157] Sūratu 'l-Fāṭir, [The Originator], 35:15.

Burden of the Shaykhs

There are many students who try to do things to benefit those around them or to benefit the shaykh, but they are derailed by doubts. They begin to question what they are doing, wondering whether it is of any real benefit, no longer sure if it is right or wrong. They think they left everything in their lives so that they could do what the shaykh wants, what the Prophet ﷺ wants and what Allāh ﷻ wants. They think this will carry them to the Divine Presence. Yet, they begin to doubt this approach, even though they know it is correct.

That is what happened to Imam Ghazālī. He was a great scholar, but he became consumed with doubts until Allāh ﷻ pulled him out.

Sayyīdinā Bayāzīd fell into the same situation. He had pursued all the different paths of worship, but none of them were opening the door to the Divine Presence for him, and so he began to doubt. When he finally found the Way to his Lord, Allāh ﷻ sent him back to *dunyā* and told him to become a trash can for His servants.

Allāh ﷻ said to Bayāzīd, "Learn to carry My servants' burdens and be a scapegoat for them. I sent the Seal of Messengers ﷺ and all his life—until he took his dying breath—he was asking, 'My nation! My nation!' Even in his holy grave, he is asking 'My nation! My Nation!' So, go and say, 'My community! My community!' Those who give their initiation, *baya*ʿ, to you, go and carry their difficulties, burdens and sins."

That is a big burden for the saints, when they seen one of their students doubting or worse, when they see one of their followers speaking badly about them. That is a great difficulty and a tremendous responsibility for them.

TWENTY-THREE

Advice for the Seeker

We ask for support (*madad*). What is *madad*, or in Turkish, *imdād*? It means to ask for help.

When there is a disaster, aid comes to the affected area. Those areas call for help, and they receive it continuously. Aircraft fly in and out 24 hours-a-day with supplies.

We, as individuals, are disaster areas. Our entire system needs rescue.

When you are sick or hurt, your body's alarm system sounds. Pain is like a ringing bell, telling you that something is wrong. You need to fix it. All of these alarms are ringing in our bodies. In the presence of the shaykh, he can see them. However, we need to ask for his help and support. If you do not ask him for aid, he will leave you to struggle more and more until you finally remember to ask. Then he sends his support to you. This is the *madad* that comes quickly to rescue you.

We as individuals must ask for *madad*. That is why you see Mawlana Shaykh Nāẓim saying, *"Dastūr yā sayyīdī madad."*[158] He is asking for the support of Grandshaykh, and from him, through all of the Grandshaykhs of the Golden Chain back to the Prophet ﷺ. That rescue must come nonstop. The aid must flow around the clock. When the *madad* comes, the aid comes with it. The *imdād* is the aid. The *madad* is the act. *Yamudduk ash-Shaykh bi madadihi*—the shaykh supports you with his spiritual aid.

This support is for us, and for all of the *murīds* of the shaykh. Each one needs something different. Each one needs a different kind of rescue, just as different disasters in different countries require different types of aid. In New Orleans, there was a hurricane and flood while in Pakistan there was an earthquake.

---

[158] Your permission O my master, your support I seek.

Each situation is different. What you, as a victim, need depends on where you are and what sort of disaster has befallen you. Each person is a disaster area unto themselves. Each one of us is contaminated by our own internal floods and hurricanes. Thus, each of us needs *madad,* support from the shaykh, and that support must be specific and private for him or her individual situation.

The Shaykh has to receive mystical inspirations (*wāridāt*). These are like heavenly telephone calls (*al-hātif ar-rabbānī*) that come to his heart and tell the shaykh what is necessary for the *murīd*. When those messages descend, they carry the manifestations that are able to rescue that person. Thus, the shaykh knows what he has to do for each of his followers. He becomes a nexus of information, and he can receive all of these messages simultaneously.

Wāridāt, inspirations come to the shaykh's heart, which is the center of information, and the shaykh will look at what kind of aid he needs to send. Then he sends it. This does not take more than one moment. He can reach all of his followers with what each one of them needs in a single second. That is heavenly power, the power of "Be, and it is" (*Kun fa-yakūn*). *Awlīyāullāh,* the power that Allāh ﷻ gave to them, there is no way to understand it.

Know Your Limits

Sayyīdinā Muḥyīddīn Ibn 'Arabī, Allāh ﷻ gave him the ability that in five minutes he could correct the heart of everyone on Earth. He was given the knowledge of all human beings, name by name, according to Grandshaykh. At the highest level of his journey, he was given the authority to turn the whole world to Islam in five minutes. Allāh ﷻ gave that power to Muḥyīddīn Ibn 'Arabī. That was his covenant (*'ahd*) with his Lord when his spirit was created, and it was revealed to him as he ascended in his journey to the Divine Presence. Yet, it never happened.

Grandshaykh explained the secret of why it never happened. It is a lesson that demonstrates that, at the higher levels, everything is in discipline and nothing exceed its limits.

In his life, Muḥyīddīn Ibn ʿArabī was imprisoned because the scholars came against him because of what he had written which appeared to them to differ with the Divine Law (Sharīʿah). They could not understand what he was writing, and they forced the king to arrest him even though the king loved the shaykh.

Out of that love, the king sent his only daughter with food to Muḥyīddīn Ibn ʿArabī. There were no guards present. She would go to the prison and deliver the food. That means that there was an acceptance from him that he is allowing his daughter to meet with him. One day, after she brought him his food, Muḥyīddīn Ibn ʿArabī married her and consummated that marriage.

At that time, it was written that he would use his miraculous power to go out from that prison, to pass through its walls and sit under a dry fig tree. Muḥyīddīn Ibn ʿArabī ibn Arabi had that power before, but it was not yet written for him to use it.

The king looked for Muḥyīddīn in the prison and could not find him. When he finally found him sitting by the fig tree he said, "What did you do? You married my daughter."

Muḥyīddīn Ibn ʿArabī looked at the withered fig tree. Suddenly, it became green, flowered and then burst forth with fruit.

"I was ordered to marry, and I was married by the Prophet ﷺ and Allāh ﷻ was Witness," he said. "That is *qadā-ullāh,* Allāh's Will. As soon as I sit by the fig tree, it gets green and gives fruit, that is the *qadā-ullāh.*"

That action was not what prevented him from transforming the whole world to Islam. It was Allāh's Order *amrullāh,* to marry the princess. The action that prevented Muḥyīddīn Ibn ʿArabī involved something else.

One night it came to his heart, "I want to spend this night with the most ascetic person on earth to speak and to exchange views about asceticism (*zuhd*)." He looked and looked. Finally, he found the most ascetic person in the world and it was a woman.

With *bismillāhi 'r-raḥmāni 'r-Raḥīm,* he was in her house, and from ʿIshā to Fajr, late night to dawn, they were both exchanging views about asceticism. Fajr prayer came. He made ablution, she made ablution and they prayed.

As soon as they said *as-salām ʿalaykum wa raḥmatullah,* the spirit (*rūḥānīyyah*) of the Prophet ﷺ appeared and said, "What is this? You are breaking my law (*Sharīʿah*). Whoever breaks my *Sharīʿah,* his hand is cut."

The first time, he was not violating *Sharīʿah,* because it was *amrullāh,* the Divine Order. The second time he stayed with the lady ascetic, who was not his wife, and so he broke the sacred law. That was what prevented Muḥyīddīn Ibn ʿArabī ibn Arabi from turning the whole world to Islam.

How many times are we breaking *Sharīʿah* every day? This shows how easy it is to break your covenant with Allāh ﷻ, your covenant with the Prophet ﷺ and your convenant with the shaykh. Even a small thing that you do not think is an issue is enough to do that. These things that we are doing are putting us in risky situations (*mankūbah*).

Fortunately, these *wāridāt,* inspirations, that are coming to the heart of the shaykh from the Prophet ﷺ inform him so that he may guide each of us and carry our burdens. Grandshaykh said, "When I am in *sajdah* in *ṣalāt an-najāt,* the *murīds* come to me one by one, and whatever *ʿibādah* I performed I share with them and take on their burdens. I go to the Prophet ﷺ saying, '*Yā Rasūlullāh,* I am taking the *murīds*' burdens.' And that is not only for those *murīds* I know (physically), but for all of those who are written as my responsibility. I carry them all in the *sajdah*."

This is not to discourage us, but to encourage us. We know we are utterly sick and in utter despair of success. We are so lost that we need support. To say, "I am not special. I am nothing," is what the shaykh likes to hear. By yourself you are nothing. Your movement is like that of an ant. When the shaykh dresses you, then you become something. We think that we need everyone to respect us and consider us this or that. That is wrong. We must think that we are more in need than everyone else.

Those who have been given authority are in far more need of support than the others. It is like the police. They take care of us all. Our safety is their responsibility. We sleep happily, but they are always dealing with problems, 24 hours a day. Those who have authority have the responsibility to check those under them.

Do Not Backbite

The Prophet ﷺ told his Companions, "Do not backbite." Grandshaykh said that anyone who heard a story about someone else two hours ago or more must not repeat it, lest they incur Allāh's Curse.

Our nature is inclined towards backbiting. We like to tell stories about people that happened, even if it was a thousand years ago. We even take pleasure in recounting the story of Adam ﷺ!

However, there are some stories that Allāh ﷻ does want us to tell. As He said in the Holy Qur'an:

لاَّ يُحِبُّ اللهُ الْجَهْرَ بِالسُّوَءِ مِنَ الْقَوْلِ إِلاَّ مَن ظُلِمَ وَكَانَ اللهُ سَمِيعًا عَلِيمًا

Lā yuḥibbu Allāhu'l-jahra bi 's-sūwi mina 'l-qawli illa man ẓulima wa kāna Allāhu samī'an 'alīma.

Allāh loveth not that evil should be noised abroad in public speech, except where injustice hath been done; for Allāh is He who heareth and knoweth all things.[159]

Allāh ﷻ does not like us to bring up anything bad, or to speak against anything publicly except under one condition:

[159] Sūratu 'n-Nisā [Women], 4:148.

When you have been oppressed (*illa man ẓulim*) or when someone accuses you of something that you did not do, then you must bring it up.

If something bad happened and it might not have affected anyone, let it go. There is no need to discuss it. However, when you have been falsely accused of something that you did not do, then you have been oppressed or wronged, Allāh ﷻ likes you to expose that. You have to defend yourself, because rumors move like the wind. They are very fast, because Shaytan carries them. That is why you must speak in such cases, because Allāh ﷻ wants you to stop them from spreading. When you bring it up and clarify the situation, you make the person who spread the false rumor repent. In this way you save him, for then Allāh ﷻ will change his bad deeds into good ones.

In his commentary, ʿAbd Allāh Yusuf Ali says:"for all wrong or injustice must be corrected openly, to prevent its recurrence." When something affects you, your family or your community, you have to bring it up. You have to defend yourself. Accompany a perfect guide and he will teach you when to bring something up and when to remain silent.

When the shaykh's followers reach a certain level, he will yell at them. That is a sign that they have become real students, not just lovers of the shaykh, *muḥibbūn*. That is why Grandshaykh used to say the time when the *murīd* should be most happy is when the shaykh shouts at him and his heart does not change towards his master.

Even if the shaykh throws the student out of his presence, the disciple's heart must not waver. He must be happy that the shaykh is still carrying him and carrying his difficulties. If he does this—if his heart does not change—the shaykh will be happen with him.

Know that when the shaykh yells at his *murīd* like this, what he is saying may be for the benefit of others among his followers. Sometimes in Arab countries, when a mother thinks her daughter-in-law is not listening to her, she will shout at her neighbor so that the girl can hear and understand. Or she might talk to a bird in a cage or even the wall in order to teach her daughter-in-law.

Awlīyā do that. They make one of their best *murīds* the target for their wrath, because they know that he or she will not run away. When the *walī* shouts at that high one, the others must listen and correct themselves. When the shaykh does this, that senior *murīd* becomes like a wagon that all of the other students can jump onto and ride. So, be that bridge for other students, so that they will learn from your behavior toward your shaykh. If they do, they can move from the rank of lover to that of *murīd*.

When Mawlana shouts at someone, you think that person is bad. In fact, he is good, because he can carry that shouting and does not run away.

Just as Allāh ﷻ does not like backbiting, the shaykh does not like having to bring out the faults of his followers. He only does so when they are oppressing themselves. That is a special understanding of the aforementioned verse of the Holy Qur'an.

Three Nails

Listen closely to what the shaykh says and you will reach the level of *murīd,* seeker. To do that, you must always remember the three pieces of advice that Grandshaykh said should be nailed into the head of every disciple.

The first is this: If the shaykh gives you a bucket and tells you to empty the ocean with it, do not look at the bucket and think, "How can I empty the ocean with this?" Go and do it. He tells you that your trust is at the bottom of the sea, but you do not know how to dive. What can you do? Go to the ocean and wade in the waves. Then learn to swim. Then learn to dive.

The second is this: If the shaykh gives you a broken shovel and tells you to dig to the bottom of the Seven Earths, do not question—start digging. It may be that you will hit a cave or a tunnel, and that will take you far.

The third is this: If the shaykh tells you that your trust is in the west and you are in the east, go as fast as you can. Even if you can only begin crawling in that direction like an ant, maybe a strong wind will come like a tornado and carry you to where you need to be. Maybe you will ride like Aladdin on a magic carpet.

Remember these three things when the shaykh yells at you, if you want to become a real *murīd*. Then the shaykh will be happy with you. If you remember these three things, they will carry you to the first plantation of the shaykh.

Three Plantations

The Shaykh has three plantations, and each one is of a higher level. In the first plantation, the shaykh grows annual crops like corn, wheat or barley. He sows his seeds there at the beginning of the season, and they grow throughout the year until they are ready to be harvested. There is no need to water them, but they only produce one crop.

These are the newcomers, the lovers who are running around. They are not training, but they love the shaykh, and so they come to see him and go. He keeps them happy.

When you are a beginner in the Way, a seeker on the path of Sufism, the shaykh will plant in your heart the seeds of *dhikrullāh*. He will tell you to recite "Allāh, Allāh" 1,500 times. You say, "That is enough. I have too many things to do in my life. I am busy with work." That is one season, and it is harvested as *dhikrullāh*. When it grows, he cuts it. Then you eat it and run away. When you come back another time, he plants the seeds again.

However, there are others who show progress and maintain their interest. If you are one of these students, the shaykh does not plant corn or wheat in your heart. He says, "Here is good soil. I will water it year-round. This student has a good heart, not a rocky heart." Such a one will advance to the level of Prepared, *musta'id*.

This is the second plantation, where Shaykh cultivates his fruit trees. There, the shaykh will plant in your heart the seeds of the fruit that he prepared in his nursery. The Shaykh plants the seed of that fruit tree in your heart and gives you treatment to prepare you before planting you in that orchard. Then the shaykh will give you more *awrād*, 10,000 "Allāh, Allāh" and 15,000 *ṣalawāt*. Those trees give fruit year after year. There is no need to replant. However, they only give fruit at harvest time.

If you are clever and ask for more, you will reach the third level, which is the level of the *murīd*. Then the shaykh will raise in you the third plantation, the orchard where he keeps those trees that bear fruit all year round. With the permission of Allāh ﷻ and His Prophet ﷺ, the shaykh will plant in your heart the Tree of Knowledge, the tree that is everlasting and ever-bearing. That eternal knowledge will be placed in your heart, and they will give you a kingdom that will never disappear. This is the Tree of Paradise that Allāh ﷻ mentioned in the Holy Qur'an:

فَوَسْوَسَ إِلَيْهِ الشَّيْطَانُ قَالَ يَا آدَمُ هَلْ أَدُلُّكَ عَلَى شَجَرَةِ الْخُلْدِ وَمُلْكٍ لَّا يَبْلَى

Fawaswasa ilayhi ash-shayṭānu qāla yā ādamu hal adulluka ʿala shajarati 'l-khuldi wa mulkin lā yablā.

But Satan whispered evil to him: he said, "O Adam! Shall I lead you to the Tree of Eternity and to a kingdom that never decays?"[160]

Allāh ﷻ told Adam ؑ not to eat from that tree because he was not yet ready for that gift. If he had not listened to Shaytan and had waited, Allāh ﷻ would have given it to him later. But he did not listen. Similarly, the shaykh may not give you something

[160] Sūrah ṬāḤā 20:120.

because you are not yet ready for it. He might prohibit something and tell you not to reach for it.

When he gives you the Tree of Knowledge, you will not just be able to teach one student or one community, you will be able to teach the whole population. Look at Mawlana Shaykh. He has students around the whole world because of the knowledge that Allāh ﷻ places in his heart.

You become like a roaring ocean that is without end. Whoever follows you, you will show them the way of *istiqāmah,* standing forth. The Shaykh will show you the Way to that ocean just as a stream flows into a river that flows into the sea. When it reaches the ocean, what happens to it? That is true submission.

Seclusions are like a river, rushing and pouring with sound and fury, but carrying you to the heart of the shaykh. That means the will of the Prophet ﷺ and the Will of Allāh ﷻ. Then they take you to the presence of the Prophet ﷺ and, finally, to the Divine Presence itself.

They never show you other than that, for the true shaykh is moderate and loving. He gives his love to all humanity. Our goal should be to produce a good harvest, not just in one season, but in every season.

May Allāh ﷻ make a Way for us. May Allāh ﷻ forgive us. *Bi-ḥurmati 'l-Fāṭiḥah.*

Glossary

'abd (pl. 'Ibād): lit. slave, servant.

'Abd Allāh: Lit., "servant of God"

Abū Bakr aṣ-Ṣiddīq ﷺ: one the closest Companions to the Prophet ﷺ, his father-in-law, who shared the Hijrah with him. After the Prophet's death, he was elected as the first caliph (successor) to the Prophet ﷺ. He is known as one of the most saintly of the Prophet's Companions.

Abū Yazīd/Bayāzīd Bistāmī: A great ninth century *walī* and master in the Naqshbandi Golden Chain.

adab: good manners, proper etiquette.

adhān: call to prayer.

al: Arabic definite article, "the"

'alamīn: world; universes.

alḥamdūlillāh: Praise God.

'Alī ibn Abī Ṭālib ﷺ: the cousin of the Prophet ﷺ, married to his daughter Fāṭimah and fourth caliph of the Prophet ﷺ.

alif: first letter of Arabic alphabet ا.

'Alīm, al-: the Knower, a divine attribute

Allāh: proper name for God in Arabic.

Allāhu Akbar: God is Greater.

'amal: good deed (pl. *'amāl*).

amīr (pl., *umarā*): chief, leader, head of a nation or people.

anā: first person singular pronoun

anbīyā: prophets (sing. *nabī*).

'aql: intellect, reason; from the root *'aqila, lit., "to fetter."*

'Arafah: a plain near Mecca where pilgrims gather for the principal rite of Hajj.

'arif: knower, gnostic; one who has reached spiritual knowledge of his Lord.

'ārifūn' bi 'l-Lāh: knowers of God

Ar-Raḥīm: The Mercy-Giving, Merciful, Munificent, one of Allah's ninety-nine Holy Names

Ar-Raḥmān: The Most Merciful, Compassionate, Beneficent, the most often repeated of Allah's Holy Names.

'arsh, al-: Divine Throne

aṣl: root, origin, basis.

astaghfirullāh: lit. "I seek Allah's forgiveness."

awliyāullāh: saints of Allah (sing. walī).

āyah/āyāt (pl. Ayāt): a verse of the Holy Qur'an.

Āyat al-Kursī*: the Verse of the Throne, a well-known verse from the Qur'an (2:255).*

'Azrā'īl: the Archangel of Death.

Badī' al-: The Innovator; a Divine Name.

Banī Ādam: Children of Ādam; humanity.

Bayt al-Maqdis: the Sacred Mosque in Jerusalem, built at the site where Solomon's Temple was later erected.

Bayt al-Ma'mūr: Much-frequented House; this refers to the Ka'bah of the heavens, which is the prototype of the Ka'bah on earth and is circumambulated by the angels.

baya': pledge; in the context of this book, the pledge of initiation of a disciple (*murid*) to a shaykh.

bismi'l-Lāhi 'r-Raḥmāni 'r-Raḥīm: "In the name of the All-Merciful, the Compassionate"; this is the introductory verse to all the chapters of the Qur'an except the ninth.

Dajjāl: the False Messiah (Antichrist) whom the Prophet ﷺ foretold as coming at the end-time of this world, who will deceive mankind with pretensions of being divine.

dalālah: evidence

dhāt: self / selfhood

dhawq (pl. adhwāq): tasting; technical term referring to the experiential aspect of gnosis.

dhikr: remembrance, mention of God through His Holy Names or phrases of glorification.

ḍīyā: light.

Diwān al-Awlīyā—the gathering of saints with the Prophet ﷺ in the spiritual realm. This takes place every night.

*duā*ʿ: supplication.

dunyā: world; worldly life.

ʿeid: festival; the two major festivals of Islam are ʿEid al-Fitr, marking the completion of Ramadan, and ʿEid al-Adha, the Festival of Sacrifice during the time of Hajj.

farḍ: obligatory worship.

Fātiḥah: Sūratu 'l-Fātiḥah; the opening surah of the Qur'an.

Ghafūr, al-: The Forgiver; a Divine Name.

ghawth: lit. "Helper"; the highest ranking saint the in hierarchy of saints.

ghaybu' l-muṭlaq, al-: the absolute unknown, known only to God.

ghusl: full shower/bath obligated by a state of ritual impurity prior to worship.

Grandshaykh: generally, a *walī* of great stature. In this text, where spelled with a capital G, "Grandshaykh" refers to Mawlana ʿAbd Allāh ad-Daghestani (d. 1973), Mawlana Shaykh Nazim's master.

hā': letter ه

ḥadīth nabawī (pl., ahadith)*: prophetic hadith whose meaning and linguistic expression are those of the Prophet Muḥammad* ﷺ.

ḥadith qudsī: divine saying whose meaning directly reflects the meaning God intended but whose linguistic expression is not Divine Speech as in the Qur'an, it thus differs from a hadith nabawī (see above).

ḥaḍr: present

ḥaywān: animal.

ḥajj: the sacred pilgrimage of Islam obligatory on every mature Muslim once in his/her life.

ḥalāl: permitted, lawful according to the Islamic Shariʿah.

ḥaqīqah, al-: reality of existence; ultimate truth.

ḥaqq: truth

Ḥaqq, al-: the Divine Reality, one of the 99 Divine Names.

ḥarām: forbidden, unlawful.

hāshā: God forbid!

ḥarf: (pl. ḥurūf) letter; Arabic root "edge."

Ḥawā: Eve.

hijrah: emigration.

ḥikmah: wisdom

ḥujjah: proof

hūwa: the pronoun "he," made up of the letters hā' and *wāw in Arabic.*

ʿibādu 'l-Lāh: servants of God

ʿifrīt: a type of Jinn, huge and powerful.

iḥsān: doing good, "It is to worship God as though you see Him; for if you are not seeing Him, He sees you."

ikhlāṣ, al-: sincere devotion

ilāh (pl. *āliha):* idols or god(s)

ilāhīyya: divinity

ilhām—Divine inspiration sent to *awlīyāullah.*

ʿilm: knowledge, science.

ʿilmu 'l-awrāq: knowledge of papers

ʿilmu 'l-adhwāq: knowledge of taste

ʿilmu 'l-ḥurūf: science of letters

ʿilmu 'l-kalām: scholastic theology.

ʿilmun ladunnī: "Divinely-inspired" knowledge

imān: faith, belief.

imām: leader of congregational prayer; an advanced scholar followed by a large community.

Injīl: New Testament.

insān: humanity; pupil of the eye.

insānu 'l-kāmil, al-: the Perfect Man; the Prophet Muhammad ﷺ.

irādatullāh: the Will of God.

irshād: spiritual guidance

ism: name

isma-Llāh: name of God

isrā': night journey; used here in reference to the night journey of the Prophet Muḥammad ﷺ.

Isrā'fīl: Archangel Rafael, in charge of blowing the Final Trumpet.

jalāl: majesty

jamāl: beauty

jamaʿa: group, congregation.

Jannah: Paradise.

jihād: to struggle in God's Path.

Jibrīl: Archangel Gabriel of revelation.

Jinn: a species of living beings, created out of fire, invisible to most humans. Jinn can be Muslims or non-Muslims.

Jumuʿah: Friday congregational prayer, held in a large mosque.

Kaʿbah: the first House of God, located in Mecca, Saudi Arabia to which pilgrimage is made and which is faced in the five daily prayers.

kāfir: unbeliever.

Kalāmullāh al-Qadīm: lit. Allah's Ancient Words, viz. the Holy Qur'an.

kalimat at-tawḥīd: lā ilāha illa-Llāh: "There is no god but Allah (the God)."

khalīfah: deputy

Khāliq, al-: the Creator, one of the 99 Divine Names.

khalq: creation

khuluq: conduct, manners.

Kirāmun Kātabīn: Honored Scribe angels.

lā: no; not; not existent; the particle of negation.

lā ilāha illa-Llāh Muḥammadun rasūlullāh: there is no deity except Allah, Muhammad is the Messenger of Allah.

lām: Arabic letter ل

al-Lawḥ al Maḥfūẓ: the Preserved Tablets.

laylat al-isrā' wa 'l-miʿrāj: the Night Journey and Ascension of the Prophet Muḥammad ﷺ to Jerusalem and to the seven heavens.

Madīnātu 'l-Munawwarah: the Illuminated city; city of Prophet Muḥammad ﷺ. Referred to as Madina.

mahr: dowry given by the groom to the bride.

malakūt: divine kingdom.

Malik, al-: the Sovereign, a Divine Name.

Mālik: Archangel of Hell.

maqām: spiritual station; tomb of a prophet, messenger or saint.

maʿrifah: gnosis.

māshāAllāh: it is as Allah Wills.

Mawlānā: lit. "our master" or "our patron," referring to an esteemed person.

maẓhar: place of disclosure.

miḥrāb: prayer niche.

Mikā'īl: Archangel of rain.

mīzān: the Scale which weighs the actions of human beings on Judgment Day.

mīm: Arabic letter م

minbar: pulpit.

miʿrāj: the ascension of the Prophet Muḥammad ﷺ from Jerusalem to the seven heavens.

Muḥammadun rasūlu 'l-Lāh: Muḥammad is the Messenger of God.

mulk, al-: the World of dominion

Mu'min, al-: Guardian of Faith, one of the 99 Names of God.

mu'min: a believer.

munājāt: invocation to God in very intimate form.

Munkir: one of the angels of the grave.

murīd: disciple, student, follower.

murshid: spiritual guide, *pir*.

mushāhadah: direct witnessing

mushrik (pl. mushrikūn): idolater, polytheist.

muwwaḥid (pl. muwaḥḥidūn): those affiriming God's Oneness.

nabī: a prophet of God

nafs: lower self, ego.

Nakīr: the othe rangel of the grave (with Munkir)

nūr: light

Nūḥ: the prophet Noah ﷺ.

Nūr, an-: The Source of Light, a Divine Name.

Qādir, al-: the Powerful, a Divine Name.

qalam, al-: the Pen.

qiblah: direction, specifically, the direction faced by Muslims during prayer and other worship towards the Sacred House in Mecca.

Quddūs, al-: the Holy One, a Divine Name.

qurb: nearness

quṭb (pl. aqṭāb): axis or pole. Among the poles are:

Quṭb al-bilād: Pole of the Lands

Quṭb al-irshād: Pole of Guidance

Quṭbu 'l-aqṭāb: Pole of Poles

Quṭbu 'l-aʿẓam: Highest Pole

Quṭbu 't-tasarruf: Pole of Affairs

al-quṭbīyyatu 'l-kubrā: the highest station of poleship

Rabb, ar-: the Lord

Raḥīm, ar-: the Most Compassionate, a Divine Name.

Raḥmān, ar-: the All-Merciful, a Divine Name.

raḥma: mercy.

rakaʿat: one full set of prescribed motions in prayer. Each prayer consists of a one or more *rakaʿats.*

Ramaḍān: the ninth month of the Islamic lunar calendar, the month of fasting.

rasūl: a messenger of God

Rasūlullāh: the Prophet of God, Muhammad ﷺ.

Ra'ūf, ar-: the Most Kind, a Divine Name.

Razzāq, ar-: the Provider

rawḥānīyyah: spirituality, spiritual essence of something.

Riḍwān: Archangel of Paradise.

rizq: provision, sustenance.

rūḥ: spirit. Ar-Rūḥ is the name of a great angel.

rukūʿ: bowing posture of the prayer.

ṣadaqa: voluntary charity.

ṣaḥīḥ: authentic; term certifying validity of a hadith of the Prophet ﷺ.

ṣāim: fasting person (pl. ṣāimūn)

salām: peace.

Salām, as-: the Peaceful, a Divine Name.

as-salāmu ʿalaykum: peace be upon you (Islamic greeting)

ṣalāt: Islam's ritual prayer.

Ṣalāt an-Najāt: prayer of salvation, done in the wee hours of the night.

Ṣamad, aṣ-: Self-Sufficient, upon whom creatures depend.

Saḥābah (sing., sahabi): the Companions of the Prophet, the first Muslims.

sajda (pl. *sujūd*): prostration.

ṣalāt: prayer, one of the five obligatory pillars of Islam. Also to invoke blessing on the Prophet ﷺ.

ṣalawāt (sing. *salāt*): invoking blessings and peace upon the Prophet ﷺ.

ṣawm, ṣiyām: fasting.

sayyid: leader; also, a descendant of Prophet Muhammad ﷺ.

Sayyidinā/ sayyidunā: our master (fem. *sayyidatunā:* our mistress).

shahādah: lit. testimony; the testimony of Islamic faith: Lā ilāha illa 'l-Lāh wa Muḥammadun rasūlu 'l-Lāh or "There is no god but Allah, the One God, and Muḥammad is the Messenger of God."

Shāh Naqshband: Khwājah Muḥammad Bahāuddīn Shāh-Naqshband, a great eighth century *walī,* the founder of the Naqshbandi *Ṭarīqah.*

shaykh: lit. "old man," a religious guide, teacher; master of spiritual discipline.

shifā': cure.

shirk: polytheism, idolatry, ascribing *partners to God*

ṣiffāt: attributes; term referring to Divine Attributes.

Silsilat adh-dhahabīyya: "golden chain" of spiritual authority in Islam

sohbet (Arabic *suḥba): association*: the assembly or discourse of a shaykh.

subḥanallāh: glory be to God.

sulṭān/sulṭānah: ruler, monarch.

Sulṭān al-Awlīyā: lit., "the king of the *awlīyā*,"; the highest-ranking saint.

sunnah: the practice of the Prophet ﷺ; that is, what he did, said, recommended or approved of in his Companions.

sūrah: a chapter of the Qur'an; picture, image.

Sūratu 'l- Ikhlāṣ: the Chapter of Sincerity, 114.

ṭabīb: doctor.

tābi'īn: the Successors, generation after the Prophet's Companions.

tafsīr: to explain, expound, explicate, or interpret; technical term for commentary or exegesis of the Holy Qur'ān.

tajallī (pl. tajallīyāt): theophanies, God's self-disclosures, Divine Self-manifestation.

takbīr: lit. "Allāhu Akbar," God is Great.

tarawīḥ: the special nightly prayers of Ramadan.

ṭarīqat/ṭarīqah: literally, way, road or path. An Islamic order or path of discipline and devotion under a guide or shaykh; Islamic Sufism.

tasbīḥ: recitation glorifying or praising God.

tawāḍa': humbleness.

ṭawāf: the rite of circumambulating the Ka'bah while glorifying God during Hajj and 'Umrah.

tawḥīd: unity; universal or primordial Islam, submission to *God*, as the sole Master of destiny and ultimate Reality.

Tawrāt: Torah

'ubūdīyyah: state of worshipfulness. Servanthood

'ulamā (sing. *'Alīm*): scholars.

'ulūmu 'l-awwalīna wa 'l-ākhirīn: knowledge of the "Firsts" and the "Lasts" refers to the knowledge that God poured into the heart of Muḥammad ﷺ during his ascension to the Divine Presence.

'ulūm al-Islāmī: Islamic religious sciences.

ummah: faith community, nation.

'Umar ibn al-Khaṭṭāb ؓ: an eminent Companion of the Prophet ﷺ and second caliph of Islam.

'umrah: the minor pilgrimage to Mecca, performed at any time of the year.

'Uthmān ibn 'Affān ؓ: an eminent Companion of the Prophet ﷺ and his son-in-law, who became third caliph of Islam. Renowned for compiling the Qur'an.

walad: a child

waladī: my child
walāyah: proximity or closeness; sainthood.
walī (pl. awliyā'): saint, or "he who assists,"; guardian; protector.
wasīlah: a means; a special station granted to the Prophet Muḥammad ﷺ as intermediary to God in the granting the petitioner's supplications.
wāw: Arabic letter و
wujūd, al-: existence; "to find," "the act of finding," as well as "being found".
Y'aqūb: the prophet Jacob ﷺ.
yamīn: the right hand, used to mean "oath."
yawm al-'ahdi wa'l-mīthāq: day of oath and covenant, a heavenly event before this life, when the souls of mankind were present before God where He took from each soul the promise to accept His Sovereignty as Lord.
yawm al-qiyāmah: Day of Judgment.
Yūsūf: the prophet Joseph ﷺ.
zīyāra: visitation to the grave of a prophet, prophet's companion or saint.

Islamic Calendar and Holy Days

The Islamic calendar is lunar-based, with twelve months of 29 or 30 days and a year of 354 days. A lunar year is shorter than a solar year, so Muslim holy days cycle back in the Gregorian (Western) calendar. This is how, for example, Ramaḍān is celebrated at different times of the year, as the annual Islamic calendar is ten days shorter than the Gregorian calendar.

Four months are sacred, in which war is prohibited, unless Muslims are attacked and must defend themselves: Muharram, Rajab, Dhūl-Qʿadah and Dhūl-Ḥijjah. Holy months include "God's Month" (Rajab), "Prophet's Month" (Shaʿbān) and the "Month of the People" (Ramaḍān), in which pious acts are rewarded more generously.

Months of the Islamic Calendar

Muḥarram
Safar
Rabīʿu 'l-Awwal (Rabīʿ I)
Rabīʿu 'th-Thāni (Rabīʿ II)
Jumāda al-Awwal (Jumādā I)
Jumādāu 'th-Thāni (Jumādā II)
Rajab
Shaʿbān
Ramaḍān
Shawwāl
Dhū 'l-Qʿadah
Dhū 'l-Ḥijjah

al-Hijrah

The first of Muḥarram marks the beginning of the Islamic New Year, chosen because it is the anniversary of Prophet Muḥammad's ﷺ historic *hijrah* (migration) from Mecca to Madinah, where he established the first, preeminent Muslim community in which he introduced unprecedented social reforms, including civil law, human and women's rights, religious tolerance, taxation to serve the community, and military ethics.

'Ashura

On tenth of Muḥarram, 'Ashūra commemorates many sacred events, such as Noah's ark coming to rest, the birth of Abraham, and the building of the Ka'bah in Mecca. 'Ashūra is a major holy day, marked with two days of fasting, on the 9th/10th or on 10th/11th based on a holy tradition (ḥadīth) of Sayyidīna Muḥammad ﷺ It is also the day of martyrdom of Sayyidīna al-Ḥusayn ؓ, the grandson of the Prophet ﷺ.

Mawlid

Mawlid al-Nabī, 12th Rabi' al-Awwal, commemorates Prophet Muḥammad's birth in 570. Mawlid is celebrated globally throughout this month in huge communal gatherings in which a famous poem "Qasīdah al-Burdah" is recited, accompanied by drummers, illustrious poetry recitals, religious singing, eloquent sermons, gift giving, feasts, and feeding the poor. Most Muslim nations observe Mawlid as a national holiday.

Laylat al-Isra wal-Mi'raj

Literally, "the Night Journey and Ascension;" 27th of Rajab is when Sayyidīna Muḥammad ﷺ physically traveled from Mecca to Jerusalem, ascended in all the levels of Heaven from a rock in the Dome of the Rock, and returned to Mecca—while his bed was still warm. In the Night Journey, Islam's five daily prayers were ordained by God. Sayyidīna Muḥammad ﷺ also prayed with Abraham, Moses, and Jesus in Jerusalem's al-Aqsa Mosque, signifying that Muslims, Christians, and Jews follow one god. This holy event designated Jerusalem as the third holiest site in Islam, after Mecca and Madinah.

Laylat al-Bara'ah

The "Night of Freedom from Fire" occurs on 15th Sha'bān. On this night God's Mercy is great; hence, the night is spent reciting Holy Qur'an and special prayers, as well as visiting the deceased.

Ramadan

Many regard Ramaḍān, the 9th month of the Islamic calendar, the holiest month of the year. Muslims observe a strict fast and participate in pious activities such as charitable giving and peace making. It is a time of intense spiritual renewal for those who observe it. Fasting is meant to instill social awareness of the needy, and to promote gratitude for God's endless favors. The fast is typically broken in a communal setting, and hence Ramaḍān is a highly social month. At night, a special Ramaḍān prayer known as "Tarawīḥ" is offered in congregation, in which one-thirtieth of the Holy Qur'an is recited by the *imām* (prayer leader); thus the entire holy book of 6,000 verses is recited in this month.

Eid al-Fitr

"Festival of Fast-Breaking" marks the end of Ramaḍān and is celebrated the first three days of Shawwāl. It is a time for charity and celebration with family and friends for completing a month of blessings and joy. In the Last Days of Ramaḍān, each Muslim family gives "Zakāt al-Fiṭr"(charity of fast-breaking) which consists of cash and/or food, to help the poor. On the first early morning of Eid, Muslims observe a special congregational prayer, such as Christmas/Easter Mass or the High Holy Days. After Eid prayer is a time to visit family and friends, and give gifts and money (especially to children). Many specialty foods and sweets are prepared solely for Eid days. In most Muslim countries, the entire three days of Eid is a national holiday.

Yawm al-Arafat

"Day of 'Arafat," the 9th Dhul-Hijjah, occurs just before the celebration of Eid al-Adha. Pilgrims on Hajj assemble for the "standing" on the plain of 'Arafat, located outside Mecca, where they contemplate the Day of Standing (Resurrection Day). Muslims elsewhere in the world fast this day, and gather at a local mosque for prayers. Thus, those who cannot perform Hajj that year still honor the sacrifice of Abraham.

Eid al-Adha

The "Feast of Sacrifice," celebrated from the 10th-13th Dhul-Hijjah, marks Prophet Abraham's willingness to sacrifice his son Isma'il on God's order. To honor this event, Muslims perform Hajj, the pilgrimage to Mecca that is incumbent on every mature Muslim once in their life if they have the means. Celebrations begin with an animal sacrifice to commemorate Sayyidīna Abraham's sacrifice. In Islam, he is known as *Khalīlullāh*, "God's friend." Many consider him the first Muslim and a premiere role model, for his obedience to God and willingness to sacrifice his only child without even questioning the command.

Other Publications of Interest

Mawlana Shaykh Nazim Adil al-Haqqani

- The Sufilive Series, Vols 1-3 (2010)
- Eternity: Inspirations from Heavenly Sources
- Breaths from Beyond the Curtain (2010)
- In the Eye of the Needle
- The Healing Power of Sufi Meditation
- The Path to Spiritual Excellence
- In the Mystic Footsteps of Saints, 2 volumes
- Liberating the Soul, 6 volumes

Shaykh Hisham Kabbani

- Cyprus Summer Series (2010)
- The Nine-fold Ascent
- Who Are the Guides?
- Illuminations
- Banquet for the Soul
- Symphony of Remembrance
- Healing Power of Sufi Meditation
- In the Shadow of Saints
- Keys to the Divine Kingdom
- The Sufi Science of Self-Realization
- Universe Rising: the Approach of Armageddon?
- Pearls and Coral, 2 volumes
- Classical Islam and the Naqshbandi Sufi Tradition
- Naqshbandi Sufi Way
- Encyclopedia of Islamic Doctrine, 7 volumes
- Angels Unveiled
- Encyclopedia of Muḥammad's Women Companions and the Traditions They Related

Hajjah Amina Adil

- Muḥammad: the Messenger of Islam
- The Light of Muḥammad
- Lore of Light / Links of Light
- My Little Lore of Light, 3 volumes

Hajjah Naziha Adil Kabbani

- Secrets of Heavenly Food (2009)
- Heavenly Foods (2001)

www.ingramcontent.com/pod-product-compliance
Lightning Source LLC
Chambersburg PA
CBHW030305080526
44584CB00012B/454
9781930409729